DECONSTRUCTING THE "DEMOCRATIC PEACE"

HOW A RESEARCH AGENDA BOOMERANGED

Michael Haas

Political Scientist

Nobel Peace Prize Nominee

Library of Congress Cataloging-in-Publication Data

Deconstructing the "democratic peace": How a research agenda
boomeranged
by Michael Haas
   p.   cm.
   Bibliography: p.
   Includes index.
   ISBN (paperbound edition): 978-0-9839626-2-5
   ISBN (hardcover edition): 978-0-9839626-3-2
   Library of Congress Control Number 2014902157

I. 1. Democracy 2. Peace 3. Political science 4 War
II. Haas, Michael

Publishinghouse for Scholars
P.O. Box 461267
Los Angeles, CA 90046

Printed in the United States of America

Table of Contents

Tables		iv
Preface		v
1	Evaluating a Research Agenda	1
2	The Main Empirical "Findings"	5
3	Problems of Research Design	11
4	Inference Problems	41
5	Faulty Theoretical Explanations	47
6	Normative Problems	97
7	Conclusion	111
Appendix: Deviant Cases		115
References		127
Index		189

Tables

3.1	Operational Definitions of "Democracy"	14
5.1	Institutional Constraints	49
5.2	Normative Explanations	56
5.3	Economic Explanations	73
5.4	Realpolitik Critiques	80
5.5	Leadership Styles	88

Preface

When George W. Bush tried to justify the Iraq War in 2003 as the first step in planting seeds for democracies within the Middle East, citing the concept of the "democratic peace," my worst fears were confirmed that academic scholarship had been perverted to justify violence. That boomerang, coming back to haunt "democratic peace" researchers, was exactly what I anticipated a decade earlier, when I presented a paper at the annual convention of the American Political Science Association in 1995.

What I then pointed out was that the concept of "democratic peace" was a fraud with dangerous implications. Whereas some researchers pretended that they could prove the existence of an absolute lack of war between democracies, they went even beyond to urge war to expand the number of democracies in the world. What they were doing was to justify the many wars waged by the United States over the recent past, covert and overt, as justifiable because they tried to leave democracies as their legacies. Wars in Bosnia and Kosovo presumably created democracies, but they ignored the fact that Washington failed to do so in Kuwait and Vietnam and even subverted democracies in Chile, Guatemala, and elsewhere.

That a country would develop democracy after losing a war is a romantic idea, but anyone who has studied the development of democracy knows that political systems change through domestic pressures from socioeconomic groups that are stakeholders in a country and seek political influence. Yet none of those who research the "democratic peace" has ever taken the time to peruse the historic development of democracies and their many forms. All that has interested "democratic peace" theorists is whether there is a number to assign to countries on a scale of "democraticness" in order to facilitate correlation with numbers representing other concepts.

By taking the sample of cases back as far as the early nineteenth century (and ever earlier), they have naïvely believed such nonsense as the fiction that the United States has been a democracy for two centuries despite the existence of slavery and Jim Crow practices up to the mid-1960s. Until women were granted the right to vote, how could most countries be classified as anything but Herrenfolk democracies, using the vocabulary of sociologist Pierre van den Berghe?

What "democratic peace" researchers have practiced is the worst abuse of behavioralist political science, namely, an irrelevant research quest. With so many world problems that could engage conscientious researchers, they shamefully withdrew into an ivory tower. Rather than seeking the causes of war, they sought explanations for peace among a narrow sample of supposed "democracies."

My paper of 1995, which is updated herein, was submitted to the editor of *The Journal of Conflict Resolution* to help those engaged in "democratic peace" research to correct serious flaws and misconceptions. Rather than seeing the need for such a publication, unlike at least one of his reviewers, the editor decided not to publish. J. David Singer, however, supported my critique. I should have sent the paper to other publication outlets, but in that very year I found myself unexpectedly pushing a wheelchair (and much more) for a paraplegic in my household, and I simply did not have any energy in the day beyond my teaching duties. Within a couple of years, the essay was placed in a book appropriate for the critique, but the book was never reviewed. Meanwhile, early retirement was the only way to find time to fulfill my human duties to my loved one, who eventually died.

What stimulated me to revise and update? When I began to attend academic conferences again after that death, I realized that hundreds of researchers were proceeding without reflecting even on partial critiques made by others. I realized that only a more comprehensive assessment would stop what had become a fantasy and a fraud.

Whether I have succeeded herein will be for other scholars to judge.

Michael Haas

DECONSTRUCTING THE "DEMOCRATIC PEACE"

HOW A RESEARCH AGENDA BOOMERANGED

1

Evaluating a Research Agenda

Some researchers of international relations have been eager to an-
nounce, after several decades and thousands of dollars of research
grants, that they have finally emerged with a robust bivariate finding
that refuses to go away when all other variables are held constant.
The finding, which has been virtually canonized as a "law" (Levy
1989:270; Russett 1989:245; Rothstein 1991:47; Ray 1992:234), is
that democracies do not make war upon one another. As the number
of democracies increase, we are promised fewer wars.

The reasons for the relationship, these scholars inform us, are
becoming increasing clear. More quantitative research is on the
agenda, and we are promised that some day we will have an explanation that will satisfy all. They point to claims by Immanuel Kant
(1795), Thomas Paine (1776:27), and Alexis de Tocqueville (1835)
that democracies are more peaceful and feel vindicated philosophi-
cally. The research agenda has been congratulated for following pre-
cepts of the philosophy of science and for making solid progress
(Chernoff 2004,2008; Van Belle 2006; Harrison 2010), though a
very different view also exists (Ungerer 2012).

Specific criticisms of the "democratic peace" generalization are found among foreign policy researchers, especially as compared with macroanalysts. Ideologically, criticisms have come from the right and the left, while political centrists generally adhere to the faith (cf. Rathbun 2012). Theoretically, John Mearsheimer (1990:49-51) and Christopher Layne (1994:48-49) have rejected the implicit neoidealism that they fear is dangerously forsaking the principles of political (neo)realism. Nils Petter Gleditsch (1992:374) has confided that integration theorists have been miffed that the functionalist logic of peace through global or regional cooperation has been upstaged, though Harvey Starr (1992, 1997) later made the connection. The lack of a theoretical context for "democratic peace" research has also been identified (Lake 1992:24; Gowa 1995). Several researchers have challenged the research on methodological grounds, including matters of definition, sampling, and quantitative procedures. Some scholars have claimed that the findings are spurious. Although a "democratic peace" finding is found in simple research designs, the effect appears to wash out when controlling for other variables (Mousseau 2013a). One critic believes that the enterprise is pseudo-scientific (Smith 2007:xiii, 108). Perhaps the most damning criticism is that the entire enterprise is counterproductive or irrelevant to major policy concerns today.

Writing nearly two decades ago, Raymond Cohen (quoted in Haas 1997a:136) noted that "the 'democratic peace' school has become something of a self-perpetuating, self-satisfied group of researchers who display greater tolerance and pay more attention to the work of those who support their thesis than to their critics." Defenders of the "democratic peace," in turn, have fired back in a Kafka-esque manner, as if ideologically under attack, methinks protesting too much (Owen 1994a,b:119-22; Russett 1993b, 1994, 1995, 1997, 2010; Doyle 1995, 1996; Ray 1995, 2005, 2013; Russett and Ray 1995; Maoz 1997; Thompson and Tucker 1997; Oneal and Russett 1999c, 2000b, 2003b; Dafoe 2011; Dafoe, Oneal, Russett 2013; Dafoe and Russett 2013). In an exchange with Samuel Huntington (2000), "democratic peace" researchers showed that they preferred to trivialize an important policy question, oblivious of the shortcomings of statistical methods without case study validation (Russett, Oneal, Cox 2000).

Accordingly, the purpose of the present book is to evaluate the research agenda in fundamental scientific terms (cf. Chernoff 2004).

What I find is that the "democratic peace" has become a dogma, not a "law," which has been advanced by researchers who have flouted some of the simplest norms of empirical, theoretical, and policy-relevant research and thus has boomeranged—inviting definitive refutations and leading to serious mistakes of public policy. Indeed, I found that a reviewer of the earlier draft of the present essay, who reocommended against publication in 1996, professed ignorance of the difference between procedural and substantive democracy (cited in Haas 1997a:129). Having failed to converge on a satisfactory explanation for an alleged bivariate finding, "democratic peace" researchers celebrate an ideology, not a research consensus, as I demonstrate herein.

Social constructionism, as an analytic philosophy, arose to explain how elites can brainwash masses by the insidious use of language. The very term "democratic peace" is a socially construction that has fooled academics into believing that there is a corresponding phenomenon. Accordingly, the purpose of the present volume is to deconstruct that concept.

The plan of the book is first to identify the basic "findings." Then problems with the research designs will be identified, followed by problems of evidence and inference. Next, shallowness of the theoretical explanations are exposed, particularly the failure to link the research to the existing paradigmatic literature. After serious normative flaws are identified, the concluding chapter asks "Quo Vadis?"

2

The Main Empirical "Findings"

The claim of a lawlike relationship between democracy and peace may be traced to Clarence Streit (1939:91), who reported that fifteen democracies had not then been involved in war with one another from 1830. However, Duncan Bell (2013) has traced Streit's thinking to a long line of English-speaking theorists who wanted to bring world peace through Anglo-American hegemony, including imperialism.

Quincy Wright (1942:841), on the contrary, found that democracies were as likely to be at war as nondemocracies. But Streit's finding was later corroborated in studies by Dean Babst (1964, 1972), Melvin Small and J. David Singer (1976:67-68), and Michael Doyle (1983:209-15). Small and Singer, however, dismissed the finding as "marginal." Later, the view arose that pairs of democratic countries (dyads) are almost universally peaceful; the dyadic peace then became the basis for what has been called the "democratic peace."

A second claim—monadic, not dyadic—was made that democracies are more peaceful than other regime types, engaging in fewer wars as well as threats of war (Rummel 1979, 1983b, 1985; Bremer 1992, 1993; Benoit 1996; Hewitt and Wilkenfeld 1996). But the "peaceful democracies" thesis has been negated in many studies (Wright 1942:841; Gregg and Banks 1965; Haas 1965:312, 1974: 229-31; East and Gregg 1967:260; Salmore and Hermann 1970:24; Banks 1972:223; Feierabend and Feierabend 1972:171; East and Hermann 1974:295-99; Russett and Momsen 1975:23; Small and Singer 1976:62; Terrell 1977; Rousseau, Gelpi, Reiter, Huth 1966: 521; cf. Zinnes and Wilkenfeld 1971:207-8). Charles Kegley and Margaret Hermann (1996a,b, 1997a; Hermann, Kegley, Raymond 1998) have reported that democracies violated the sovereignty of other democracies in half the military interventions during the Cold War (cf. Carpenter 1992; Tures 2001). Rudolph Rummel, however, vigorously stated the "peaceful democracy" thesis again (1983b, 1995), faulting some of the contrary studies for irrelevance or sloppy computations (Rummel 1985, 1993, 1995).

While Rummel remained adamant that democracies are more peaceful than nondemocracies, some studies announced that democracies engage in fatal clashes with nondemocracies at much higher rates than either pairs of democracies or pairs of nondemocracies (Maoz and Abdolali 1989:23; Morgan and Schwebach 1992:312; Weart 1994:303; Gleditsch 1995; Henderson 2002:ch3), a finding disputed by Stuart Bremer (1992:329). But other scholars have reasserted the generalization that democracies are as warlike as nondemocracies (Chan 1984; Weede 1984; Vincent 1987a; Domke 1988:ch4; Bremer 1992, 1993; Haas 1994:ch6; Oneal and Russett 1997). Although Errol Henderson (2002:ch4) noted that democracies were more involved in colonial and imperial wars than nondemocracies, he found that overall nondemocracies were more likely to engage in "extrastate wars," that is, those involving nonstate entities, such as China's attack on Tibet in 1950 and the American attacks on Al-Qaeda terrorists.

Several studies have observed that autocracies and democracies are more peaceful than regimes undergoing change in regime type in either direction (cf. Mansfield and Snyder 1995:5), though other studies have found that transitional states are much less likely to be involved in militarized conflicts in the few cases when they undergo smooth transitions (Ward and Gleditsch 1998; Gleditsch and Ward 2000; cf. Casper 1995; Casper and Taylor 1996) or have recently become democracies (Enterline 1998; Hensel, Goertz, Diehl 2000). Recent autocracies, however, are war prone (Maoz 1989, 1996; Enterline 1998). Anocracies (regimes midway between democratic and autocratic extremes) are evidently the most prone to engage in external conflict (Gleditsch and Hegre 1997; Enterline 1998). Paul Senese (1999) found that regime maturity has a pacifying effect, but moreso in regard to nondemocracies than democracies.

In an experimental study, democracies attacked other democracies when the level of threat was sufficiently high (Mintz, Geva, Redd, Carnes 1997). According to another study, democracies are more likely to go to war with anocracies than autocracies (Bennett and Stam 2000:677). Yet another finding is that autocracies are more likely to challenge democracies than other autocracies (Reiter and Stam 2003:336).

However, there has been a monadic revival. When the dependent variable is conflict initiation rather than war, the data appear to show that democracies are more peaceloving than other regime types: Various studies have reported that democracies are less likely to threaten war, military actions short of war, or to start wars (Babst 1972; Rummel 1983b, 1995, 1997; Chan 1984; Weede 1984, 1992; Maoz and Abdolali 1989:24; Morgan and Schwebach 1992:312; Bueno de Mesquita and Lalman 1992:152; Bremer 1992, 1993; Russett 1993b:21; Ray 1995:11-21,33, 2000, 2003; Benoit 1996; Rousseau, Gelpi, Reiter, Huth 1996; Elman 1997c:15-18; Gleditsch and Hegre 1997:205; Oneal and Ray 1997; MacMillan 1998, 2003; Rioux 1998:282; Leeds and Davis 1999; Russett and Starr 2000; Russett and Oneal 2001:95-96; Schultz 2001:137), especially against other democracies (Morgan and Schwebach 1992:314; Maoz and Russett 1993; Russett and Maoz 1993; Dixon 1993, 1994; Hensel, Goertz, Diehl 2000; Huth and Allee 2002; Caprioli and Trumbore 2006). Several analyses have found that democracies resolve crises, deescalate disputes, and otherwise conduct foreign policy more peacefully than nondemocracies (Geller 1985:154-57; Brecher, Wilkenfeld, Moser 1988:11,196-97; Maoz and Abdolali 1989:18; Bercovitch, Anagnoson, Wille 1991:10; Bueno de Mesquita and Lalman 1992:154-58; Maoz and Russett 1993; Russett and Maoz 1993; Dixon 1993, 1994; Leng 1993:28; Burley 1994; Raymond 1994). Getting down to cases, as suggested by Joseph Nye (1993:40), Layne (1994) provided specific examples when democracies went to the brink of war and backed down.

But serious questions have continued to be raised about the monadic level (Henderson 2002; Pickering 2002; Buhaug 2005; Chojnacki 2006; Quackenbush and Rudy 2009), and there is no consensus regarding the proposition that democracies are less likely to initiate wars against nondemocracies than the reverse (Small and Singer 1976:64-66; Domke 1988:ch4; Chan 1984:639; Bremer 1993; Reiter and Stam 2003; Bueno de Mesquita and Ray 2004:117). The reverse appears to be the case (Quackenbush and Rudy 2009:281). The distinction between dyadic and monadic behavior of democracies continues to confuse the literature.

Nevertheless, when democracies go to war, many researchers have agreed, their adversaries are almost exclusively nondemocracies (Maoz and Abdolali 1989). In two studies, the "democratic peace" finding remained when such factors as alliances, capabilities, contiguity, domestic violence, economic growth, political stability, and wealth were held constant (Maoz and Russett 1993; Russett and Maoz 1993). The "democratic peace" also has been applied to indigenous societies (Ember, Ember, Russett 1992). Although Bruce Russett and William Antholis (1992) found that democracies fought one another during the Peloponnesian wars, such anomalies were later questioned by Spencer Weart (1994:311), who has noted examples of the "democratic peace" among the Achaean, Boeotian, Castilian, Dutch, Hanseatic, Lithuanian, Peloponnesian, South African, and Swiss leagues (see Appendix).

Accordingly, most scholars have restated the "democratic peace law" as follows: "Democracies rarely fight other democracies" (Ray 1993). Thus, instead of a "law" based on comparisons between democracies and nondemocracies, the "law" is seen as ironclad with respect to dyadic pairs of democracies (Gleditsch 1992:372, 1995: 318).

Yet developed socialist countries, both inside and outside the former Iron Curtain, have almost never fought (Braumoeller 1997; Oren and Hays 1997). But a "socialist peace" has not impressed the "democratic peace" research mainstream. In one study, however, the more assets owned by a state, the more likely that country will go to war (McDonald 2010). Besides, the conflict between Cambodia and Vietnam in the late 1970s is an important case deviating from the "socialist peace" thesis (Haas 2012b:ch1).

Other studies find ambiguous or negative support for the hypothesis that democracies are less likely to escalate from mere crises and disputes into serious displays of military force and war (East and Hermann 1974; Senese 1997a; Ray and Wang 1995; Ray 1995:17-21). However, there is consensus that democracies are less likely to initiate serious militarized international disputes (Gochman and Maoz 1984:596-97; Bremer 1993; Maoz and Russett 1993:632; Russett and Maoz 1993:86; Enterline 1998). Once war is ongoing, democracies have rallied to join other democracies in the fray more than autocracies have banded together (Gleditsch and Hegre 1997).

Numerous studies, of course, claim that regime type is not the most important variable accounting for war. Huntington (1989:7) claimed that most democracies historically have been noncontiguous or contemporaneously have been allies of the United States and thus have been unable or unwilling to project power to one another. Bremer (1992:327, 1993:245; cf. Gleditsch 1992, 1995) found geographic contiguity was the most important variable, though regime type still had considerable explanatory power. But when other researchers have held contiguity constant, the "democratic peace law" has remained (Rummel 1983b; Maoz and Russett 1993:632; Russett and Maoz 1993:84-87). Kenneth Waltz (1993:44) argued that the need for deterrence solidarity during the Cold War preserved the peace; however, Erich Weede (1983, 1989), who once held similar views, later recanted (Weede 1992:382). Henry Farber and Joanne Gowa (1995) provided data to support Waltz, but their study was disputed by William Thompson and Richard Tucker (1997).

Bremer (1992, 1993) found that major powers are more likely to go to war, whether they are democracies or not. Another study reported that stable regimes are more likely to avoid war than unstable regimes, regardless of regime type (Maoz and Russett 1993:86). Alternative causes of war or peace abound, such as previous levels of foreign conflict (Zinnes and Wilkenfeld 1971:178). Kegley and Hermann (1995a, 1996a,b, 1997a) have found that democracies are least likely to experience interventions but more likely to intervene in anocracies than in autocracies, and that such interventions have been increasing, particularly if the anocracy is unaligned, unstable, developing into an autocracy, or is highly militarized. Their research has been faulted, however (Lemke and Regan 2004; Gleditsch, Christiansen, Håvard 2007). Another study found a positive relationship between nondemocratic dyads and the likelihood of violence but no such relationship for democracy dyads (Hewitt and Wilkenfeld 1998). For Gowa (1999:3), the Cold War entirely accounted for the "democratic peace," so the phenomenon is now "extinct."

The "democratic peace" thesis, thus, must be contextualized. The probability of international conflict may be low between two democracies, and other factors may have higher explanatory power in accounting for the behavior of all states, whether democratic or otherwise. However, flaws in the design of research on the subject seriously limit the generality of the "democratic peace" thesis, as the next chapter reveals.

3

Problems of Research Design

In an eloquent statement, Bremer (1992:310-11) once delineated several problems in research on the "democratic peace" proposition. I did so as well (Haas 1995, 1997). Alas, our criticisms have made no impact. Let me lay out a comprehensive review of the way in which "democratic peace" research has been designed by focusing on problems of definition, sampling, and the deviant cases that have been swept under an ivory tower rug. As a result, the research has boomeranged—that is, led to numerous autocorrelations and refutations.

Definitions

In a common research project, involving more than one hundred scholars focused on democracy, one might suppose that they would define the key term with considerable care and sophistication. Yet most empirical researchers of the "democratic peace" fail to do so. They do not, for example, specify various types of democracy consistently, thereby jeopardizing the conceptual validity of their measures (cf. Merritt and Zinnes 1991:209-14). I count at least 25 different elements of "democracy" (Table 3.1; Index), thus severely limiting the cumulatively of the research. A major canon of empirical research, that an interesting study should be replicated before proceeding to further analysis, thus, has not always been followed. When a challenge to the "democratic peace" thesis emerges, nevertheless, Russett and associates often perform replications, leading to counter-replications (cf. Gartzke 1998, 2000; Oneal and Russett 1999b), but without attempting to compare alternative definitions of "democracy" within their results. Some researchers have made up qualifying adjectives for "democracy," thereby confusing results.

Throughout political science, the term "democracy" has been defined in many ways (cf. Bollen 1980, 1991, 1993; Inkeles 1991; Davenport 2007:100-10), and the meaning has evolved historically (Owen 1994b). Democracy may be viewed as procedural (observance of political constraints and rights), or substantive (control of elites by nonelites), or social (providing material equality). In addition, some studies include "Herrenfolk democracies," that is, countries which restrict voting from minorities or women (van den Berghe 1967). "Illiberal democracies" recognize political rights but not civil rights (Zakaria 1997). The political science literature also refers to communitarian democracy, consociational democracy, developmental democracy, economic democracy, elitist democracy, participatory democracy, pluralist democracy, and protective democracy (Bachrach 1969; Lijphart 1984; Dahl 1985; Held 1987; Hudson 1995). But, in the "democratic peace" literature, "democracy" is treated as a number (a variable), not as a sophisticated multidimensional concept.

None of the "democratic peace" researchers previously studied democracy in any depth before undertaking their analyses. Their citations rarely include some of the major distinguished essays on democracy (e.g., Sartori 1962; Macpherson 1963; Pickles 1970; O'Donnell 1978; Pennock 1979; Held 1987; Przeworski 1991; Huntington 1991; Pateman 1994), with the occasional exception of Robert Dahl, whose concept of "polyarchy" is sometimes mentioned, though not his more theoretical works (Dahl 1956, 1985)—and not his ten-point scale of polyarchy or his eight institutional guarantees (Dahl 1971). Yet Dahl's "polyarchy" is the merger of procedural with substantive democracy, combining the concepts of majority rule with minority rights. Dahl's proposed scale, indeed, was "jettisoned" (Merritt and Zinnes 1991:230) when a new scale was drawn up by Michael Coppedge and Wolfgang Reinecke (1991). Huntington (1991:37), meanwhile, identified 27 variables that could be used in a democracy scale, but he has had no takers. The lack of nuance toward the basic concept of "democracy" is an indicator of how shallow the research has been (cf. Munch and Verkuilen 2002; Rengger 2006). Any tests including subtypes of "democracy" would almost certainly invalidate the "findings."

As presumed equivalents of "democracy," some researchers have insisted on counting "libertarian regimes" (Rummel 1983a), "liberal regimes" (Doyle 1983, 1986; Owen 1994b), "coherent regimes" (Geller 1985:154-57), "clear democracies," (Russett and Antholis 1992) or "open systems" (East and Hermann 1974; Mansfield and Snyder 1995). Russett (1993b:15) specifically rejected economic liberty from his definition. John Owen (1994b:89) defined a "liberal democracy" as a state with liberal ideas and liberalism as the dominant ideology. In most of the research, a single measure (from the Polity dataset developed by Ted Gurr) has been used. Given the multifaceted nature of the term "democracy," a single measure not only fails on grounds of lack of proof of unidimensionality but also boomerangs into the trap of the well-known fallacy of composition.

Few scholars have grasped the obvious possibility of using various definitions to contextualize findings. Operationalizations of "democracy" vary (Table 3.1). Babst (1972:55) dichotomized governments based on whether they are freely elected, by which he meant an independent regime with an executive chosen by direct election by secret ballot from opposing candidates at regular intervals or chosen by an elective legislature elected in the same manner, with freedom of speech. Countries with freedom of the press, as rated by the University of Missouri's School of Journalism, are considered "politically free" (East and Gregg 1967:200) or "accountable" (Salmore and Hermann 1970:19). Bruce Russett and Joseph Momsen (1975:23) have stressed electoral regularity.

Rummel (1983b) used a trichotomy collapsed from the scales of Freedom House (1978-) for political rights, civil liberties, and economic freedom, thus rating Scandinavian social democracies as less "free" than individualistic Anglo-American democracies, though a few years later he reclassified both types as "libertarian" by dropping

Problems of Research Design

the economic freedom component (Rummel 1985:426). Kegley and Hermann (1996a,b) have also used Freedom House codings. Yet Raymond Gastil's initial methods were challenged on grounds of reliability and validity that he was fired by Freedom House, and researchers have found economic freedom uncorrelted with political democracy (Hewitt 1977; Lange and Garrett 1985, 1987).

Table 3.1. Operational Definitions of "Democracy"

Type of Democracy	Definitional Component	Studies Utilizing the Definitional Component
procedural: elections	competitive elections	Babst (1972:55); Feierabend & Feierabend (1972:160); Small & Singer (1976: 55); Rummel (1983b, 1997); Doyle (1986); Domke (1988:ch4); Maoz & Abdolali (1989); Morgan & Campbell (1991); Bremer (1992); Morgan & Schwebach (1992); Schweller (1992:240); Weede (1992); Dixon (1993,1994); Maoz & Russett (1993b); Russett & Maoz (1993); Owen (1994b:89); Raymond (1994); Oneal, Oneal, Maoz, Russett (1995); Enterline (1998); Polity I-IV; Vanhanen (2000): Boix, Miller, Rosato (2013)
	directly chosen executive	Babst (1972:55); Banks (1972:218); Rummel (1983b); Bremer (1992, 1993); Leng (1993); Polity I-IV; Cheibub & Gandhi (2004)
	indirectly chosen executive	Babst (1972:55); Rummel (1983b)
	extent of franchise: 10%+	Small and Singer (1976:55); Rummel (1983b)
	30%+	Schweller (1992:240)
	50%+	Ray (1995)
	"wide"	Weede (1992); Russett (1993b:16-19); Rummel (1997); Reiter & Tillman (2002); Ferejohn & Rosenbluth (2008); Polity I-IV
substantive	regular intervals of elections	Rustow (1967); Babst (1972:55); Banks (1972:218); Feierabend & Feierabend (1972:160); Russett & Momsen (1975: 23); Small & Singer (1976:55); Chan (1984); Morgan & Campbell (1991); Morgan & Schwebach (1992); Schweller (1992:240); Weede (1992); Russett (1993b: 16-19); Owen (1994b:89); Lemke & Reed (1996)

procedural: conditions of elections	secret ballot; ballots not stuffed	Babst (1972:55); Weede (1992); Russett (1993b:16-19); Rummel (1997)
	2/3 of adult males have equal rights	Weart (1994:301-3); Rummel (1997)
	economic freedom	Rummel (1983b)*; Doyle (1986)
	freedom of assembly	Feierabend & Feierabend (1972:160); Rummel (1983b, 1997); Schweller (1992:240); Weede (1992); Kegley & Hermann (1996a,b)
	freedom of the press	East and Gregg (1967:200); Salmore & Hermann (1970:19); Feierabend & Feierabend (1972:160); Rummel (1983b); Schweller (1992:240); Weede (1992); Van Belle (1997, 2000); Van Belle and Oneal (2000); Choi & James (2004, 2005)
	freedom of religion	Rummel (1997)
	free speech	Babst (1972:55); Feierabend & Feierabend (1972:160); Schweller (1992:240); Weede (1992); Owen (1994b:89); Kegley & Hermann (1996a,b); Rummel (1997)
	political suppression absent	Feierabend & Feierabend (1972:160); Small & Singer (1976:55); Rummel (1983b); Weede (1992)
	right to run for office	Weede (1992)
	few voting regulations	Ember, Ember, Russett (1992:579); Vanhanen (2000): Boix, Miller, Rosato (2013); Polity I-IV
procedural: limits on executive power	decentralized bureaucracy	Bremer (1992); Dixon (1993, 1994); Domke (1988:ch4); Maoz & Abdolali (1989); Morgan & Campbell (1991); Morgan & Schwebach (1992); Maoz & Russett (1993); Russett (1993b: 14-15); Russett & Maoz (1993); Raymond (1994); Oneal, Oneal, Maoz, Russett (1995); Enterline (1998)
	effective, independent legislature	Babst (1964, 1972); Feierabend & Feierabend (1972:160); Small & Singer (1976: 55); Chan (1984); Doyle (1986); Leng (1993); Bremer (1992, 1993); Russett & Antholis (1992:419-20); Schweller (1992: 240); Ray (1993, 1995); Lemke & Reed (1996)

procedural: limits on executive power (continued)	election losers leave office	Ray (1995:100); Polity I-IV
	executive power limited	Maoz & Abdolali (1989); Morgan & Campbell (1991); Bremer (1992); Morgan & Schwebach (1992); Dixon (1993, 1994); Maoz & Russett (1993, 2002); Russett (1993b:14-19); Domke (1988:ch4); Oneal, Oneal, Maoz, Russett (1995); Raymond (1994); Enterline (1998); Polity I-IV
	government scope limited	Domke (1988:ch4); Maoz & Abdolali (1989); Morgan & Campbell (1991); Bremer (1992); Morgan & Schwebach (1992); Dixon (1993, 1994); Maoz & Russett (1993); Russett (1993b:14-15, 1995); Russett & Maoz (1993); Raymond (1994); Oneal, Oneal, Maoz, Russett (1995); Rummel (1997); Enterline (1998)
	independent judiciary	Pritchard (1988); Feierabend & Feierabend (1972:160); Doyle (1986)
	strong local government	Feierabend & Feierabend (1972: 160)
substantive: public control of elites	at least half vote	Ray (1993,1995)
	"high level" of participation	Ember, Ember, Russett (1992:579); Russett & Antholis (1992:418-19); Polity I-IV
	public effectiveness in policies	Feierabend & Feierabend (1972: 160)
social democracy	welfare state provisions	Oren and Hays (1997)

*Disavowed later (Rummel 1985:426)

Rummel (1983b) also used the three-point scale of Richard Pride (1970:688-89,704) and a six-point scale from Ivo and Rosalind Feierabend (1972:160). He reported results similar to those that used Freedom House codings.

The Pride scale is based on selection of the chief executive through elections or by an elected parliament, with a legal opposition contesting elections, universal suffrage, and the absence of political suppression. The Feierabends's scale is based on the right to vote in frequent and fair elections, press freedom, freedom of the opposition, effectiveness of the public and legislature in policy-making, independence of the judiciary, strength of local government, and general civil and political rights, thus combining procedural and substantive democracy.

Stephen Quackenbush and Michael Rudy (2009) compared definitional formulations from four sources—Polity IV (Marshall and Jaggers 2000), Freedom House (2008), Tatu Vanhanen (2000), and José Cheibub and Jennifer Gandhi (2004), though they found little difference between results based on the four alternative measures. Gretchen Casper and Claudiu Tufis (2003) used different but highly correlated operationalizations and found disparate results (cf. Seawright and Collier 2014; Wilson 2013).

But there are other compilations of democracies. In the spirit of Kant, Doyle (1983:212, 1986) generated a list of "democracies" based on Freedom House criteria of economic and political freedom, an effective legislature, as well as whether female suffrage is granted within a generation of its being demanded. To be on his list, sovereign states must have market economies, citizens must enjoy juridical rights, and governments must be representative. G. Bingham Powell (1982) has a list of "polyarchies," following criteria from Dahl (1971). Weede (1992) identified twenty democracies from two sources (Dahl 1971:248-49; Powell 1982:3-5); the first source was based on public contestation and the right to vote and run for office, whereas the second applied to competitive, regular elections, freedom from coercion, with secret ballots and a wide franchise and freedom to run for office, along with freedom of speech, press, assembly, and organization. Russett (1993b:15) rejected civil rights from his notion of democracy.

As discussed in some detail within two essays (Gleditsch and Ward 1997; McLaughlin, Gates, Hegre, Gissinger, Gleditsch 1998), Gurr (1978; Gurr, Jaggers, Moore 1989) constructed a democracy scale based on sixty or so characteristics, with a focus on six components. Gurr's original scale, widely used in some of the earliest tests of the "democratic peace," is currently superseded by a database (Polity IV) that has ten-point scales for both democracy and autocracy for the years from 1800, with a neutral point between. The term "anocracy" applies to countries rated between -5 on the autocracy scale and +5 on the democracy scale; democracies are above, and autocracies are below. However, the ratings on individual items may be incomplete, so judgments allow for equivalencies, possibly making the enterprise inconsistent. Despite the fundamental obscurity of its components, Polity IV has been the main measure of "democracy" over the past decade. As a result, most researchers do not know what their data actually measure, an incredible flaw that mars all recent "democratic peace" research (Munch and Verkuilen 2002). Instead, Douglas Van Belle (1997; Van Belle and Oneal 2000) substituted press freedom for Polity IV and was satisfied with his unidimensional measure (cf. Choi and James 2006).

To ascertain the empirical validity of the Gurr data, William Domke (1988:78) obtained a high correlation with the variable "competitive and free norm" from the *World Handbook of Political and Social Indicators* (Taylor and Hudson 1972:57). Randolph Siverson and Juliann Emmons (1991:292) found Gurr's data to be highly correlated with a scale of democracy devised by Kenneth Bollen (1980). Two other efforts have been undertaken to validate "democracy" scales (Domke 1988:78; Siverson and Emmons 1991:292), finding that two alternative scales were positively intercorrelated, though both referred to procedural, not substantive, democracy. Other efforts have also found high intercorrelations with alternative measures (Bollen 1980:381; Arat 1991; Coppedge and Reinicke 1991; Benoit 1996; Hadenius 1992:41, 43, 71, 159-63; Vanhanen 1993:317-19, 1997:31-40; Jaggers and Gurr 1995:473-76; Alvarez, Cheibub, Limongi, Przeworski 1996:18-21; Eyerman and Hart 1996; Gasiorowski 1996:477-78; Coppedge 1997:180). Kegley and Hermann (1996b:314) found that Freedom House and Polity data captured "somewhat different dimensions." However, Freedom House data has been out of the mainstream (Munch and Verkuilen 2002: 30).

Russett's earlier studies accorded equal weight to various aspects of democracy, but in some later studies he and associates reverted to a dichotomous measurement by drawing an arbitrary cutting point, reporting that a dichotomized variable yielded more statistically significant findings than a continuous scale (Oneal, Oneal, Maoz, Russett 1996). However, Farber and Gowa (1997; cf. Gowa 1999:103)

found no difference between "deep" democracies and all other democracies. One benefit from contrasting alternative measures is the
is to discover whether the "democratic peace" may only apply to
democracies at the high end of the scale (Gleditsch 1992; Mansfield
and Snyder 1995, 1996), but that research path has not been trod.

Meanwhile, Randall Schweller (1992:240) combined Freedom
House codings with the definition of Singer and Small, though he
raised the suffrage level to 30 percent at the suggestion of Doyle. In
addition to the Polity data, Bremer (1992, 1993) used a dichotomy
based on popular elections for the chief executive and legislative effectiveness, relying on data from Steve Chan (1984), a source utilized as well by Douglas Lemke and William Reed (1996) and Russell Leng (1993). For James Lee Ray (1993, 1995), the criteria for
"democracy" are peaceful change of government following free elections that involve at least half of the population. For Owen (1994b:
89), citizens in a democracy have a voice over policies of war due to
free speech and regular competitive elections. Weart (1994:301-3)
studied "democratic republics," that is, polities where at least two-
thirds of adult male citizens have equal political rights, but even that
requirement could include Herrenvolk democracies.

Russett and Antholis (1992:419-20) identified fifth century BCE
Greek "democracies" as states that had a representative assembly
which made independent decisions, had a democratic faction in power, are so classified by expert historians, and were colonies of democracies that practiced democracy. They then compared clear democracies, questionable democracies, and nondemocracies, and a
category of states with an unknown regime type. Even "clear democracies" had fewer constitutional restraints than would be acceptable
in a coding of modern states, they noted. Carol Ember, Melvin Ember and Russett (1992:579) lowered the definitional threshold in preliterate societies to equivalence "democracy" with a high level of political participation.

One of the few efforts to measure differences in "democraticness" between dyads contrasted two of the five components—executive constraints with institutionalization (Partell and Palmer 1999:
395). Two studies used only executive constraints (Kiser, Drass,
Brustein 1995; Davenport 2004:549). According to Kristian Gleditsch and Michael Ward (1997:380), executive constraints mostly
defined degree of "democracy," and the other components contribut-

ed little. In other words, the five components could be used separately, but most researchers cut corners and thus prefer not to do so. Some even use a mysterious measure multiplying concentration, a component of democracy, by the democracy score. Lately, how to operationalize define "democracy" has become a very esoteric but shallow debate (Russett 2011; Dafoe and Russett 2013; Dafoe, Oneal, Russett 2013; Mousseau 2013a; Mousseau, Orsun, Ungere 2013).

Although a democracy scale might include a wide range, from well-established democracies, to recently-established democracies, to proto-democracies, to nondemocracies taking steps toward democratization, researchers thus have instead preferred dichotomies and trichotomies (democracy, anocracy, autocracy). Indeed, efforts appear to have been undertaken to cook the scales so that certain countries will be excluded from the rank of "democracy," as Russett (1993b:16) expressed the worry that "lowering the standards" would increase the likelihood "that some events will be labeled wars between democracies—events that many writers contend are, at most, exceedingly rare." Accordingly, some scholars have refused to allow a country to be counted as a democracy until various criteria are met criteria for at least three years in a row (Rummel 1997; Russett 1993b:16; Schweller 1992:240; Weart 1994:305, 1998; Schwartz and Skinner 2002), though Ray (1998, 2003) was less insistent about the need for democracy to "mature."

As several researchers have pointed out, Germany was one of the most progressive states in 1914, having granted universal free health care and universal suffrage (examples of social and procedural democracy). But Germany of that era is coded as a "nondemocracy" in many studies of the "democratic peace" phenomenon (Mearsheimer 1990:51; Sørensen 1992:411; Oren 1995), often because coding rules have changed (Gates, Knutsen, Moses 1996:4). Several scholars have protested that Germany was as much a democracy in 1914 as the democracies that fought on the other side in World War I (Doyle 1983:216-17; Oren 1995; Kegley and Hermann 1996a,b; Peceny 1997). Udo Oren (1995) has attacked Russett's definition of "democracy" as Americentric (cf. Spiro 1994; Gowa 1995). For Cohen (1994), the definition of "democracy" pertains to North Atlantic countries and is very subjective.

What is perceived as a democracy may be subject to bias when states are in conflict. Despite Polity's classification of Spain as a semi-democracy on objective grounds in 1898, Russett (1993b:19) reclassified Spain so that the Spanish-American War would not be an exception to the "democratic peace" thesis; his reasoning was that U.S. policymakers *perceived* Spain as a nondemocracy, but ironically Spain also considered the United States to be illiberal (Owen 1997b). Mark Peceny (1997) has pointed out that the Spanish-American War was one of conquest. Indeed, one reason for seizing the Philippines was the fear that otherwise a German squadron of ships, then engaged in helping the Spanish to hold back the Americans, was poised to do so as soon as Madrid surrendered (Lind 2006:82-83).

Although the Athens-Syracuse war is excused as Athenian misperception of Syracuse as a nondemocracy (Russett and Antholis 1992:425), Tobias Bachteler (1997:320) disagreed strongly. Azar Gat (2006:6) has also objected to the "inchoate democracy" rationalization used by Russett and Antholis to exclude interdemocracy wars so that the "democratic peace" thesis will be unchallenged.

But were Russett to take his qualification about perceptions seriously, then every war must be analyzed in terms of perceptual evidence, not just one or two cases. Indeed, the United States government deliberately misperceived other democracies as "dictatorships" to justify covert intervention in Guatemala and Iran during 1954 and 1953, respectively, and similar cases (Peceny 1997; Schwartz and Skinner 2002; cf. Rosato 2003). Thus, Russett's qualification would facilitate the identification of even more anomalies to the "democratic peace."

Classification of the United States as a "democracy" is also problematic. Because of the systematic exclusion of African Americans in many states of the United States until the Voting Rights Act of 1965, the United States has been a Herrenvolk democracy for most of its existence, and in 2013 the Supreme Court struck down the linchpin of that legislation. Some "democratic peace" researchers, nevertheless, blithely count Herrenvolk democracies as pure democracies.

What is also bothersome is that countries maintaining colonial control by force are counted as "democracies." Consider the fate of China after the First Opium War of 1839, as European powers and Japan gobbled up territorial enclaves as if picking feathers from a turkey. Similarly, after 9/11 the United States has cooperated with other governments, mainly democracies, to torture prisoners in black sites and conduct secret raids of suspected terrorists around the world (Haas 2009). How can such countries be called "democracies" when they violate the principles of the International Covenant on Civil and Political Rights with impunity?

Democracy is an ideal type, attained by no country, though some countries are arguably more democratic than others. Were we to use the standard that a state must have procedural, substantive, and social democracy to be placed high on the scale, then no democracies were even possible until women gained the franchise, public opinion matched vote counts, and citizens enjoyed the right of nonpoverty through the establishment of welfare states.

In sum, there are several operational definitions of democracy. They stress procedure more than substance. Except for some speculative theory (Mousseau 2009; Lees 2013), social democracy is mostly ignored. Problems in coding certain countries are evident, and there are "shifting thresholds" (Spiro 1994:58; Davenport 2007:100-10). Measurement problems have been identified in several studies (Chan 1983, 1994; Bueno de Mesquita and Lalman 1992; Ray 1993, 1995; Oren 1995; Henderson 2002:ch2), suggesting that definitions are being tweaked to conform to desired results. One exhaustive analysis of several operationalizations, including Polity IV, is that they have failed on various methodological grounds (Muncha and Verkuilen 2002). More than a dozen alternative measures of democracy, however, inexplicably remain unutilized (Lipset 1959; Cutright 1963; Adelman and Morris 1967; Neubauer 1967; Rustow 1967; Smith 1969; Dahl 1971; Flanigan and Fogelman 1971:461; Dick 1974; Jackman 1975; Frakt 1977; Hewitt 1977; Bollen 1980, 1991, 1993; Schoultz 1981b; Muller 1988; Spalding 1988; Arat 1991; Coppedge and Reinecke 1991; Gasiorowski 1991, 1996; Hadenius 1992; Alvarez, Cheibub, Limongi, Przeworski 1996). Only Karen Rasler and William Thompson (2005), Quackenbush and Rudy (2009), and Erik Gartzke (2007) have used the data of Vanhanen (2000) to cross-check results. The latest dataset (Boix, Miller, Rosato 2013) appears to be an update of Vanhanen.

The possibility that the databases and scales are multidimensional has never been tested. Given the variety of concepts included in the term "democracy" (Table 3.1), the unidimensional assumption is clearly insupportable.

The task of operationalizing "democracy" more clearly, consistently, and honestly remains. A simple factor analysis would clarify the dimensionality of components of democracy, but no researcher has done so, even Rummel, who pioneered the use of factor analysis in political science. As noted below, some researchers have attempted to explain that the "democratic peace" exists because of constitutional or structural constraints without decomposing the Polity variable into its five components. Their claim is tautological: Structural constraints (legislative checks on the executive) is one of the five definitional components in the Polity data in the first place!

Statistical Methods

Rather than treating "democracy" as a multidimensional concept with many subdimensions that might differentially predict war and peace outcomes, "democratic peace" researchers primarily use logit analysis, which is designed for dichotomies, using the "democracy" score of the least democratic in each pair. Even though the Polity dataset has a 21-point scale for "democracy," the design of "democratic peace" research often requires a cutoff point on the scale so that some countries can be called democratic and others nondemocratic. One research study dichotomized the sample into "high democracies" and "low democracies," but again used the same scale (Bliss and Russett 1998). Findings based on dichotomous variables are inherent shallow. By using pooled data from pairs of countries, two studies claimed to find heterogeneities in the data (King and Zeng 2001a,b; Beck, King, Zeng 2004).

Case Studies

Most studies on the "democratic peace" tend to be statistical. Case studies have been examined when researchers have found deviations from generalizations (Ray 1995; Russett 1993b). Both forms of research are legitimate, but case studies have more inherent validity, since statistical regularities may be artifacts of operationalizations, research techniques, and the quality of data. Those seeking to refute the "democratic peace" thesis often use case studies, which have served to erode the confidence that the "democratic peace" is anything but a statistical oddity (Brecher and Wilkenfeld 1997; Elman 1997d; Kacowicz 1998; Peceny 1999; Clark and Nordstrom 2003).

However, a recent study may set the trend. After demonstrating a connection between democracy and territorial disputes, Douglas Gibler and Jaroslav Tir (2014) offer a case study about Central Europe and the former Yugoslavia as a validation exercise after they present quantitative cross-sectional results.

Sample of Countries

Sampling bias is a perennial problem in the social sciences, as one can prove a thesis by excluding inconvenient cases. Certain types of countries are curiously included or excluded from analysis in the "democratic peace" literature. There is much agreement that there have been too few democracies for most of the research to be statistically meaningful (Doyle 1983; Mearsheimer 1990:50; Wayman 2002). For Arend Lijphart (1984), there were only 21 stable democracies before the end of the Cold War.

Some countries are included in the samples even though they are not democratic. The inclusion of Herrenvolk regimes, such as apartheid South Africa, as "democracies" is unacceptable. Countries that maintain colonies or imperial possessions are also included in the sample. Although colonies sometimes practice democracy, according to Russett and Antholis (1992:419-21), no researchers of more contemporary eras included the colonies of Britain, France, the Netherlands, or the United States, whether the colonies practiced democracy or not, but they accepted all four countries as "democracies" even when the colonized had strong objections. Thus, some of the bloodiest wars fought by democracies, involving colonial suppression of Third World countries, have been excluded from the sample of cases. Interestingly, Russett and Antholis (1992) found no confirmation of the "democratic peace" hypothesis in their study of the Greek city-states, which admitted colonies of democracies into the sample.

Most scholars exclude nonsovereign states, though Lewis Richardson's *Statistics of Deadly Quarrels* (1960b) included nonsovereign entities in a sample of contemporary cases to study causes of war. So did Arthur Banks (1972), David Wilkinson (1980), and Edward Mansfield and Jack Snyder (1995).The colonies that became the United States exhibited some characteristics of democracy before being recognized collectively as an independent state by European countries, but they have not been separately counted. To be "sovereign," to satisfy one democratic theorist, a country must be internationally recognized (Russett 1993b:17). But no researcher has ever included the Kingdom of Hawai'i, fully democratic and recognized diplomatically by Britain, France, and the United States from 1840. In another study, indigenous cultures are included (Ember, Ember, and Russett 1992).

Mini-states are sometimes excluded. Small and Singer (1982; cf. Reiter 2001) excluded states with less than 500,000 persons; their "systemic wars" were between countries that were recognized by both Britain and France, whereas wars involving countries not recognized by both countries were called "extra-systemic." Gurr's data initially imposed a requirement of 1,000,000 persons but later was lowered to 500,000. Other studies relax population exclusion criteria. The Kingdom of Hawai'i, with a population of about 100,000 at the end of the nineteenth century (Haas 2012a:Table 8), has not been on any list of countries sampled.

Such sampling clearly has Catch-22 proportions: For example, democracies engaging in colonialism need not be embarrassed by their brutal suppression of political freedom. Findings from such research are thus culture-bound, implying a double standard in which colonial powers are allowed to be democracies while they were preventing their colonies from becoming democracies. As Ray (1998: 89) once said, the use of a restrictive sample of democracies "might be disparagingly termed public relations"—that is, a way to cook the data to ensure that the thesis will survive scrutiny.

Regions

The image of peaceful Europe is often in the minds of researchers of the "democratic peace." However, two studies have demonstrated quite different results for various regions (Crescenzi and Enterline 1999; Goldsmith 2006). Regional zones of peace have interested many other scholars (Haas 1989, 2013; Weart 1994; Kacowicz 1995; Bachteler 1997; cf. Gowa and Mansfield 1993; Gowa 1994; Henderson 1999:222-26). The implication is that studies involving all countries from all regions have missed important cultural and regional differences.

Dyads

Some studies have appropriately restricted the sample to contiguous country dyads or to dyads in which one country is a major power (Weede 1992; Russett 1993b:20-21; Maoz and Russett 1993; Russett and Maoz 1993; Oneal, Oneal, Maoz, Russett 1996; Lemke and Reed 1996; Russett and Oneal 2001), though wars involving major powers may be on the decline today (Mueller 1989:5). However, many disputes involve noncontiguous countries (Mitchell and Prins 1999). Schweller (1992:236) analyzed wars involving only major power "preventive wars," that is, aggression "motivated by the fear that one's military power and potential are declining relative to that of a rising adversary." Weede (1992) excluded dyads of countries that are allied to superpowers so that he would only have only pairs of countries that could potentially project power toward one another.

Russett and Zeev Maoz (1993:74) excluded two types of "implausible" dyads—those between Belgium and the Netherlands and their respective former colonies, as well as countries joining collective security actions in Korea and Vietnam. Why the exclusion they did not say, but they noted that sampling bias did not result, as the cases were deemed not democracy-democracy dyads.

The dyadic approach has been faulted on several methodological grounds (Green, Kim, Yoon 2001; Croco and Teo 2005). Quackenbush and Rudy (2009:273) restricted their sample to politically active dyads in which one country initiates action toward another.

Sample of International Conflicts

"International conflict" can be measured along a continuum from diplomatic protests to verbal threats to acts of coercion to armed violence (wars) by one state against another (cf. Most and Starr 1983: 139). Intensities of events (aggressiveness, casualties, duration, troop strength), which may be scaled, are sometimes counted along with numbers of events (cf. Duvall 1976:72-74). Depending on which measures are used, findings may differ (cf. Mansfield 1988). Accordingly, some researchers exclude "big wars" (Bueno de Mesquita 1990; Kugler 1990; Midlarsky 1990; Thompson 1990). One study (Kiser, Drass, Brustein 1995) uses data from 1400-1700 for four European countries (Dupuy and Dupuy 1997; Kohn 1987).

Wars. The focus in most early studies is on wars, which are usually defined as "state-supported organized violence across political boundaries" (Weart 1994:301). But not all wars qualify. Some scholars insist upon a minimum of battle deaths—100 deaths (Russett 1967; Russett and Momsen 1975; Butterworth 1976; Weede 1992), 200 deaths (Weart 1994:3011), 317 deaths (Richardson 1960b:73; Banks 1972; Wilkinson 1980), 950 deaths (Russett 1993b:12-13), or—the most widely used source—1,000 deaths (from Small and Singer 1982). Rummel (1983b) also consulted *Freedom at Issue* to ensure a wider sample.

Another cutoff figure relates to the number of troops involved— 500 (Kiser, Drass, Brustein 1995), or 1,000 (Small and Singer (1982:ch4) or 50,000 (Babst 1964, 1972). The list of Istvan Kende (1982) has no casualty or troop minimum; in one study, his data were compared with Singer and Small (Benoit 1996). But evidence has arisen that democracies only enter wars in which they expect few casualties (Valentino, Huth, Croco 2010). In other words, limiting the sample based on levels of war deaths may bias results.

Yet another factor is whether a "war" is counted as having one data point for a year or two data points within the same year. Results differ considerably, according to Scott Bennett and Alan Stam (2000), who point out many other flaws in the research designs of "democratic peace" research.

Levels of conflict. Wars and similar phenomena have been scaled by various researchers. Stephen Salmore and Charles Hermann (1970) and Rummel (1983b) have examined the full range of foreign conflict, from verbal to physical violence, with the number of casualties at the top of the scale. Some studies (East and Gregg 1967; Feierabend and Feierabend 1972; Haas 1974; Terrell 1977) utilized the Dimensionality of Nations data of Rummel (1972:279). Salmore and Hermann used the World Event/Interaction Survey (McClelland and Hoggard 1969), which was later refined into a 15-point scale by Edward Azar (1980). Rummel (1987:114), however, objected to Azar's data because lesser forms of conflict can sum to values for higher forms of conflict. Instead, he compared data that he collected from databases of Small and Singer (1976) and Wayne Ferris (1973). According to Jack Vincent (1987a:104), Rummel's scaling criteria enabled countries that inflict a single battle death to get a higher coding than countries that "threaten . . . nuclear destruction, strengthen . . . military forces, make threatening military movements, go on alert, and call for a general mobilization." Maurice East and Phillip Gregg (1967) regressed their measure of political freedom onto threats and treaties. Singer's Correlates of War dataset has been standard for many studies.

Overt military interventions. Combat-ready military actions undertaken by regular armed forces of a country inside a foreign territory already in conflict (Tillema 1991) have been studied by Kegley and Hermann (1995a, 1996a,b, 1997a). They have asserted that interventions are the most frequent type of military force in use in the post-Cold War era. But interventions are not counted as "wars" in other studies. From 1945-1999, Jun Koga (2011) found that autocracies tended to intervene to obtain lucrative resources, whereas democracies intervened on behalf of those of the same ethnic group. Of course, before 1945, democracies were intervening to obtain colonial prizes.

Covert military operations. When carried out by democracies, "black operations," as they are sometimes called, have received much less attention. Noam Chomsky, a voice in the wilderness on the subject for quite some time, provided evidence in *Deterring Democracy* (1991) to link Washington's desire to impose hegemony on other countries with efforts to restrict debate on the subject and thus to a lesser attainment of democracy inside the United States. Steven Van Evera (1992:291) identified about a dozen instances when the United States acted to subvert democratic governments during the Cold War to prevent "Communists" from coming to power. David Forsythe (1992) cited documentation for six such cases involving violence (Iran in 1953, Guatemala in 1954, Indonesia in 1957, Brazil from 1961, Chile in 1973, Nicaragua in 1984) and three nonviolent operations (Guyana in 1953, Costa Rica in 1955, Ecuador in 1960). Georg Sørensen (1992:404) added the case of the Dominican Republic in 1965. Others have presented a variety of cases (Schraeder 1992a,b; Stedman 1993; Rosas 1994; Kegley and Hermann 1995a). The number killed by covert operations, whether by assassination, direct intervention, or paid mercenaries (Ransom 1992; Schraeder 1992a), has yet to be fully documented, though some of these cases may lie above the 1,000 threshold used for wars.

Interestingly, Russett (1993b:121-23) tried to discount covert operations against democracies as an exception to his "democratic peace" thesis, reasoning that the cases of Brazil, Chile, Guatemala, Indonesia, Iran, and Nicaragua involved countries that were "unstably democratic" and that the operations were not "wars," according to his criteria. Nonetheless, one reason for the instability was Washington's covert operations, which were promoted so that regime change would be accepted by the populations.

Militarized interstate disputes (MIDs). More recently, the unit of analysis has been explicit, government-sanctioned threats, displays, or actual uses of military force (Jones, Bremer, Singer 1996). The original dataset was developed by Azar (1980). The latest compilation includes about 5,000 MIDs from 1816 (Maoz 2005). Because there are so few wars, use of MIDs enhances the sample for "democratic peace" research. After all, some 89 percent of MIDs have escalated into war (Maoz 1982). Those studying MIDs have admitted that violent threats often occur between democracies (Maoz and Abdolali 1989; Weede 1992; Bremer 1993; Maoz and Russett 1993; Enterline 1998), but at a lower rate than disputes involving nondemocracies (Maoz and Abdolali 1989:24; Morgan and Schwebach 1992:312), and they have claimed that democracy-democracy disputes almost never escalate into war (Morgan and Schwebach 1992:314; Maoz and Russett 1993; Russett and Maoz 1993; Dixon 1993,1994; Partell and Palmer 1999; cf. Ellis, Mitchell, Prins 2010). The definition "socially organized armed combat between members of different territorial units," used for preliterate cultures, is approximately equivalent to MIDs (Ember, Ember, Russett 1992:580).

MIDs are now used more often than wars in "democratic peace" research, though there are some discrepancies in the database (Partell and Palmer 1999:393-94), leading Fredick Pearson and Robert Baumann (1993-1994) to develop a separate International Military Intervention dataset. Other databases have been used (Blechman and Kaplan 1978; Fordham and Sarver 2001). In one study, the researchers validated the MID compilation by cross-checking with *Facts on File*, *Keesing's Contemporary Archives*, and the *New York Times Index* (Mitchell and Prins 1999:173n6), finding that about half of the conflicts were about territorial disputes. Another source is the

SERFACS dataset of Frank Herman (1994:489-90). Senese (1999) developed a category scheme of 21 types of MIDs and collapsed them into a three-point scale (verbal threat, display of force, use of force), with war as the fourth scale item. Results appear the same for fatal and nonfatal MIDs (Mousseau 2013a). Gibler and Tir (2014) have developed a database distinguishing between conflicts involving military actions and perceived threats based on unresolved territorial problems.

Another database for MIDs is the Issue Correlates of War Project (Hensel 2001; Hensel, Mitchell, Sowers, Thyne 2008). The compilation includes territorial disputes from 1816 to 2001 and maritime/riparian disputes from 1900 to 2001. Asian disputes from 1945 to the present are in *Asian and Pacific Cooperation* (Haas 2013). One study contrasted conflict resolution methods by democracies and nondemocracies (Ellis, Mitchell, Pins 2010). Arbitration cases are found in Jackson Ralston (1929) and Alexander Stuyt (1972).

Dispute resolution efforts. One version of "democratic peace" theory could be stated as follows: When two democracies have conflicts, such as trade disputes between Japan and the United States, there is a tendency to resolve conflicts peacefully. Accordingly, the reasons for peaceful resolution will become most evident by examining specific negotiations rather than macropolitical correlations. One such database would appear to consist of conflict management situations, such as the compendium of Robert Butterworth (1976), another the International Crisis Behavior database of Michael Brecher, Jonathan Wilkenfeld, and Sheila Moser (1988; Wilkenfeld, Brecher, Moser 1998), both covering the Cold War era. Layne (1994) and Owen (1993, 1994b) identified several more disputes, mostly for the nineteenth century. William Dixon (1993, 1994) has utilized the entire database, as updated by Hayward Alker and Frank Sherman (1986). Gregory Raymond (1994) supplemented Butterworth with several sources (Darby 1904; Levine 1971; Ralston 1929; Stuyt 1972). Maoz and Russett (1993:628; Russett and Maoz 1993:75), using the Brecher-Wilkenfeld-Moser dataset to cross-check MID data, reported on 260 cases among the 959 MID cases and 359 ICB cases. Several studies, indeed, show that respect for international legal norms (Dixon 1993, 1994; Raymond 1994; Burley 1994), support for multilateralism (Weiss, Forsythe, Coate 1994; Risse-Kappen 1995a), and foreign aid generosity (Hook 1995; Hook, Kegley, Hermann 1995) are linked both to democracies and to peaceful behavior.

Summary. Research on the "democratic peace" covers many types of foreign conflict. Covert operations and interventions appear to provide data contrary to the thesis. However, wars to impose colonialism and wars of national liberation have been excluded from the sample by definition. Although Layne (1994) and Owen (1994b) engaged in process tracing to ascertain exactly which interactions occurred in crises, most researchers are content to dissect cases into the barest of components, leaving the actual rationale for peace or war in a black box. The exclusion of internal wars by definition, David Spiro (1994:59) has objected, is "what is wrong with liberal theory."

Sample of Years

Given that wars are rare events, limited historical eras do not provide a basis for solid generalizations, as Bremer (1992:310) has cautioned. Most scholars, however, study the Cold War era primarily. Russett and Maoz (1993:73-74) have given ample reasons for believing that the "democratic peace" would be less likely in much earlier eras, but never tested their assumption. Rummel's tests initially covered the year years 1976 to 1980, and he later employed data from 1816 to 1974. Data from the Correlates of War project, which provides a database from 1816 to 1980 (Small and Singer 1982), has been used in many studies, but only a few researchers have analyzed a long time sweep (Babst 1964, 1972; Small and Singer 1976; Rummel 1983b; Domke 1988; Morgan and Schwebach 1992; Schweller 1992:252; Russett 1993b:ch1, Raymond 1994). Antholis and Russett (1992) surveyed 434 to 405 BCE in their study of Greek city-states. The study of preliterate cultures (Ember, Ember, Russett 1992) did not specify a time frame.

Small and Singer (1976) and Chan (1984) counted war-years. Rummel's principal unit of analysis, the conflict dyad-year (Rummel 1983b), has been accepted by many others (Vincent 1987a,b; Maoz and Abdolali 1989; Bremer 1992, 1993; Ember, Ember, Russett 1992; Morgan and Schwebach 1992; Russett and Antholis 1992; Weede 1992; Maoz and Russett 1993; Russett 1993b:ch1; Oneal, Oneal, Maoz, Russett 1996).

Dyad sample. The use of dyads can affect the sample size considerably. In one case, according to Vincent (1987a), Rummel computed a correlation based on 6 cases. In other studies, the number of dyads has ranged from 40 (Leng 1993) to 202,778 (Bremer 1992), though in the latter study only 85 dyad-years involved war (.0004 percent of the cases). And most wars involve contiguous countries. Further limiting wars to instances of first initiation (Bremer 1992) means that the only World War II dyad in the sample is Germany-Poland (Rakenrud and Hegre 1997).

According to Spiro (1994:65-76), the hypergeometric probability of war between democracies is such that the total wars studied by "democratic peace" researchers is not statistically significant. Mearsheimer (1990:50-51) and Layne (1994:7) have further noted that the world has had few democracies and few wars, so the case for the "democratic peace" is weak, especially since there are so many deviant cases.

There has been a tendency to use conflict cases without control groups. Relationships that hold with conflict dyads may also apply to nonconflict dyads, and findings may be spurious (Bremer 1992:310; cf. Most and Starr 1983). Accordingly, some studies have compared actual number of democracy-democracy wars with expected values (Maoz and Abdolali 1989; Bremer 1992, 1993; Russett and Antholis 1992; Weede 1992; Maoz and Russett 1993; Russett and Maoz 1993). Weede (1992) also contrasted democracy-democracy dyads that consist of Western alliance partners with those outside the Western alliance structure.

Longitudinal studies. Most research designs are satisfied with snapshots of conflicts—that is, they aggregate all cases into a single sample. However, some studies have employed cross-temporal analyses or examine dispute escalation (Banks 1972; Vincent 1987a,b; Rummel 1987; Domke 1988; Wilkinson 1980; Dixon 1993, 1994; Maoz and Russett 1993; Russett and Maoz 1993). Methodological criticism has emerged as a result (Beck, Katz, Tucker 1998; Green, Kim, Yoon 2001; Beck and Katz 2001; Oneal and Russett 2001). Farber and Gowa (1995) separated their sample into pre- and post-1945 eras, finding no "democratic peace" in the earlier era. Then they found no "democratic peace" before 1914, when democracies were rare (Farber and Gowa 1995; Gowa 1999).

In short, despite much sophistication in data manipulation, the scope of findings is largely restricted to the Cold War era, when democracies banded together to contain the Soviet bloc. If conflicts between democracies evolve peacefully over time, as the "democratic peace" thesis expects, more cross-temporal research designs are needed in the future.

Deviant Cases

A significant problem is to deal with cases where democracies have been at war with one another, thus deviating from the supposed "law." Rummel (1983b:29) found only one "clear case of violence or war unqualified by very unusual or mitigating circumstances" that would serve to falsify the dyadic proposition. "Democratic peace" researchers have been eager to use any picayune reason to explain away any apparent cases that contradict the "democratic peace law," an "intellectual suppleness" to which Layne (1994:40; cf. Schwartz and Skinner 2002:159) has objected. Thus, the number of wars between democracies was reduced from 10 to 8 in Polity III compared to Polity IIId, and the number of MIDs involving democratic dyads was cut from 167 to 150 cases (McLaughlin, Gates, Hegre, Gissiner, Gleditsch 1998:239). Accordingly, a review of possible anomalies is in order (see Appendix).

Many scholars seek to wipe the slate of wars between democracies clean. Babst (1964, 1972) led the way by excluding the War of 1812 because the British parliament did not choose the prime minister until 1832. He excluded Germany as a democracy in 1914 because the head of state chose the head of government. Babst also refused to accept the American Civil War and the Boer Wars because one party was nonsovereign. Rummel (1983a:29-30) dismissed the Israeli attack on the *USS Liberty* in 1967 because Israel was too socialist. Doyle (1983:213) threw out the Ecuador-Perú conflict of 1863 because their democracies were less than three years old. Similar examples of cognitive dissonance pervade those desperate to keep the "democratic peace" alive.

After stating the hypothesis that "democratically governed states rarely go to war with each other," Russett and Antholis (1992:1) counted 36 dyads from 14 cases apparently involving democracies in Hellenic times. Rather than accepting these cases as disproof of the hypothesis, they instead concluded that the data "neither clearly confirms nor clearly disconfirms the hypothesis" because the evidence is ambiguous regarding the number of casualties, some regimes were colonies, and a faction was allied with undemocratic Sparta (ibid., p.424).

John Ferejohn and Frances Rosenbluth (2008:21) found that democracies during the Renaissance were more prone to war than nondemocracies. They cited the writing of Niccolò Machiavelli (1517), who argued that democracies can better mobilize popular support. They applied the same logic to Athenian aggressiveness, the fact that Rome became more warlike after citizens were given the vote. Britain increased its empire after the franchise was extended, and American presidents have repeatedly ignored constitutional checks on executive power

The Yanomamo settlements on the Brazil-Venezuela border has been admitted as one possible exception, though participatory deliberation is infrequent (Ember, Ember, Russett 1992:584). The Cuna, a democratic community living on an island off Panamá, were often attacked by Spain (ibid., p. 593), but fought a brief independence war with Panamá in 1925 (Howe 1998). The Mapuche of Chile have also been identified as a democratic people (Russett, Ember, Ember 1993:113). Although some indigenous cultures were randomly selected by the authors for the study, some had already been coded without a random selection process, perhaps suggesting that there might be a sampling bias, with more than two exceptions.

Bremer (1992:329) has attributed two more anomalies to faulty coding by Gurr and associates: Belligerents in the Franco-Thai War of 1940 are classified as democracies in the Gurr database, but Bremer noted that the classification of France as a democracy is incorrect, as the Vichy regime came to power just before entering the war. The Second Kashmir War of 1965, similarly, followed a sharp reduction in Gurr's democratic score for Pakistan.

In the Six-Day War of 1967 between Israel and its neighbors, democratic Lebanon used its air force rather than using its infantry as cannon fodder to sacrifice sufficient casualties for inclusion in a social science sample. The American war to defeat the constitutionally-established Malolos Republic of the Philippines is excluded because the latter regime did not have time to hold an election, but ignores the fact that Washington first recognized the republic as independent in 1898 and then crushed the new regime through massive bloodshed by 1901 (Hall 1964:768; Kessler 1992:270).

Ray (1995:104-22), citing many researchers, listed 21 possible exceptions. After reiterating some of the above disqualifications, he winnowed out several more cases—the Anglo-Dutch War of 1780-1783 and Anglo-French War of 1792-1802 (because so few were eligible to vote in England), the Swiss Civil War of 1847 (because only about 100 persons died), World Wars I and II (because the German states had executives with considerable power). The rest involved nonpeaceful transfers of power—Belgian Independence War of 1830-1831, Ecuadorian-Peruvian War of 1981, and the wars of succession in the former Soviet Union and Yugoslavia (see Appendix).

While Spiro (1994:59-62) sought to refute the rationale for some of the various exceptions delineated above, Layne (1994:14-38) found exceptions to "democratic peace" theory by process tracing of the *Trent* Affair (Britain and the United States, 1861), Venezuela crisis (Britain and the United States, 1895-1896), Fashoda crisis (Britain and France, 1898), and the Ruhr crisis (France and Germany, 1923). Layne also footnoted (ibid., p. 6) other possible cases (Anglo-French relations, 1832-1848; Franco-Italian relations, late 1880s-early 1890s; Samoan crises of 1889 and 1899; Moroccan crises of 1905-1906). Owen (1994b:114-19), however, differed from Layne's interpretations in two cases, thereby demonstrating that prior researcher bias may have much to do with what is or is not considered anomalous.

Weart (1994:315-16, 1998) has provided one of the longest list of deviant cases. His fascinating narrative finds democratic-type consultation processes not only in the classical Athenian era but also in the Middle Ages and early modern Europe, including many anomalies not mentioned by other scholars. In his first article, he provided reasons for rejecting democratic dyads at war for various reasons. In his book, he was more inclusive, finding democratic processes within states that are not democratic in the modern sense.

Another long list of militarized disputes between democracies, 97 in all, is contained in the Polity dataset (Mitchell and Prins 1999). Wars between the United States and democratic indigenous peoples of North America certainly deserve some attention (Stannard 1992; Tebbel and Jennison 1960, Utley and Washburn 1977). Weart (1998:306) identified the war waged by the State of Georgia on the

Cherokee Nation, which led to the "Trail of Tears." The Comanche, for example, held annual meetings for deliberation, had recognized boundaries (Comanchería), were sophisticated negotiators, and were diplomatically recognized by México, Texas, and the United States (Hoebel 1940; DeLay 2008). The 1890 massacre at Wounded Knee is perhaps the best known incident of a democracy attacking an indigenous democratic people, the Lakota, with about 300 murdered in a single major confrontation (Brown 1971).

Other anomalies have yet to confront the literature. In one deviant case, the American consul assigned to the Kingdom of Hawai'i ordered Marines to land in Honolulu during 1893, the capital city of a progressive democratic state, internationally recognized as the world's first to have compulsory universal primary education for all citizens. The marines soon placed Queen Lili'uokalani under house arrest, lowered the Hawaiian flag, raised the American flag, and a group of expatriates, mostly Americans, awaited word from Washington that the islands were to be placed under the jurisdiction of the United States. Rather than resisting with bloodshed, thus qualifying as a war in future compendia by researchers of international relations, the reigning queen and Native Hawaiian majority expected the act of war to be disavowed. Indeed, President Grover Cleveland, explicitly considering the consul's action to violate international law, recalled the consul, gave the order for American troops to lower the Stars and Stripes and to return to their ships. Although the American flag came down, troops remained in Pearl Harbor. The expatriate conspirators proclaimed a Republic of Hawai'i in 1895 and lobbied Congress and the next president, William McKinley, for annexation. In 1898, annexation was effected by a joint resolution of both houses of Congress because there were insufficient Senate votes to adopt a treaty of annexation, again in violation of international law and without a plebiscite. Hawai'i has remained militarily occupied by the United States ever since, never allowed a plebiscite on the question of independence (Dudley and Agard 1990), though a majority of voters accepted statehood in 1959.

According to the terms of the Geneva Accords of 1954, Vietnam was to be temporarily partitioned at the Perfume River for two years. The Democratic Republic of Vietnam, which supported democratic elections to determine whether the country would be unified, continued to operate in the North. From 1954, the United States stepped in to prevent elections in the South, supporting instead a regime that soon proclaimed itself without popular elections. The North then sought to liberate the South by force (Kahin 1986:ch3). In the process, the United States bombed democratic Cambodia from 1964 and continued doing so until covert aid toppled the government in 1970; Cambodians killed from American aggression are estimated at from 275,000 to 826,000 (Kaplan 1999:A33; Herold 2010; Haas 2012b). The Cambodian case is perhaps the most egregious of all the deviant cases.

In 1961, Britain announced a decision to give up the colonies of Sabah and Sarawak, and Singapore—also without a plebiscite—to democratic Malaya, which had been granted independence in 1948, thereby creating Malaysia by 1963. As two colonies, hitherto known as North Borneo, were adjacent to Indonesian provinces on what Jakarta calls the island of Kalimantan, democratically-elected President Sukarno, seeking to cement his slim majority in a multiparty state with free elections, dispatched troops to the borders of the provinces, still under British rule. Border clashes occurred until 1966. No one consulted with international relationists on how many persons to kill in order to qualify the militarized dispute as a war, but democracies were indeed fighting (Gordon 1966:ch3). And the issue is still not settled (Grant 2013).

In 2001, some American officeholders had what to them seemed a bright idea: If they could create democracies, they could bring peace. After attacks on Afghanistan and Iraq under various pretexts, precarious democratic forms of government were established. But both are experiencing civil war and problems of terrorism.

Meanwhile, Israel and the United States threaten war with Iran, which has had a democratically elected if illiberal government from 1989. Tehran, meanwhile, refuses to recognize the sovereign state of Israel as legitimate. But was the United States illiberal before the Voting Rights Act of 1965? Is Israel illiberal for its occupation of the Palestinian territories?

Another bizarre case involves Israel, which has had serious security problem from the beginning in 1948. In 1993, Israel accepted the Oslo Accords, which recognized a Palestianian Authority for administrative control of Israeli-occupied Palestine territory. In 2005, Israel evacuated the Gaza Strip, which thus became the only part of Palestine to have a semblance of autonomous sovereignty. Then in 2006, those governed by the Palestianian Authority were allowed to hold parliamentary elections as a preliminary to the establishment of a separate sovereign state. When Hamas gained a slim majority of parliamentary seats, the peace process virtually ended. During subsequent violence, Hamas ejected Fatah from the Gaza Strip despite the establishment of a coalition government with Fatah, the other Palestinian political partner. Egypt then moved its embassy from the Gaza Strip to the West Bank. Hamas, with arms smuggled through tunnels from Egypt, then began to fire artillery on Israeli targets, leading to countermeasures including invasions in 2008 and 2012. Nevertheless, the Palestine State was officially declared sovereign by the United Nations in 2012. Violence across borders continues.

Most "democratic peace" researchers have been quick to dismiss anomalies. Analyzing some of the deviant cases, one study found that hostile actions by one democracy are likely to be shorter, and at a lower level of hostility (fewer casualties), and reciprocated proportionally if at all (Wayman 2002). But the same study indicated that democracies have been so few historically that generalizations from the findings can only be considered tentative.

Those who spend some time to address each case find reasons for exclusion and move on, not stopping to think that democracies have acted in much the same manner—that is, not having the slightest qualms of conscience while butchering native populations at home and abroad. Preferring to deal only with "coherent," "mature," and "stable" democracies, when the same regimes prevent coherence, maturity, and stability abroad, can be seen as clearly ethnocentric, an attempt to ask darker-skinned peoples to go to the back of the bus while serious research is in progress.

The anomalies listed in the Appendix may or may not be numerous enough to reverse the sign of a correlation coefficient, but they do call into question the fundamental design of existing research on the "democratic peace." Small and Singer (1976) found 11 democracy-democracy dyads among 325 total war dyads and dismissed the idea of a "democratic peace." The 85 democracy dyads-years in the sample of Bremer (2002) are dwarfed by the number of unexplained deviant cases in the Appendix!

Surveys

Very few studies have employed surveys (Layne 1994; cf. Owen 1993, 1994b; Senese 1997a; Braumoeller 1997). One study argued that public opinion was primarily responsible for being skeptical about entering wars, but did not use survey data (Reiter 1995). Gordon Henderson (2006) has made a particularly eloquent plea for the use of more survey data in "democratic peace" research, as such evidence is required if the Kantian paradigm of peaceful republics is to be fully tested. The logical implication of his jeremiad is that the Kantian agenda has been castrated because the public has largely been left out of consideration. The survey research of Michael Tomz and Jessica Weeks (2013), thus, is greatly welcomed. Their finding that the contemporary public in Britain and the United States opposes military aggression toward another democracy is a breakthrough, though an opinion study limited in time and place.

Conclusion

The search for statistical regularities is only one route to knowledge. Another route is to build knowledge up from individual cases, as Russett (1970) himself argued some time ago. Rather than sweeping more than 100 cases that contradict the "democratic peace" under a definitional rug, intellectual honesty requires an explanation for why dozens of democracy-democracy fatal dyads are found along with democracy-democracy peace dyads, and why democracies are so warlike (cf. Meehan 1968). Although the Wikipedia website for "democratic" theory lists several anomalous cases, advocates of the "democratic peace" have not bothered to contradict them. "Democratic peace" theorists have encouraged attention to regime type and militarized conflict, but their quest has boomeranged, as many skeptics have thus multiplied the number of deviant cases beyond their ability to respond.

But the simple democracy→peace "finding" is assumed without reflection on problems of inference. Those problems are identified in the following chapter.

4

Inference Problems

In the social sciences, where experiments are rare, causation is difficult to establish. For a "law" to be accepted, there must be agreement that a certain amount of evidence permits a particular inference (cf. Lerner 1960). When a strong correlation is found between two variables, alternative explanations for the relationship must be ruled out before causation can be inferred. Yet Russett and associates have claimed to be disinterested in causality (Dafoe, Oneal, Russett 2013: 202-3)! Since a "law" requires causality, and explanations without causality are mostly pre-theories or tendency statements, the most inveterate "democratic peace" researchers have inflicted serious damage to their pretensions to have a theory (cf. Beck and Jackman 1998). And now several alternative models compete among "democratic peace" researchers:

Sufficient Relationship (democracy → peace)

Let us assume that the relationship to be explained is a bivariate relationship with no exogenous or intervening variables, as many researchers have implied. "Democratic peace" researchers, thus, would make democracy a sufficient condition for peace. Indeed, Nils Gleditsch (1995:318) has claimed that a democratic dyad is "a near perfect sufficient condition for peace," and Russett (1996:177) has agreed. Do they really believe that the world was never at peace until two democracies first emerged on the planet?

Necessary But Not Sufficient Relationship
(democracy+X → peace).

If democracy is a helpful condition to create peace but insufficient by itself, then the question is what other elements are needed. The concept of a "capitalist peace" could presumably supply that X if democracies alone are capitalist, but capitalism has long become accepted in undemocratic countries. Singapore is firmly committed to capitalism, is not democratic, and is quite peaceful (Haas 1999, 2014b).

Bivariate Relationship (democracy$_1$ → peace$_1$)

If democracy is one factor in accounting for peace, but some democracies are more peaceful than others, the best way to proceed is to employ Louis Guttman's (1951) facet theory approach by dimensionalizing both concepts in order to determine which subdimensions of "democracy" are consistently related to which subdimensions of "peace." For example, does one particular aspect of democracy consistently correlate with peaceful behavior in relation to MIDs but not wars? As noted above, one might contrast procedural democracy, substantive democracy, and social democracy, and a second facet might dimensionalize types of conflict from nonlethal to lethal. Yet no such exercise has yet emerged.

Another way of dimensionalizing democracy is ontological— that is, "democracy" could be defined in terms of ideas and norms rather than behavioral and institutional practices. As Owen (1994b: 102) has suggested, facets of democracy may interact in some complex way. Since democracies go to war as frequently as nondemocracies, one facet of "democracy" might account for peace with other democracies, and a second facet might account for war with nondemocracies. But no such study exists.

Intervening Relationship (democracy → X →peace)

If there is an important intervening variable, then there would be no correlation between democracy and peace—no "democratic peace." Given the high correlation presumably derived thus far between democracy and peace, one might expect researchers to avoid this line of inquiry. Nevertheless, there is some speculation of this sort, as noted in the chapter to follow on theoretical explanations.

Exogenous Relationship (X → democracy; X → peace)

If the same variable accounts for both democracy and peace, then the democracy→peace relationship is a spurious, trivial finding (cf. Gleditsch 1992:371-72). But what variable might be independently responsible for both the incidence of democracies and the incidence of peace? Russett (1993b:10), for example, has suggested that deterrence operating during the Cold War accounted for lack of wars between democracies from 1946 to 1989. Did the Cold War also encourage Western countries to become more democratic by divesting themselves of their colonies and enforcing civil rights for minorities? Some observers believe so (Fraser 2013). Weede (2004) has argued that economic development and trade interdependence are exogenously associated with both democracy and an absence of foreign war, though his finding is disputed (Goemans 2004; Kim and Rousseau 2005).

For Michael Mousseau (2000, 2005, 2013b), capitalist contract-intensive economies, being more profitable, replaced clientelist economies in what Karl Polanyi (1944) called the "great transformation." To sustain an economy based on impersonal contracts rather than personal relationships requires a rule of law of the sort best provided in democratic systems. Similarly, contract-based global trade is best assured when the world system is peaceful. Thus, the rise of contract-intensive economies may account for both the flourishing of democracy and the flowering of peace. Similar results are found in other studies (Gat 2005; Gartzke 2007; Choi 2011). Mousseau (2013a) has further clarified that the "democratic peace" washes out when controlling for contract-intensive economies. In another study, Gibler and Tir (2010) found that settled boundaries are the basis for both the viability of democracies and the rise of peaceful relations from 1945 to 2000.

Probabilistic Relationship

If democracies have higher propensities toward peace than nondemocracies (say, .02 and .09, respectively), then the probability of a
peaceful outcome between two democracies will be higher
($.9^2=.0081$) than the probability of a peaceful outcome between a
democracy and a nondemocracy (.0018), which in turn will exceed
the probability of peace between two nondemocracies (.0004). Such
statistical probabilities (Farber and Gowa 1997:407) are confounded
by the finding thus far observed that the probability of a peaceful relationship is no higher for the nondemocracy-nondemocracy dyad
than for the democracy-nondemocracy dyad. Nevertheless, some
"democratic peace" proponents have identified the relationship as
probabilistic without stating the probabilities (Slantchev, Alexandrova, Gartzke 2005). They presumably expect that a multiple re-
gression equation will prove that democracy is the major factor
alongside minor factors, but aside from research by Gartzke (2000),
such regressions are rare. However, the best predictor of international conflict between two countries today is whether the same two
countries had conflicts in the past—and how frequently that conflict
erupted before (Crescenzi and Enterline 2001; Mousseau, Hegre,
Oneal 2003:296; Rasler and Thompson 2005).

Reverse Relationship (peace → democracy)

When Woodrow Wilson urged peace in order to make the world
"safe for democracy," his vision was of a reverse causal relationship,
albeit with the principle of self-determination as another precondi-
tion for the flourishing of democracies. Some scholars have argued
that democracies thrive during times of peace, whereas tense international environments prompt governments to stifle domestic disunity
in order to be ready for foreign threats (Hintze 1906; Wright 1942:
841; Tilly 1985; Bueno de Mesquita, Siverson, Waller 1992; Midlarsky 1995; Desch 1996; Gates, Knutsen, Moses 1996; Thompson
1996; Wolfson, James, Solberg 1998; James, Solberg, Wolfson
1999; Reiter 2001; Rasler and Thompson 2005). Other studies have
claimed to refute that proposition (Mousseau and Shi 1999; Oneal
and Russett 2000b). But even if the correlation is reversed from expectations of most "democratic peace" researchers, the positive correlation remains, though evidence for the "democratic peace" has

boomeranged again.

The establishment of a security community or a zone of peace, even when pursued by nondemocracies, may create the conditions of reduced mutual threat such that the military role will be less necessary for state survival. Three researchers have thus far found the reverse hypothesis as a function of both efforts (Thompson 1996; Haas 1989, 2013; cf. Maoz 2001).

Inverse Relationship (democracy → war)

No researcher has found that the increase in democracies worldwide has resulted in more wars, though Huntington (1991) predicted that as democracies increase, so will their conflicts over vital interests. Some studies find that transitional democracies have more wars than either democracy-democracy or nondemocracy-nondemocracy dyads (Mansfield and Snyder 1995, 1996, 2002, 2005; Ward and Gleditsch 1988; Braumoeller 2004), and others do not (Enterline 1996; Oneal and Ray 1997; Oneal and Russett 1997; Thompson and Tucker 1997).

Recursive or Simultaneous Relationship
(peace →democracy → peace)

A more complex chain of events might agree with both the bivariate and reverse models (Reuveny and Li 2003). However, if the "democratic peace" hypothesis is to be taken seriously, such relationships should fit within more complex cross-temporal theories with many conceptual elements and causal arrows. A review of theoretical explanations is therefore the next part of the critique.

No Relationship

There is a possibility that there is really no relationship between the two conceptual variables whatsoever. Indeed, Russett (1967:ch12) once discovered that there was no relation between foreign conflict behavior and statistically-derived profiles of nations. In a factor analysis of human rights data, I found that variables related to human rights, including indicators of democracy, ended up on a different (noncorrelated) factor from indicators of international conflict (Haas 1974:ch6). If there is no correlation, then the relationship is spurious because of either intervening or exogenous factors.

But the fact that democracies go to war as much as nondemocracies remains a paradox. Sebastian Rosato (2003) has suggested that something else must explain the apparent connection between democracy and peace. Moreover, "democratic peace" researchers have not explored why countries become democracies in the first place; factors favorable to democracy might also be favorable to peace.

Nevertheless, the thrust of recent research has been to find a theoretical explanation for such a peculiar bivariate relationship. Such research is marred both by the way "theory" is conceived and by the fact that contradictory findings have emerged, as noted in the following chapter.

5

Faulty Theoretical Explanations

A principal difficulty with the democracy-peace connection is that the "finding" has been presented within an atheoretical context as a "law" of international relations, though as an anomaly to those studying international conflict. For those advancing the "democratic peace," including philosopher John Rawls (1999:128), the finding is a triumph for idealist and institutionalist liberalism, a rejection of Morgenthauian realism and Waltzian neorealism. But that "victory" in the ideological battle within international relations is theological, not empirical or scientific.

In deductive science, theories are supposed to precede empirical research. "Democratic peace" researchers have inductively tried to discover a theoretical explanation without first subscribing to a clear paradigm. The result has been confusion more than clarification, as the present chapter indicates in spades. Each time a new explanation is proposed, that line of inquiry boomerangs, as contrary studies soon emerge.

Jerrod Hayes (2011) has identified three stages in the "democratic peace" agenda. The first wave, during the last years of the Cold

War, sought to establish the quantitative basis for claiming that there was a "democratic peace." In the second wave, the decade of the 1990s, when the Cold War evaporated, researchers sought an explanation for the supposed finding, but again used statistical methods. In the third wave, case studies have competed with statistical studies to disprove or solidify the original finding, with more focus on psychological elements.

But none of the "theories" reviewed below has received widespread consensus. Rosato (2005) has argued that most of the explanations reviewed below are monadic, not dyadic. Several scholars have sought to refute the various explanations because of the monadic view that democracies are as warlike as nondemocracies (Brock 2006; Daase 2006; Müller 2004). My problem with the search for an explanation is that "democratic peace" researchers do not even understand how to develop paradigms or theories based on paradigms, as I demonstrate below:

Institutional Constraints

"Democracy" can be defined in terms of various constraints ensuring that governmental decisions occur after wide consultation, such that nonleaders substantively control leaders (Dahl 1971). A common explanation, to which Immanuel Kant (1795) subscribed, is that representative forms of governance have more checkpoints, allowing various institutions, interests, and the public to veto decisions for war (democracy→constraints→peace). But which ones? Unfortunately, sophisticated definitions of "democracy" have not characterized research on the "democratic peace."

Researchers differ on the types of constraints that are most likely to inhibit foreign violence, but procedural definitions of democracy predominate (Table 5.1). Russett and Antholis (1992:427-28), however, found that some democracies fought one another in Hellenic times despite procedural restraints on Athens and other democratic states. And the fact remains that nondemocracies also have procedural restraints of various sorts.

Table 5.1 identifies the different types of institutional constraints on the left. The next two columns list studies that agree or refute that constraint as an explanation for the "democratic peace."

Table 5.1. Institutional Constraints

Constraint	Studies in Agreement	Refutations
constitutional separation of powers	Babst (1972:55); Small & Singer (1976:54); Geller (1985:181); Morgan & Campbell (1991); Bueno de Mesquita & Lalman (1992:ch5); Lake (1992); Maoz & Russett (1992,1993); Ray (1993,1995); Russett (1993b:38-40); Dixon (1994); Muller & Seligman (1994); Carmant & James (1995); Kiser, Drass, Brustein (1995); Miller (1995); Gates, Knutsen, Moses (1996); Oneal, Oneal, Maoz, Russett (1996); Rousseau, Gelpi, Reiter, Huth (1996); Gaubatz (1999); Partell & Palmer (1999); Frost (2000:9-11,114,181,323); Reiter & Stam (2002); Bueno de Mesquita, Smith, Siverson, Morrow (2003); Lipson (2003:6); Siverson (2005); Ferejohn & Rosenbluth (2008); Danilovic & Clare (2011)	Morgan & Schwebach (1992:313); Layne (1994); Weart (1994:304); Dussel (1997); Elman (1997a,b); Malin (1997); Matthews (2007); Reiter & Tillman (2002); Rosato (2003); Rousseau (2005:339); Brock (2006); Daase (2006); Müller & Wolff (2006:54); Ferejohn & Rosenbluth (2008); Downes & Lilley (2010)
limited government	Rummel (1979, 1983a,b); Manicas (1989); Weart (1994); Danilovic & Clare (2011); McDonald (2010)	Braumoeller (1997); Oren & Hays (1997); Gartzke & Hewitt (2010)
civil society	Morgan & Campbell (1991); Snyder (1991); Morgan & Schwebach (1992); Mintz & Geva (1993); Verdier (1994); Risse-Kappen (1995a); Owen (1994b, 1997a:9,37-39,45-47); Peceny (1997); Van Belle (1997); Schultz (1998)	Mueller (1973); Ostrom & Job (1986); Hagan (1993:ch5); Layne (1994); Weede (1995); Prins & Sprecher (1999); Rosato (2003:596); Leblang & Chan (2003); Lipson (2003:74)
transparency	Bueno de Mesquita & Lalman (1992); Russett (1993b:39); Fearon (1994); Reiter & Stam (1994); Risse-Kappen (1995a); Starr (1997); Schultz (1998); Bueno de Mesquita, Siverson, Woller (1999); Schultz (1999); Russett & Oneal (2001);	Jervis (1976); Layne (1994); Doyle (1997: 292); Finel & Lord (2000:166-67; Russett & Oneal (2001); Müller &

Table 5.1 (continued)		
transparency (continued)	Oneal, Russett, Berbaum (2003); Cooper (2003); Levy & Razin (2004); Choi & James (2005)	Wolff (2006:50,53); Henderson (2009); Potter & Baum (2010)
civilian control of the military	Gibler (2007,2010,2012); Choi & James (2005,2008); Gibler & Tir (2010)	Layne (1994, 1997); Elman (1997b)
substantive democracy (non-leaders control leaders)	Babst (1972); Small & Singer (1976); Stoll (1984); Ostrom & Job (1986); Russett (1989,1990:128, 1993b:38); Morgan & Campbell (1991); Morgan & Schwebach (1991); Risse-Kappen (1991:510); Bremer (1992); Bueno de Mesquita & Lalman (1992); Ember, Ember, Russett (1992:588-92); Lake (1992); Mintz & Geva (1993); Ray (1993, 1995); Fearon (1994,1997); Holsti (1996); Rousseau, Gelp, Reiter, Huth (1996); Braumoeller (1997); Elman (1997c); Oneal (1997); Schultz (1998, 2001); Smith (1998b); Bueno de Mesquita, Siverson, Woller (1999); Gaubatz (1999); Kull & Destler (1999); Gelpi & Griesdorf (2001); Russett & Oneal (2001); Reiter & Tillman (2002); Lipson (2003:6); Prins (2003); Lagazio & Russett (2004); Owen (1994b); Oneal & Russett (2005); Lektzian & Souva (2009); Choi (2010b); Tomz & Weeks (2013)	Owen (1993, 1994b:100,103); Layne (1994, 1997); Farber & Gowa (1995); Holsti (1996); Foyle (1999); Gowa (1995,1999); Ray (1995); Chan (1997:75); Friedman (1997); Kacowicz (1997); Rock (1997); Senese (1997a); Foyle (1999:264-65); Kull & Destler (1999:232-34); Schultz (1999); Barkawi & Laffey (2001:13); Ireland & Gartner (2001); Huth & Allee (2002); Schwartz & Skinner (2002:158); Rosato (2003:594-95): Rousseau (2005:339); Daase (2006); Müller & Wolff (2006:44); Danilovic & Clare (2011)

Constitutional constraints. Division of authority, separation of powers, and regular competitive elections are the key for many scholars. Aware of each other's constraints, democracies are presumed unlikely to march into war. Limited (libertarian) government is crucial for another school of thought (Lake 1992; Rummel

1983a,b; cf. Manicas 1989). In contrast, leaders who are difficult to dislodge from power are arguably more involved in war (Miller 1995). One view is that war mobilization is so slow for democracies that surprise attacks are unlikely (Russett 1993b:38-40). But secret attacks have been neither constrained nor slow in democracies (Rosato 2003; Downes and Lilley 2010).

In a comparative study, T. Clifton Morgan and Sally Howard Campbell (1991:187) reported that procedural constraints associated with democracy (using Gurr's data on competitive elections, legislative checks on the executive, and freedom of opposition parties to contest elections) were associated with less war involvement only for major powers from 1816 to 1976. Gradual reform to establish structural constraints is a more solid basis than revolutionary restructuring in peaceful democratization (Muller and Seligman 1994).

Russett and Maoz constructed a composite measure of procedural constraints from Gurr's measures of concentration of power, degree of executive constraint, decentralization (federal rather than unitary systems), and the inability of government to regulate economic and social life (Maoz and Russett 1993; Russett and Maoz 1993). They concluded, "Institutional constraints prevent escalation to war, but they do not by themselves prevent states from becoming involved in lower-level conflicts. . . . Constraining institutions . . . may in fact encourage [tough bargaining] so long as each side knows that its adversary will be tightly constrained from escalating the dispute all the way up to war" (p. 90). Thus, *perception* of constraints of other countries is the key variable, not the constraints themselves, a judgment shared in a study of the Franco-British Crisis of 1840 (Rendell 2004). Yet most "democratic peace" studies blackbox perceptions, preferring aggregate numbers and correlations.

Morgan and Valery Schwebach (1992:313-17) found democracies to be less likely to engage in militarized conflict if they have some decision-making constraints, namely, popular executive selection, political competitiveness, and separation of powers. But they also found that unconstrained autocrats were less likely to escalate to war than autocrats that had to cater to domestic elites. Indeed, they found that some autocrats were more constrained than some democrats. Another study found that the widening of the franchise improved constraints on decisionmakers to enter wars (Ferejohn and Rosenbluth 2008). But Dan Reiter and Erik Tillman (2002) found no relation between dispute initiation and either executives checked by legislatures or by political parties.

Peter Partell and Glenn Palmer (1999) have found that countries with constrained executives, whether democratic or not, tend not to escalate their disputes to the use of force. But Charles Lipson (2003: 6) has pointed out that when laws have been passed that restrain governments to use force, much effort is required to repeal the laws; constitutional constraints are even more of a barrier than statutes. For Lothar Brock (2006), nondemocracies are as unlikely to make quick decisions as democracies because they, too, encounter institutional resistance.

Limited government. The libertarian ideal of government with minimal power is an attractive explanation for Rummel (1979, 1983). But few researchers have invoked the same explanation. For Erik Gartzke and Joseph Hewitt (2010), economic liberty (free markets), not political liberty, is the key.

Civil society. Interest groups have also been viewed as a source of constraints. However, strong opposition parties have not always been found to exercise constraints on war. A party unsure of reelection may try war to get the public to rally around the flag (Russett 1990: 133-34). But public opinion can fluctuate widely.

Presidential systems with fewer political parties are less peaceful than parliamentary systems with coalition governments according to one study (Leblang and Chan 2003), a finding contradicted by two other studies (Prins and Sprecher 1999; Ireland and Gartner 2001). Parliaments may consist of coalitions of parties or majorities; in the latter case, the minority cannot stop a determined majority (Elman 1997a,b).

Yet British commercial elites having strong trade interests with Germany pressed British decisionmakers not to antagonize Berlin before World War I (Papaoanou 1996). The arms industry in democracies and nondemocracies is always happy to argue the case for war. A serious study of the role of interest groups in preventing war has yet to appear (cf. Weede 1995; Lipson 2003:74).

Transparency. Russett (1993b:39) has argued that democracies are unsuited to making surprise attacks because the transparency of democratic decision making enables objections by those opposed. Because of a free press, informing the public to beware plans for war, decision makers in democracies feel constrained from implementing decisions (Peceny 1997; Van Belle 1997). Indeed, Seung-Whan Choi and Patrick James (2006) discovered that openness was a better predictor of dyadic peace than regime type. Yet Errol Henderson (2009) found that open democracies outside Europe were not restrained from fighting each other, and of course open democracies employ the CIA and MI5 as instruments of violence.

But Bernard Finel and Kristin Lord (2000:166-67) point out that the "yellow press" is quite capable of slanting the news jingoistically; an obvious example is the Hearst press and the Spanish-American War. Although Louis Terrell (1977:106) discovered that the best predictor of foreign conflict behavior between two states was contiguity, his next best predictor was similarity in the "openness" of their polities. Yet democracies engage in covert military adventures precisely because otherwise they would be accountable (Doyle 1997:292; Russett and Oneal 2001). Robert Jervis (1976) has long pointed out the main fallacy of the transparency argument—that wars are often caused by misperceptions (cf. Henderson 2002).

Civilian control of the military. If there is a hostile neighboring state, the military will be increased to meet the challenge, but only a democracy can control the military to avoid conflict. But if "democracy" is defined as a government in which the military are subordinate to the civilian leaders, then the observation is tautological.

Substantive democracy. Popular control of decisions to go to war, should be the most important constraint in "democratic peace" theorizing. For Russett (1990, 1993b), democracies must appease many audiences or constituencies about the cost and necessity for war; that is, they face "audience costs," but he did not use public opinion data to support his claim. Presumably, a democracy may signal another democracy or even nondemocracy that the the public supports war in defense of vital interests, whereupon the latter will back down and compromise will emerge (Letkzian and Souva 2009). For Philip Potter and Matthew Baum (2010), however, the audience must learn about the issues through a free press; if the government manipulates the press, as in the prelude to the Iraq War, public support for war is a sham. Surveys reported by Michael Tomz and Jessica Weeks (2013) found that costs are much less important than morality—abhorrence of war—among the public.

However, other evidence is that the public often clamors for war while elites are more cautious or the reverse—that elites can whip up support from the public by appealing to nationalism (Yoon 1997; Owen 1994b:100,103; Foyle 1999). Charles Ostrom and Brian Job (1986) have argued that bold action for war creates public support.

On the other hand, democracies tend to have centrist politicians and a public that does not always want the instability wrought by war (Lipson 2003:6), though polarized democracies have been more likely to choose war (Müller and Wolff (2006:54). The more "veto players" in parliament, the less likely will the party in power to choose war (Choi 2010b).

War is costly, so one argument is that voters will stop leaders from running up the cost of government by embarking on war. During election campaigns, unless they are nervous about reelection, democratic leaders presumably will not make warlike actions (Smith 1998a,b; Huth and Allee 2002), as most undecided voters are more interested in pocketbook issues (Stoll 1984; Yoon 1997), though survey data show that voters in democracies are very interested in foreign policy (Jentleson and Britten 1998). The time to get support for war in democracies is after the election (Gaubatz 1999). However, Ostrom and Job (1986) have argued that bold action creates public support. And the costs of war are not spread across the public but concentrated in poor communities that lack political power. Mearsheimer (1990:49) has asserted that the public, susceptible to nationalistic appeals, rarely thinks about the costs of war, and some survey data agree (Tomz and Weeks 2013).

Contrary to the view that democratic leaders uniquely oppose war to avoid policy failure and thus defeat at the next election, undemocratic leaders who lose wars are as likely to be deposed as democratic leaders are defeated in elections under the same circumstances (Rosato 2003; cf. Downes and Lilley 2010). Gowa (1995) has also proved that nondemocratic leaders are less likely to go to war if they depend upon citizens or the nobility for taxes or depend on other review bodies for support (Kiser, Drass, Brustein 1995).

When democratic leaders suspect that their actions might be risky or unpopular, they might avoid action. Alternatively, they have pursued covert action (Morgan and Bickers 1993; Geva, deRouen, Mintz 1993; Kegley and Hermann 1995b). One example is the secret support by President Ronald Reagan for the Khmer Rouge to keep Vietnamese military power in Cambodia at bay (Haas 1991b, 2012b).

Thus, substantive democracy is both proposed and dismissed as a factor. Ember, Ember, and Russett (1992:588-92) found that the wider the political involvement in politics within indigenous cultures with substantive democracy, the less external conflict. Thomas Risse-Kappen (1991:510), comparing France, Germany, Japan, and the United States, concluded that in a democracy one set of elites can cite a peaceloving public opinion to block pressures to go to war emanating from another set of elites, whereas Owen (1994b:91; cf. Ray 1995), in process tracing of four cases, discovered that substantive democratic constraints "were nearly as likely to drive states to war as to restrain them."

Nevertheless, the argument that democracies will not go to war with one another because of the role of constraints is tautological, since "democracy" can be defined as a form of government with procedural and substantive constraints on decision makers. If democracies are supposedly less likely to go to war with other democracies because of various constraints, then why does evidence show that they are more likely to initiate war with nondemocracies (Bennett and Stam 1998; Lipson 2003:4)? Accordingly, the structure of the argument must be that some aspects of procedural democracy are related to peaceful foreign behavior, whereas other unspecified aspects are unlikely to account for peace. Looking at cases in which democracies were on the brink of war, Layne (1994) found that there was no evidence of either procedural or substantive constraints, but his evidence was questioned by Russett (1995). Then Kenneth Schultz (1999) rebutted Russett with more data. Yet the evidence is contradictory, both for procedural and substantive democracy. Since all governments have restraints on their operation, the concept of restraints washes out as too crude an explanation (Gowa 1999), especially since leaders may differ in their perception of whether the various structural barriers really constrain them (Owen 1997a; Keller 2005). David Rousseau (2005:339) concluded that constraints operate on both democracies and nondemocracies when disputes arise, but they only held back democracies when the situation escalates.

Political Culture

A common view is that democratic states have a unique culture (Kant 1795; Doyle 1986:1160-61). The content of "democratic culture" is variously defined, and it is unclear in the literature whether the democratic culture is a subdimension of democracy, a correlate of democracy, part of the definition of democracy, or an attitude separate from the procedural or substantive operation of democracy. Whereas Michael Ireland and Scott Gartner (2001) found constraints to be more important than culture in accounting for the "democratic peace," Owen (1994b:119) and Ray (1995:36-37) have considered the two explanations to be complementary.

For many scholars, attitudes and culture are more important than constraints in keeping the "democratic peace" going (O'Donnell 1978; Przeworsky 1991:178; Russett 1993b, 1995; Muller and Seligman 1994; Inglehart and Welzel 2005; Xenias 2005 "Culture" is usually defined as an integrated set of norms, so the search for a democratic culture should measure attitudes and beliefs, though Thomas Risse-Kappen (1995a) has focused on the ability of democracies to create friendships with other democracies. It is unclear whether the causation is democratic culture→democracies→peace or democracies→democratic culture→peace, as "democratic peace" researchers assume but do not directly really measure cultural norms (Table 5.2).

Table 5.2. Normative Explanations

Norm	Studies in Agreement	Refutations
liberal political principles	Rummel (1983a,b); Bueno de Mesquita & Lalman (1992: ch5); Owen (1994b); Ray (1995); Risse-Kappen (1995a); Weart (1998); Mitchell, Gates, Hegre (1999); Russett & Oneal (2001); Williams (2001); Mitchell (2002); Oneal, Russett, Berbaum (2003); Rasler & Thompson (2005); Danilovic & Clare (2007); Mitchell, Kadera, Crescenzi (2009); Crescenzi (2011); Gartzke & Weisiger (2013)	Müller & Wolff (2006:45)

norm of "bounded competition"	Dixon (1993, 1994); Russett (1993); Maoz & (1993b); Dixon & Senese (2002)	(2003); Mueller (2004); Müller Gowa (1999:19-26)
common culture	Merritt & Zinnes (1991); Maoz & Russett (1993); Weart (1994:309)	Bueno de Mesquita & Lalman (1992); Weart (1998); Russett, Oneal, Cox (2000); Letzkian & Souva (2009); Haas (2013)
cultural similarity	Haas (1974:ch5); Nincic & Russett (1979:73); Wilkinson (1980:104); Oren (1995)	Raknerud & Hegre (1997); Beck & Jackman (1998); Götze (2006)
individualism	Owen (1994b:100); Russett & Oneal (2001:66-67); Williams (2001); Henderson (2006)	Regens, Gaddie, Lockerbie (1995)
political similarity (UN voting patterns)	Kim & Russett (1996); Gleditsch & Hegre (1997); Oran & Hays (1997); Raknerud & Hegre (1997); Oneal & Russett 1997, 1998, 1999c); Gartzke (1998, 2000); Lai & Reiter (2000); Mousseau (2000, 2003); Werner (2000); Peceny, Beer, Sanchez-Terry (2002); Mousseau, Hegre, Oneal (2003); Beck, King, Zeng (2004); Quackenbush & Rudy (2006)	Oneal & Russett (1999c); Reuveny & Li (2003:341)
regional affinity	Russett & Antholis (1992); Mitchell & Prins (1999); Maoz (2001:165); Gleditsch (2003); Cederman & Gleditsch (2004); Senese (2005); Thompson & Tucker (2005); Enterline & Greig (2006: 155); Gleditsch & Ward (2006); Weede (2007) Vasquez & Elmon (2011)	Maoz & Russett (1992); Kacowicz (1997); Legro (1997); Malin (1997); Russett, Oneal, Cox (2001); Reiter & Stam (2002)
alliance solidarity	Small & Singer (1976); de Vries (1990); Siverson & Starr (1991:93); Ostrom & Job (1996); Maoz & Russett (1992, 1993); Dixon (1993, 1994); Russett (1993b); Farber & Gowa (1995);	Bueno de Mesquita (1981); Kim (1989); Mearsheimer 1990; Ray 1990; Siverson & Emmons (1991); Siverson & Starr (1991); Bremer (1992); Maoz & Russett (1993:632); Russett & Maoz (1993:86);

alliance solidarity (continued)	Raymond (1995); Oneal, Oneal, Maoz, Russett (1996); Maoz (1997); Oneal & Ray (1997); Gartzke (1998); Mousseau (1998); Leeds & Davis (1999); Maoz (2001:165); Lai & Reiter (2000); Henderson (2002:ch6); Kinsella & Russett (2002)	Spiro (1994); Rousseau, Gelpi, Reiter, Huth (1996); Simon & Gartzke (1996); Farber & Gowa (1997:411); Raknerud & Hegre (1997); Senese (1997a); Wilkinson (1980:37); Mousseau (1997); Ray (1998); Gowa (1999:100); Bennett & Stam (2000); Lai & Reiter (2000); Cedarman & Rao (2001); Gelpi & Griesdorf (2001); Russett & Oneal (2001); Kinsella & Russett (2002); Oneal, Russett, Berbaum (2003:381); Ray (2003); Goldsmith (2006:552); Wright (2010); Haas (2013)
international organization cultures	de Vries (1990); Holsti (1991:307); Russett & Atholis (1992); Hewitt & Wilkenfeld (1995); Russett (1997a); Russett, Oneal, Davis (1998); Oneal & Russett (1999c); Mansfield & Pevehouse (2000); Maoz (2001:165); Russett & Oneal (2001:ch5); Oneal, Russett, Berbaum (2003:381); Boehmer, Garzke, Nordstrom (2004); Dembinski, Hasenlever, Wagner (2004:547-48); Lagazio & Russett (2004); Bearce & Omori (2005); Eilstrup-Sangiovanni & Verdier (2005); Pevehouse & Russett (2006); Dorussen & Ward 2008); Vasquez (2012:52)	Wallace & Singer (1970); Goldsmith (2006:544-45); Lipson (2003:74); Boehmer, Gartzke, Nordstrom (2004); Daase (2006); Dorussen (2006); Hafner-Burton & Montgomery (2008); Haas (2013)
mutual respect and trust	Russett (1993b:5-11,35,59-74); Owen (1997a); Cederman (2001); Levy & Razin (2003); Rosato (2003:590-91); Sobek (2005)	Layne (1994); Muller & Seligman (1994); Rock (1997); Friedman (2008); Letzkian & Souva (2009)

moral constraint	Geva, deRouen, Mintz (2003); Mintz & Geva (2003); Tomz & Weeks (2013)	Morgenthau (1948); Brock (2006); Daase (2006); Smith (2007); Haas (2013)
negotiation propensity	Bueno de Mesquita & Lalman (1992); Leng (1993:28-29); Russett (1993b:33); Dixon (1994); Raymond (1994); Brecher & Wilkenfeld (1997); Mousseau (1998); Weart (1998); Leeds & Davis (1999); Mitchell (2002); Mitchell, Kadera, Crescenzi (2009); Ellis, Mitchell, Prins (2010); Crescenzi, Kadera, Mitchell, Thyne (2011)	Huth & Allee (2002); Müller & Wolff (2006:47); Letzkian & Souva (2009)
human rights	Gleditsch, Ravlo, Dorussen (2003); Maoz (2004); Danilovic & Clare (2007)	Daase (2006); Smith (2007); Haas (2009)
pacific settlement principles	Morgan & Campbell (1991: 189); Dixon (1993, 1994); Maoz & Russett (1993); Raymond (1994); Bachteler (1997); Mitchell (2002)	Freedman (1997); Kacowicz (1997); Legro (1997); Malin (1997)
economic liberal principles	Bueno de Mesquita & Laman (1991:ch5); Owen (1994b, 1997a); Mousseau 1997:75, 76, 1998, 2000, 2003, 2005, 2009, 2013a); Gartke (2007); Gartzke & Hewitt (2010)	Braumoeller (1997); Schwartz & Skinner (2002); Friedman (2008)
social market principles	Oren & Hays (1997); McDonald (2010); Mousseau (2009, 2013a); Lees (2013)	
cosmopolitanism	Archibugi (2008)	Lipson (2003:74); Goldsmith (2006)

For a democratic culture to exist, there must be elites or a public that subscribes to values that support democratic politics. One might therefore expect that research pursuing this line of inquiry would be mining opinion polls (e.g., Stouffer 1955; Almond and Verba 1963). Not so for Maoz and Russett (1993), who have operationalized cultural values as regime longevity and level of domestic political violence! Among those who have cited surveys, the hypothesis of a peaceful public in a democracy has been exposed as false (Layne 1994; cf. Owen 1993, 1994b; Senese 1997a, 1999).

Liberal political principles. As a common culture, to which democracies may subscribe, the argument is that the principles have
taken root to such an extent that conflicts, whether internal or external, are viewed as resolvable through peaceful means: In democracies, new leaders are selected in elections, whereas coups are required in nondemocracies. Accordingly, some researchers no longer
refer to the "democratic peace" but instead to a "liberal peace"
founded on trade patterns, as noted later in the section on economic
explanations for the "democratic peace."

A corollary is that liberal democratic principles of conflict resolution are so attractive that they "spill over" to nondemocracies.
Since the founding of the World Trade Organization in 1995, a
peaceful mechanism has existed for resolution of trade disputes
based on liberal democratic norms; both democracies and nondemocracies have taken advantage (Bearce 2003:352). But norm adherence
and diffusion is not supported by survey data, which are blackboxed,
so the spillover hypothesis is entirely speculative, based on correlations alone.

"Norm of bounded competition." As hypothesized by Dixon
(1993, 1994) as "tolerance, compromise, and fair play," a satisficing
habit in domestic politics that is presumably carried over to the international system. However, he admitted that he did not measure
norms; instead he used the Gurr data for a scale of "institutionalized
democracy." His conception is similar to the postulate of "regulated
competition" (Maoz and Russett 1993).

However, if democracies uniquely adhere to such norms, Rosato
(2003) has pointed out, then why do they go to war as often as nondemocracies? If the norms are identical with the definition of "democracy," then the explanation is simply a tautology, as in the auto-
correlated concept of "pacifist democracy" (Müller 2004).

Commonality of culture. Weart (1994:309 has claimed that pairs
of democracies as well as pairs of oligarchies avoid war when they
believe that they share a common culture. In identifying an "oligarchic peace" in which nobles blocked kings from foreign adventures,
Weart (1998) claimed to have answered the puzzle that both democracy-democracy and nondemocracy-nondemocracy dyads are more
peaceful than democracy-nondemocracy dyads. Ray (2005), howev-

er, has disputed the idea of an "autocratic peace."

But cultural commonality was an element in the security (no-war) communities involving both democracies and nondemocracies identified by Karl Deutsch and associates (1957). Similarly, the Association of South-East Asian Nations (ASEAN) was specifically to set up in 1967 to end violent conflict involving Indonesia-Malaysia and Malaysia-Philippines. Known in the early years as the "dictators' club," ASEAN scholars trumpet a common diplomatic culture known as the "Asian Way" that is in sharp contrast with what leaders perceive as the formalistic diplomatic style practiced by Anglo-European countries (Haas 2013). Today, some ASEAN members are democracies and some are nondemocracies, yet they have forged a common ASEAN culture that has served to softpedal many border disputes.

After the Cold War, Huntington famously argued, the main sources of conflict would be "clashes of civilizations." However, when data were assembled to see whether his futurist theory was borne out, the data (including very few post-Cold War years) revealed that most conflicts were intracivilizational (Russett, Oneal, Cox 2000). Huntington (2000), however, objected that he was making a prediction, not stating a correlation.

Cultural similarity. Rather than cultural commonality, perceived cultural dissimilarity was the key antecedent variable that explained 95 percent of the variance in a five-variable causal model of decisions for violence (Haas 1974:ch5). Democratic leaders may feel cultural affinity, but so may undemocratic leaders. Using Richardson's data, David Wilkinson (1980:104) discovered a mild tendency for country similarity to predict to mutually peaceful behavior. ASEAN countries have very dissimilar cultures but share the ASEAN Way, an operational code, in common. According to Brian Lai and Dan Reiter (2000), Cold War alliances were composed of countries sharing similar cultures. But similarity is something perceived rather than an objective matter (Oren 1995).

Individualism. The cultural trait similar among democracies is said to be individualism. The argument is that the self-interested public restrains democratic leaders, who in turn calm jingoistic publics as support for war appears to reach a tipping point. Self-discipline is thus assumed to be shared by all democratic leaders who want to be reelected, as the public expects leaders to act rationally for the country. In a study of six times when the United States declared war, however, James Regens, Ronald Gaddie, and Brad Lockerbie (1995) found no clear correlation between reelectability of members of Congress and their votes for or against a declaration of war.

Political similarity. Rather than cultural similarity, political similarity, according to some researchers, is the key explanation. After all, democracy dyads are about as peaceful as autocracy dyads. Several scholars have reported that similarity of political and economic institutions encourages peace—a "democratic peace" and an "autocratic peace" (e.g., Peceny, Beer, Sanchez-Terry 2002). Scott Bennett (2006; cf. Kinsella 2005) discovered that political similarity for both democracies and autocracies was evident in reducing conflicts primarily for the most bloody wars, not for all wars, though he found democratic dyads more peaceful than autocratic dyads, and other combinations were more likely to be at war. But if a factor accounts for peace for both autocracies and democracies, then that factor must be ruled out as a definitive cause of the "democratic peace."

Instead of regime type similarity, several studies have discovered that countries with similar United Nations voting patterns—with policy similarity—are unlikely to go to war with one another. The direction of causation is in dispute, however. Gartzke (1998) was among the first to identify the correlation. After criticisms of his research (Oneal and Russett 1997, 1999c), Gartzke returned to the data and found that UN voting similarity was more predictive of peace than regime type (Gartzke 2000). Mousseau (2000, 2003; Mousseau, Hegre, Oneal 2003) has also found a high level of UN voting similarity among market-oriented democracies, which in turn tend to be at peace.

Regional affinity. For some European researchers, the regional location of countries suggests a common cultural thread. The argument is that most wars are fought among contiguous states, but not among contiguous democracies (Russett and Antholis 1992; Mitchell and Prins 1999; Senese 2005). Countries with settled borders are less likely to be involved in conflicts (Gibler 2007; Vasquez and Elmon 2011). The *Caroline* incident (Canada vs USA, 1837) may not fit that presumption, but "democratic peace" scholars always find some way to delete such cases from their samples. Although countries with the highest scores on democracy had few territorial disputes from 1946, they had other disputes, such as the Cod Wars (Mitchell and Prins 1999:174). ASEAN brought regional peace to Southeast Asian democracies and nondemocracies, but diplomacy not regional affinity has been crucial (Haas 2013). Arie Kacowicz (1997) has described similar developments in South America and West Africa. Meanwhile, Maoz and Russett (1993) have claimed that the "democratic peace" finding remains when contiguity is held constant.

Alliance solidarity. Common norms that decrease conflicts among their members may be cultivated within alliances (Kinsella and Russett 2002). Some studies have found that democracies are more likely to ally together than nondemocracies and remain allied for longer periods of time (Siverson and Emmons 1991; Spiro 1994; Ray 2003). But regime type did not correlate with alliance membership until the Cold War (Simon and Gartzke 1996; Lai and Reiter 2000).

Although allies are more likely to fight together on the same side of a conflict than non-allies, especially after war has already begun, the relationship evidently vanishes when controlling for regime type (Mearsheimer 1990; Ray 1990; Siverson and Emmons 1991:304; Bremer 1992:315,328; Spiro 1994; Raknerud and Hegre 1997), as some allies are more reliable than others (Clare 2013). Policy conformity is not the same thing as common norms, as the Locarno Peace Pact demonstrated (Wright 2010).

However, if democracies are on the same side, and alliances are formed to meet common threats, then democracies will inevitably be at war as a result of their alliances: Competing alliances breed wars (Kim 1989). Indeed, evidence shows that democracies are more likely to be in war together than nondemocracies (Mousseau 1997). The reason for joining, may not be regime type or an agreement on basic principles but instead common national security interests (Maoz 2001:165; Russett and Oneal 2001:214), as Morgenthau (1948) would have expected.

Moreover, allies have often fought one another (Bueno de Mesquita 1990; Siverson and Emmons 1991; Oneal, Russett, Berbaum 2003:381). One explanation is that allies were close only during the Cold War (Simon and Gartzke 1996). Yet peace despite small-scale incidents exists within nondemocratic ASEAN members, which have formed a voting bloc within UN bodies.

Although Ray (1998) has objected that alliance solidarity would predict to peace within the Communist bloc, his counterexamples (Cambodian-Vietnamese War and Sino-Vietnamese incursions) demonstrate that he did not realize that the Sino-Soviet split fueled both cases or that Hanoi called for UN intervention. Nevertheless, he indicated that there were three wars among Western alliance partners—the Football War (El Salvador vs Honduras) in 1969, the Turkish invasion of Cyprus in 1974, and the Falklands/Malvinas War of 1982.

Alliances may forge economic ties that make war unlikely. Two studies found that common alliance membership facilitates increased trade between partners (de Vries 1990; Simon and Gartzke 1996), but another study did not (Siverson and Emmons 1991).

International organization cultures. Inside international organizations bilateral ties are sometimes cemented that would otherwise be difficult to establish, and such organizations provide an environment in which third-party mediation is more likely (Dorussen and Ward 2008). Democracies are supposedly more likely to join international organizations (Russett and Oneal 2001:213; Mansfield and Pevehouse 2003). But the claim that democracies disproportionately join international organizations is questionable: Some international organizations only allow democracies to join and expel or suspend members after coups, and the sample of organizations studied does not appear to adequately represent those from Africa and Asia (Haas 2014a:ch13). Bruce Russett and John Oneal (2001:160) obtained a sample of only 293 intergovernmental organizations, (ibid., p. 160), but I found 50 in Asia at that time, and none were then composed solely of democracies (Haas 1989, 2013). Russett and Oneal, nevertheless, in agreeing that the number of international organizations has a positive effect on peace, found that the effect was less than the impact of democracy and trade.

The argument is that peace flows from the mode of discourse in international organizations, where equality of states is assumed, a culture similar to that which prevails in democracies. Accordingly, multilateral discussion on matters of high politics is predicted to mitigate conflicts. But that does not mean that international organizations will be more effective in conflict resolution (Hewitt and Wilkenfeld 1996).

Not all intergovernmental organizations develop a common culture that provides peaceful mechanisms; there must be a mandate for conflict resolution, structures that have mediatory capabilities, and member cohesiveness (Boehner, Gartzke, Nordstrom 2004; Bearce and Omori 2005). ASEAN, nevertheless, developed a common culture before member countries became democracies (Haas 2013).

Mutual respect and trust. Another attitudinal basis for peaceful interaction is mutual respect and trust (Owen 1997a). Machiavellian states, which breed distrust among other countries, are more likely to end up at war (Sobek 2005). The development of a commonality of culture takes time. Russett (1993b:5-11,35,59-74) has speculated that democracies gradually learned from the experience of cooperating together, notably during the World Wars and the Cold War, that they could rely on one another. But some research has found more covert democracy-democracy conflict (Rosato 2003:590-91). Gilat Levy and Ronny Razin (2003), in a game-theoretical analysis (without evidence) found that democratic leaders are more likely to trust one another, whereas a nondemocratic leader is likely to be distrusted by a democratic leader. Examining specific conflict situations, two studies found a lack of trust involving Britain, France, Germany, and the United States during the nineteenth century, and two studies cautioned that interpersonal trust is not necessarily present even in democracies (Layne 1994; Muller and Seligman 1994; Rock 1997). A detailed case study of the Munich Crisis of 1938 reveals that President Franklin Roosevelt trusted Adolf Hitler's promises and did not consider the existence of a fascist regime to be an indicator of Hitler's possible perfidiousness (Farnham 2003).

Moral constraints. According to Gil Friedman (2008), moral constraints prevent democracies from attacking other democracies. He has argued that democracies respect the rights of their own citizens and therefore extend that thinking to respect the rights of citizens in other democracies. For evidence of his hypothesis, he has cited experimental surveys (Geva, deRouen, Mintz 2003; Mintz and Geva 2003). A recent public opinion survey validates Friedman's thesis (Tomz and Weeks 2013).

But moral constraint is not unique to democracies. Aristocrats during the nineteenth century, in forming the Concert of Europe, established a moral constraint from attacking one another (Morgenthau 1948[1985]:260-64). A mixture of democracies and nondemocracies may also do so: A culture of trust applies to ASEAN, whose leaders have achieved conviviality through such activities as karaoke sessions together (Haas 2013). Everyone knows that war is immoral except when a country's vital interests are involved (Brock 2006).

Negotiation propensity. Democratic leaders tend to handle disputes in a peaceful rather than a coercive manner. Several researchers have found democracies respond to foreign conflict by cooperative negotiations more than violence, reporting that democracies are more likely than authoritarian regimes to use reciprocating rather than tit-for-tat negotiating styles. But the most dramatic shift toward negotiation as a means to replace violent conflict resolution began with the Peace of Westphalia, hardly an era of numerous democracies. Paul Huth and Todd Allee (2002) have found many nuances in the use of negotiations by democracies. The outcome of the Locarno peace agreement was war (Wright 2010).

Human rights commitment. Uniquely, democracies are founded on the basis of human rights, whereas most nondemocracies have human rights problems. One claim is that after imperial powers divested themselves of their colonies, they became more accepting of the rights of sovereign non-European peoples (Gleditsch, Ravlo, Dorussen 2003). But the argument is tautological, as most definitions of democracy demand more than a minimum standard of human rights. One study operationalized "human rights" by a single variable—the absence of politically motivated executions (Oneal, Oneal, Maoz, Russett 1996:22), an element embedded in the very concept of democracy. The practice of extraordinary rendition and torture in the years immediately after 9/11, involving several European countries and the United States, destroyed the figleaf that democracies universally respect human rights (Haas 2009). Efforts to impose democracy by war also belie the claim (Daase 2006; Smith 2007).

Commitment to pacific settlement principles and international law. As illustrated by the creation of "zones of peace," democracies may have a more legal orientation to international affairs than nondemocracies, thus explaining why pairs of democratic countries resolve conflicts peacefully. Sara Mitchell (2002) has traced the authorship of the pacific settlement idea to democracies, which have sold the idea to nondemocracies. Thus, ASEAN countries formed their organization in 1967 because of such a commitment, in particular the Zone of Peace, Freedom, and Neutrality Declaration of 1971, after the United States bombed democratic Cambodia and was at war in Vietnam, having refused to allow a plebiscite throughout the latter country. Bachteler (1997) has characterized the Delian League as a zone of peace, though both democracies and nondemocracies joined. In addition, Kacowicz (1995, 1997; cf. Maoz 2001) has identified eight historical zones of peace as simply no-war commitments, while others are strategic security communities; many involve nondemocracies that might use force to repress domestically but respect international law abroad. For the commitment to have meaning, international legal principles must be ingrained and mediatory institutions operating.

Economic liberal principles. According to Mousseau, a free market is based on reciprocal respect for contracts, which in turn demands both democracy and peaceful international commerce (cf. Lipson 2003:6). The specific liberal principles are from John Maynard Keynes, not Frederick Hayek (Mousseau, Orsun, Ungerer 2013, Mousseau 2013a). Similar to economist Joseph Schumpeter (1943 [2003]:296), Mousseau has argued that voters in democracies insist on the equal enforcement of contracts, whereas nondemocratic leaders inevitably must appease their political elites by showing them favoritism in the economy. However, in one study his operational measure is percapita life insurance policies, while in another he uses level of development as operational indicators; neither are survey-based. One study found that scope of economic freedom, a concept assumed similar to liberal culture, explained the "democratic peace" only for developed countries (Gartzke 2007), but the findings of Mousseau (2013a) made that variable less determinative.

According to survey data, adherents of economic liberalism in the former Soviet Union are more aggressive than non-liberals (Braumoeller 1997). If marketplace culture or Keynesianism exogenously account for both democracy and peace, then the relationship between democracy and peace is spurious. But marketplace norms are rules of fair competition, and economic competitors will necessarily be out for profit, so such norms can encourage conflict (Schwartz and Skinner 2002). Friedman (2008), similarly, has objected that the norm of self-interest, embedded in economic liberalism, ensures that democracies will go to war to advance their interests.

Social market economy principles. Mousseau (2013a) has found that countries with larger public sector budgets have fewer external conflicts, but of course they are located within Europe, which remained at peace during the Cold War. Another study found that democracies have lower percentages of their budget devoted to military spending, thus devoting more attention to education and other matters (Fordham and Walker 2005).

Cosmopolitanism. Kant's proposal for a league of republics was in fact premised on cosmopolitanism, that is, a universal culture (Delahunty and Yoo 2010). One argument is that democracies respect minorities and women to an extent that nondemocracies do not. Democracies think in terms of the advance of diversity, whereas nondemocracies fear differences and dissent. But Herrenvolk democracies are decidedly conformist. Indeed, as noted below, the "democratic peace" may best be explained as racist.

According to the "English School," world cosmopolitanism is bringing about world peace. Yet Lipson (2003:74) and Benjamin Goldsmith (2006) have argued that there is no "democratic peace" among democracies outside the North Atlantic region, obviously unaware of the peace within the nations of the South Pacific and discounting the long history of war within Europe.

Summary. In sum, cultural explanations appear to be ad hoc (Bueno de Mesquita, Siverson, Smith 1999:792). For Gowa (1995, 1999), national interests determine norms, not culture. The existence of covert violence also negates highfalutin cultural explanations (Forsythe 1992; James and Mitchell 1995). Since democracies do go to war with one another on occasion, cultural explanations seem farfetched (Lipson 2003:3). What is lacking is analysis of how norms are invoked by political leaders while deliberating foreign policy options. Quantative exercises necessarily cannot capture decision making processes.

The economic culture approach of Mousseau (2013a) is so potent that Russett and associates have sought every possible means of refutation (Dafoe 2011; Dafoe, Oneal, Russett 2013; Dafoe and Russett 2013). His theory is explained in more detail below.

Domestic Stability

Several studies have demonstrated that domestic conflict measures are better predictors of foreign conflict than indicators of institutional aspects of democracy (Haas 1965, 1968; Ostrom and Job 1986; Russett and Maoz 1993; Maoz and Russett 1992, 1993; Morgan and Bickers 1992; Russett 1989, 1993b:35). The argument is that democracies differ fundamentally from nondemocracies in that the latter tend to have more domestic conflict and a paucity of successful coping mechanisms (democracy→domestic tranquility→peace). In a strange remark, Maoz and Russett (1992:262) ejaculated that stability is "obviously correlated with democracy," clearly unaware of how stable authoritarian and totalitarian rule has been over the centuries. Nevertheless, several studies have reported not only that democracies have a lower level of domestic violence than nondemocracies (Rummel 1997; Harff 2003; Russett and Maoz 1993:86-93; Oneal, Oneal, Maoz, Russett 1996:22) but also that pairs of countries with minimal domestic violence will have low levels of conflict with each other.

Similarly, Ember, Ember, and Russett (1992:585), in a study of indigenous cultures, found that peaceful societies had an absence of political fission (the tendency for disgruntled persons to move to another community). In other words, some voted with their feet against remaining in the group (cf. Bateson 1958), in effect becoming refugees.

When governments lack adequate problem-solving resources to deal with serious domestic problems, they are at least two scenarios. One is a coup d'etat or reelection defeat (cf. Crozier, Huntington, Watanuki 1975:ch5; Revel 1984). The second option is foreign conflict or war to divert attention from economic or political problems (Haas 1965; Wilkenfeld 1968; Zinnes and Wilkenfeld 1971; Hazelwood 1973). A major study concluded that democracies are more likely to engage in "diversionary" foreign conflict, whereas autocracies can more easily engage in repression (Gelpi 1997; cf. Oakes 2012). However, another study found that military regimes are more likely to rely upon diversionary war to retain control than single-party regimes; the latter are much less fragile (Lai and Slater 2006).

However, some early studies of "diversionary theory" found no relationship between domestic and foreign conflict (Rummel 1963; Tanter 1966; Wilkenfeld 1972; cf. Maoz and Abdolali 1989). Later studies of "diversionary theory" have focused on whether *economic* conditions decline, using war to divert blame from leaders, who might otherwise be held responsible for poor economic management, toward foreign governments (Haas 1968; Ostrom and Job 1986; James 1988:ch5; Levy 1989; Mintz and Russett 1992; Morgan and Bickers 1992; Geva, deRouen, Mintz 1993; Mintz and Geva 1993; James and Rioux 1998; Miller 1999; deRouen 2000; Davies 2002). Despite the state of the economy, however, American presidents with higher approval ratings from 1949 to 1976 were reluctant to use force (cf. Ireland and Gartner 2001), while those with lower public approval were more likely to do so in bad economic times (Ostrom and Job 1986; cf. Russett 1990:133-34; James and Oneal 1991).

A second version of diversionary theory is that *political* dysfunctions in solving domestic problems may be so frustrating that wars are launched to divert the attention of the public from inadequacies of democratically-elected leaders (Russett 1990:133-34; James and Oneal 1991; Van Belle 1993; Gates, Knutsen, Moses 1996:1; Miller 1995; Hess and Orphanides 2001; Fordham 2002). Several studies have argued that sources of political discontent are much more important than objective economic conditions in producing diversionary action (MacKuen 1983; Russett 1990:136), but they contradict the argument that democracies build in decisional constraints against war. If the domestic conflict is violent, war is more likely to be the response than is the case with nonviolent protest (Davies 2002).

T. Clifton Morgan and Kenneth Bickers (1992) found that American leaders with divisions in their political parties have whipped up war fever within the public to justify aggressive action abroad, confirming two studies (Mueller 1973; Ostrom and Job 1986). However, William Baker and John Oneal (2001) found that the public only "rallies round the flag" when leaders cultivate them to do so. Democracies with fewer constitutional constraints on the executive or with ethnic political parties are more likely to participate in diversionary wars (Carment and James 1995). However, diversionary wars do not succeed in their aims for American presidents (James and Oneal 1991), who are often defeated because long wars become unpopular.

In a comprehensive study of diversionary theory, Jeffrey Pickering and Enizet Kisangani (2005) have distinguished between stable and consolidating autocracies and democracies, four regime types in all. They found that stable autocracies, where there is a unity among elites, rarely respond to mass unrest by diversionary action; after all, they can crack down on dissent. Consolidating autocracies react to elite unrest more than mass discontent, and only engage in diversionary action when mass unrest skyrockets. Their research contradicts previous findings that democracies becoming autocracies are involved in a high level of foreign conflict (Enterline 1996,1998; Maoz 1998; Ward and Gleditsch 1998).

Pickering and Kisangani (2005) also reported that leaders in stable democracies respond to mass political unrest by immediate shows of force abroad and engage in more diversionary conflict than all other regime types, supporting Alistair Smith (1998b). One explanation, noted above, is perhaps that the public may be more likely to support war than their leaders (Mueller 1973; cf. Geva, deRouen, Mintz 1993:222). Because partisan support is more crucial than general public support for leaders in stable democracies (Morgan and Campbell 1991), diversionary war may result when the party in power is being challenged by members of its own political party (Picking and Kisangani 2005:38; cf. Morgan and Bickers 1992; Morgan and Anderson 1999). However, Brandon Prins and Christopher Sprecher (1999) have concluded that domestic unrest in parliamentary systems decreases the possibility of diversionary external conflict.

According to many studies, countries transitioning to democracy are more often at war than either democracies or nondemocracies (Haas 1965, 1968; Wilkenfeld 1968:57; James 1988:114; Enterline 1998; Mansfield and Snyder 1995, 1996, 2002, 2005; Mousseau 2000; Snyder 2000). One reason is that they must cope with internal conflict due to a loss of power by old elites. However, other studies have found that there is no positive or negative relationship with foreign diversionary conflict: Oneal, Russett, and Michael Berbaum (2003:384), for example, have demonstrated that the likelihood of foreign conflict wears off by the seventh year of the transition. Two studies contradict those who have found that democratizing countries have higher levels of foreign conflict than the other regime types (Pickering and Kisangani 2005; Thompson and Tucker 1997). As noted earlier, a key element may be the smoothness of the transition to democracy, as countries with rough transitions are more likely to encounter foreign conflict (Ward and Gleditsch 1998; Gleditsch and Ward 2000; cf. Casper 1995; Casper and Taylor 1996). Another factor may be whether the democratizing country is surrounded by nondemocracies (Enterline 1996; Oneal and Ray 1997; Oneal and Russett 1997; Thompson and Tucker 1997). But the evidence is not conclusive on either side. Graeme Davies (2002) found no correlation between countries undergoing democratic transitions and their likelihood to be engaged in war.

Aside from diversionary theory, a country may be at war because external powers have attacked. According to Weede (1996), domestic tranquility in both democracies and nondemocracies provides little opportunity for external intervention and thus for war. Similarly, Russett and associates have found that nondemocracies without domestic violence and regime instability are more peaceful than nondemocracies with domestic violence (Oneal, Oneal, Maoz, Russett 1996). Evidently countries experiencing internal strife are more likely to be attacked (Davies 2002; Lemke and Regan 2004:162-63). Huth and Allee (2002) found that countries already involved in a foreign dispute are vulnerable to a military threat.

In short, there appears to be a consensus on the proposition that domestic conflict is somehow linked to participation in wars. But the proposition applies differentially to democracies, transitional democracies, and nondemocracies. Besides, James and Oneal (1991) have found that the severity of a foreign threat is more important than domestic discontent in explaining why a country ends up at war.

Prosperity

Kant argued that warmaking is inherently unprofitable and thus will be avoided by representative governments where the population seeks increased prosperity (democracy→prosperity→peace). As this "commercial liberal" argument goes, democracies are free-traders and thus view state interaction in terms of contractual rather than status considerations (cf. Schumpeter 1919 [1951]:66-72; Doyle

1983:350-51, 1986:1152-54; Lake 1992). A "capitalist peace" model has been advanced as an alternative to the "democratic peace" (Gartzke 2007), but that thesis appears to subvert or supplant rather than support the "democratic peace" (Table 5.3). In some studies the term "liberal peace" has emerged, presumably because democracies are free and open capitalist states.

Table 5.3. Economic Explanations

Factor	Studies in Agreement	Refutations
liberal economic principles	Bueno de Mesquita & Lalman (1992:ch5); Braumoeller (1997: 389); Mousseau (2000, 2002, 2003, 2005, 2013a,b); Souva (2004)	Lipson (2003:74); Goenner (2004)
level of economic development	Haas (1965:313); Cooper (1982); Russett (1989,1990); Merritt & Zinnes (1991); Bremer (1992, 1993); Maoz & Russett (1993: 632); Dixon (1993,1994): Russett & Maoz (1993:86); Weede (1995); Morrow, Siverson, Tabares (1998); Verdier (1998); Hegre (2000); Mousseau (2000, 2003, 2005:65); Gartzke (2000, 2007); Gat (2005: 89-96, 2006:600-5); Goldsmith (2006); Gartzke & Hewitt (2010)	Mearsheimer (1990:46); Maoz & Russett (1992: 257); Risse-Kappen (1995b); Ember & Ember (1992); Dixon (1994:26); Oneal, Oneal, Maoz, Russett (1996:18); Mousseau (2000, 2003, 2005); Mousseau, Hegre, Oneal (2003:296-99); Choi (2011)
economic growth rate	Burkhart & Lewis-Beck (1994: 906); Russett, Oneal, Davis (1995); Gartzke (1998)	Haas (1968); Oneal & Russett (1998); Russett & Oneal 2001:153); Maoz & Russett (2002); Egan (2010)
cost of war	Gilpin (1981:ch4); Rummel (1983b:28); Ostrom & Job (1986); Yoon (1989); Russett & Antholis (1992); Dixon (1993); Goldsmith (2007)	Zinnes, North, Koch (1961); David (1991); Bueno de Mesquita, Siverson, Woller (1992); Bueno de Mesquita & Lalman (1992: 154-58); Rock (1997); Lipson (2003:3); Gowa (1999); Henderson (2002); Brock (2006); Tomz & Weeks (2013)

economic interdependence	Angell (1910); Gasiorowski & Polacheck (1982); Polachek (1980, 1992, 1997, 2003); Dixon (1984); Domke (1988:136-37,168); de Vries (1990); Lake (1992); Polachek & McDonald (1992); Brawley (1993); Dixon & Moon (1993); Farber & Gowa (1994, 1995); Mansfield (1994:235, 2000); Verdier (1994:294); Barbieri (1996, 1997); Oneal, Oneal, Maoz, Russett (1996); Weede (1996); Oneal & Ray (1997); Oneal & Russett (1997, 1998, 1999c, 2001:ch4); Gartzke (1998); Bliss & Russett (1998); Polachek, Robst, Chang (1999); Bennett & Stam (2000); Hegre (2000); Mousseau (2000); Gartzke, Li, Boehmer (2001); King & Zeng (2001a); McDonald (2001); Russett & Oneal (2001); Henderson (2002:ch6); Kinsella & Russett (2002); Gleditsch (2002); Heagerty, Ward, Gleditsch (2002); Beck (2003); Dorussen & Hegre 2003); Hegre, Gissinger, Gleditsch (2003); Mansfield & Pollins (2003); Oneal & Russett (2003a,b); Oneal, Russett, Berbaum (2003:382); Polachek (2003); Weede (2003,2004); Bennett & Stam (2004:ch5); Lagazio & Russett (2004); Rasler & Thompson (2005:77); Goldsmith (2006:544); Pevehouse & Russett (2006)	Galtung (1964); Russett (1967); Wallensteen (1973); Kahler (1979-1980); Buzan (1984); Gasiorowski (1986); Pollins (1989a,b); Russett & Antholis (1992: 429); Dixon & Moon (1993:17-21); Gowa & Mansfield (1993:416); Buzan (1994); Gowa (1994, 1999:14-19); Mansfield (1994); Weart (1994:304); Barbieri (1996); Oneal & Ray (1996); Oneal, Oneal, Maoz, Russett (1996); Copeland (1996, 2000); Beck, Katz, Tucker (1998); Barbieri & Levy (1990); Greene, Kim, Yoon (2001); Beck (2003); Gartzke & Li (2003); Mansfield & Pollins (2003); Morrow (2003); Mousseau, Hegre, Oneal (2003:263, 297); Schneider & Schulze (2003); Goemans (2004); Kim & Rousseau (2005) Mousseau (2005:70,77); Goldsmith (2006:547)
trade communities	Mansfield, Pevehouse, Bearce (1999/2000); Mansfield & Pevehouse (2000, 2003); Gartzke & Li (2003); Eilstrup-Sangiovanni & Verdier (2005)	Lai & Reiter (2000)

Liberal economic principles. As noted above in the section on norms, principles of capitalism may provide the appropriate cultural context for war avoidance, and indeed many democracies prosper by following those principles. But the degree of acceptance of liberal principles may, in turn, be a function of levels of economic development, growth rates, and trade interdependence.

At least one study has corroborated the finding that lower levels of economic development hinder the rise of liberal institutions and values (Souva 2004), and another has demonstrated that higher levels of economic development bring support for liberal economic principles (Mousseau 2003). Surveys in the former Soviet bloc countries have confirmed that those with liberal views are less likely to be warlike and less aggressive than their illiberal leaders (Braumoeller 1997:389). Lipson (2003:74) is skeptical about the role of liberalism, as he would like to have evidence that business interests pressure for peace. The arms industry does the opposite!

Economic development. The level of economic development has been found to correlate positively with peacefulness. Although some believe that the economically developed aggressors of World Wars I and II refute such a notion, in one study countries with high levels of democracy and high levels of economic development (both together, not separately) are more likely to treat each other peacefully (Morrow, Siverson, Tabares 1998; Verdier 1998).

However, for Mousseau (2000), only during the Cold War were the most developed democracies were at peace with one another, and he also found that poorer democracies were more likely than prosperous democracies to go to war (Mousseau 2005:65). Hårvard Hegre (2000) found that the finding was more robust with democracies than nondemocracies.

Nevertheless, dependency theorists believe that the seeds of war are sewn by world economic inequality (Galtung 1964). Several studies have found that wealth of the country is unrelated to war involvement. Dixon (1994:26) has determined that economic development is unrelated to the propensity to utilize negotiations to resolve conflicts. Although Gartzke (2007) strongly differed from Dixon, a replication of his analysis found that both the "democratic peace" and the "capitalist peace" are valid, but that democracy is not a function of capitalism (Choi 2011).

According to Richard Cooper (1982) and Azar Gat (2005:89-96, 2006:600-5), post-industrial society limits the ability of democracies to fight wars. Increasingly, workers are hired in the service industry, unsuited for the manual labor required in factories as well as in combat, whereas women tend to vote against war policies. Post-industrial society has lower birthrates to provide a supply of human cannon fodder. The sexual revolution and desire for comfortable lives also dampen enthusiasm for war.

Growth rates. High economic growth is sometimes thought to encourage governments to become more democratic. But when social change is too rapid or there are economic downturns after periods of growth, the result can be domestic turmoil, from which a diversionary war may emerge (Haas 1968). Gartzke (1998) found that democracies with high growth rates do not go to war with each other (cf. Russett, Oneal, Davis 1995), but Oneal and Russett (1998b) found that growth rates were not correlated with war propensities. According to Daniel Egan (2010), economic growth in the age of globalization undermines democracy by promoting domestic inequality.

Cost of war. In democratic polities, the costs of spending the people's money may caution against war, as voters will demand a reallocation of resources on a more equal basis, such that military spending will be seen as wasteful. War costs involve economic, military, and "soft power" factors; the latter refers to measures that enchance a state's reputation and respect abroad (Nye 2004).

Although cost factors apply both to democracies and nondemocracies alike (Bueno de Mesquita, Siverson, Woller 1992; Lipson 2003:3), one calculation is that the economic costs of going to war have been higher for democracies than nondemocracies (Bueno de Mesquita and Lalman 1992:154-58), whereas Stephen David (1991) has suggested that the political costs of losing a war are even more severe for leaders of undemocratic states.

Yet cost considerations were rarely brought into discussions as the prospect of World War I occupied elites (Zinnes, North, Koch 1961). Gowa (1999) has also disputed whether cost factors play any role in decisions of democratic countries for war; after all, they tend to be more prosperous than nondemocracies (Henderson 2002). Survey data would have to show that in democracies reasons of morality outweigh costs when the public contemplates military action against another democracy. War costs are a strategic consideration, as noted below.

Economic interdependence. Trade is often presumed to bring peace by providing a win-win situation for trade partners, who will avoid war to gain profit and wealth. Those who believe that trade brings peace refer to their view as the "liberal peace." Yet the evidence is mixed (Morrow 2003). World War I occurred despite a high level of trade interdependence (Kahler 1979-1980). During the Cold War, Barry Buzan (1984) noted that free trade in pursuit of profit sometimes led to diplomatic and military conflict, and Athenian wars were sometimes motivated for profit (Russett and Antholis 1992: 429). One study has demonstrated that democracies are more likely to lower trade barriers for one another (Mansfield, Milner, Rosendorff 2000), but that does not necessarily mean that the mutual volume of trade will be very high (Gowa and Mansfield 1993).

In selecting trade partners, security needs are a factor (Gowa 1994; Pollins 1989a,b), and indeed much of the expensive trade is in armaments. Countries with few commodities to export, known as "trade dependent" in the literature (Frank 1967) have been found to have more foreign conflict in one study (Gasiorowski 1986) but less foreign conflict in another (Oneal, Oneal, Maoz, Russett 1996:21). For Gerald Schneider and Gunther Schultze (2003), the import/export sector must have more political clout than the military-industrial complex for trade to be a factor inhibiting external violence.

Regressing trade data onto foreign conflict events data, Solomon Polachek (1980) reported that the more trade between pairs of some thirty countries (mostly European and Middle Eastern) from 1958-1967, the less foreign conflict and the more cooperation, though he did not employ regime type as a control variable. Similar results have been reported in other studies (Polachek 1992; Mansfield 1994). Domke (1988:136,168) discovered that the higher a country's percentage of exports, the fewer decisions to go to war, a relationship stronger among democratic countries. In a replication, dyads with high trade interdependence, including one very dependent on the other, are more likely to be peaceful than contiguous dyads not commercially linked, even if neither pair is democratic (Oneal, Oneal, Maoz, Russett 1996).

Other studies have found no connection between trade interdependence and dyadic "democratic peace." Gowa and Mansfield (1993:416; Gowa 1994) found no extraordinary democratic trade dyads embedded within patterns of world trade, and the same was true in earlier studies (Russett 1967; Wallensteen 1973). Similar results emerged when the sample consisted of U.S.-Warsaw bloc trade from 1967 to 1978, though the effect was greater for the Warsaw bloc than for the United States (Gasiorowski and Polachek 1982). Mousseau (2005:70,77; Mousseau, Hegre, Oneal 2003:283) has noted that countries with high economic development have small percentages of foreign trade and interdependence; the correlation between developed democracy and percentage of foreign trade is nearly zero.

William Dixon and Bruce Moon (1993:17-21), however, reported that exports are more likely to flow between countries that have similar United Nations voting patterns than between democracies. In two studies, interdependent trade patterns were found related to peace, but democracy washed out as an explanatory variable (Oneal, Oneal, Maoz, Russett 1996; Oneal and Ray 1997). But that finding so threatened the "democratic peace" thesis that the data were re-run to find that democracy predicted peace, with trade only a helpful variable (Oneal and Russett 1997)!

Trade expectations may complicate the pattern. Dale Copeland (1996, 2000) assembled several case studies to prove that countries expecting to trade less in the future are more likely to be involved in conflict. Although a statistical test did not find the same results (Oneal, Russett, Berbaum 2003:385), case studies trump statistical studies. Nevertheless, one study found that trade is not especially disrupted by the intervention of foreign conflict (Barbieri and Levy 1999, 2003), yet others found that trade lessens when conflict arises (Anderson and Carter 2003; Oneal, Russett, Berbaum 2003:386).

As noted above, Weede (1995,2003,2004) has argued that free trade and economic interdependence cause both economic development and democracy: Trade of capitalist countries establishes the right to property, which in turn supports democracies averse to war. The interconnectedness of the world economic system has been identified as a major reason why there are only minor wars in the post-Cold War era (Wallerstein 1993; Hardt and Negri 2000). For some observers, the findings suggest that the "democratic peace" may have a successor—the "capitalist peace." However, capitalism is a worldwide phenomenon that was extended after the Cold War to the entire globe, and war continues. History is filled with many examples of wars involving capitalist and mercantilist states.

Michiel de Vries (1990) has found that economic interdependence is also related to a high level of diplomatic, institutional (international organization memberships), and political-military (alliance) relations. In other words, trade interdependence is not separate from the international organization norms explanation. Similarly, one study reported that the "democratic peace" was promoted by both memberships in intergovernmental organizations among democracies and economic interdependence (Lagazio and Russett 2004).

Trade communities. What is at stake in war—disruption of lucrative trade—must be faced when countries contemplate military or peaceful resolution to conflicts. Trade communities range from treaty-based common markets, customs unions, free-trade agreements, and monetary unions to preferential trade agreements. Three studies have found that democracies are more likely to join trade communities and then prefer peaceful options (Mansfield, Pevehouse, Bearce 1999/2000; Mansfield and Pevehouse 2000, 2003), a view held by Europeans who are understandably proud of efforts at European integration (e.g., Eilstrup-Sangiovanni and Verdier 2005).

However, such communities need not involve democracies but could be between autocracies, as was the case when the Soviet bloc integrated socialist states that were at peace. Erik Gartzke and Quan Li (2003) have cautioned that states compete for trade; what may mitigate war between trade partners is the establishment of common markets, preferential trade agreements, and the like. Lai and Reiter (2000), however, found that trade was not the unifying component in alliances between democracies.

Power Status

Realpolitik theorists, whether realists or neorealists, have scoffed at the "democratic peace" thesis. Their arguments have not been successfully refuted by "democratic peace" researchers (Table 5.4).

In Table 5.4, power elements are on the left. The column labeled "critiques" lists studies opposing the "democratic peace"; proponents, which provide "refutations," outnumber the latter. Explanations vary from hegemony theory to post-Cold War logic to military cooperation, power calculations and transition, to contiguity theory.

Table 5.4. Realpolitik Critiques

Power Element	Critiques	Refutations
hegemony	Haas (1970); Waltz (1979, 1993); Kim (1989); Bremer (1993); Mearsheimer (1990); Lake (1993); Kacowicz (1995); Russett, Oneal, Cox (2000)	Lipson (2003:74)
Cold War strategy	Singer & Small (1979:77); Weede (1983); Mearsheimer (1990); Russett & Antholis (1992); Russett & Maoz (1993:73-74); Cohen (1994); Farber & Gowa (1995); Gowa (1997: 3, 2011); Mitchell, Gates, Hegre (1999); Mousseau (2000); Henderson (2002:ch6); Rosato (2003)	Weede (1992): Gochman (1996): Maoz (1997); Oneal & Russett (1997, 1999b); Thomson & Tucker (1997); Cederman & Rao (2001); Dixon & Senese (2002); Lagazio & Russett (2004); Park (2013)
military integration	Jervis (2002:7); Dembinski, Hasenclever, Wagner (2004); Ireland & Gartner (2001); Müller (2001:496)	Huth & Allee (2002)
power calculations, including expected utility	Howard (1984:14-15, 22); Ostrom & Job (1986); Mearsheimer (1990); James & Oneal (1991); Morgan & Campbell (1991:205-6); Bremer (1992); Russett & Antholis (1992: 429); Mintz & Geva (1993); Layne (1994:38, 1997); Rousseau, Gelpi, Reiter, Huth (1996); Senese (1997); Gowa (1999); Mitchell & Prins (1999); Partell & Palmer (1999); Huth & Allee (2002); Oneal, Russett, Berbaum (2003:379); Senese & Vasquez (2004); Keller (2005); Rasler & Thompson (2005: 86); Elman (1997a); Ganguly (1997); Kacowitz (1997); Malin (1997); Owen (1997b); Rock (1997); Quackenbush & Rudy (2006); Hayes (2009, 2012)	Bueno de Mesquita, & Lalman (1992); Maoz & Russett (1993); Russett & Maoz (1993); Fearon (1994); Dussel (1997); Freedman (1997); Werner & Lemke (1997); Maoz (1998); Cederman & Rao (2001); Gelpi & Griesdorf (2001); Lipson (2003:74)
power transition	Organski (1958); Kim (1989, 1990); Kacowicz (1996); Lemke & Reed (1996, 2001); Benson (2004)	Schweller (1992)
deterrence	Bueno de Mesquita, Morrow, Siverson, Smith (2004); Siverson & Emmons (1991); Bueno de Mesquita	Hewitt & Wilkenfeld (1998); Huth &

deterrence (continued)	& Lalman (1992); Lake (1992, 2003); Schweller (1992:252); Bremer (1993); Fearon (1994, 1995); Bueno de Mesquita & Siverson (1995); James & Mitchell (1995); Rousseau, Gelpi, Reiter, Huth (1996); Stam (1996); Gartzke (1998); Hart & Reed (1998); Reiter & Stam (1998a,b); Smith (1998b); Bueno de Mesquita, Siverson, Woller (1999); Partell & Palmer (1999); Schultz (1999:253-55,2001); Finel & Lord (2000); Henderson (2002:ch6); Reiter & Stam (2002)	Allee (2002); Potter & Baum (2010)
major power strategy	Bremer (1992:328,330); Gochman & Maoz (1984:596-97); Morgan & Campbell (1991); Maoz & Russett (1993b:632); Russett & Maoz (1993:85-86); Gowa (1999:9); Ireland & Garner (2001); Huth & Allee (2002); Kinsella & Russett (2002); Bueno de Mesquita, Morrow, Siverson, Smith (2004); Senese (2005)	Bennett (1997): Krause (2004)
percentage of democracies	Russett (1993a); Mitchell, Gates, Hegre (1999); Mitchell (2002); Rummel (2002); Maoz (2004); Rasler & Thompson (2005:195)	Harff & Gurr (1988); Maoz & Abdolali (1989); Russett (1995); Starr (1991); Brecher & Wilkenfeld (1997); Maoz (2001:143)
contiguity	Small & Singer (1976); Terrell (1977:106); Weede (1984, 1992); Huntington (1989:7); Holsti (1991); Siverson & Starr (1991:92); Bremer (1992:327, 1993:245); Goertz & Diehl (1992); Russett & Antholis (1992); Bremer (1993); Dixon (1993, 1994): Raymond (1994); Vasquez (1995); Mitchell & Prins (1999); Kinsella & Russett (2002); Senese & Vasquez (2004); Kacowicz (1995); James, Park, Choi (2006); Gibler (2007, 2012); Ward, Siverson, Cao (2007); Gibler & Braithwaite (2013)	Rummel (1983, 1993); Bremer (1992, 1993); Maoz & Russett (1993: 632); Russett (1993b); Russett & Maoz (1993:84-87); Gleditsch (1995); Enterline (1998); Gibler & Tir (2014)

Hegemony. Dominance by one country, even if a nondemocracy, always has the power to keep the peace (Waltz 1979, 1993). A world with many major powers has been demonstrated to be unstable compared to bipolar and unipolar world systems (Haas 1970). Nonmajor powers ally with a major power so that they will be less vulnerable to outside threats. An alternative, rarely found historically, is for a lot of nonmajor powers to ally with one another in a united front, but competing alliances increases the chance of war (Kim 1989). One example of peacemaking by an alliance of nonmajor powers was ASEAN's solid support for Thailand while Vietnamese troops, occupying Cambodia, were on the Thai border (Haas 2013). Soon after the end of the Cold War, many scholars argued that the United States provided the hegemony to keep the peace (Mearsheimer 1990; Lake 1992), but wars continued nevertheless. Despite several India-Pakistan conflicts and India's involvement in the Sri Lankan civil war, one study attributed relative peace in South Asia to democratic India's role as a subregional hegemon (Russett, Oneal, and Cox 2000). But the fact that India keeps the peace by waging war is the very flaw in hegemony theory: To maintain hegemony, a superpower must be prepared to use military force to keep the rest of the world in line (Lipson 2003:74)!

Cold War strategy. Democracies kept the peace, many researchers agree, because of their Cold War policies. The "democratic peace" did not exist in the multipolar world before 1945, they argue. The Cold War accounted for the reluctance of democracies to break ranks (cf. Russett and Antholis 1992; Russett and Maoz 1993:73-74). Weede (1983) once attributed the "democratic peace" to the need of Western alliance partners to stick together in order to deter the Soviet Union, although he later disavowed such an explanation (Weede 1992). Other studies found that democracies stuck together to cope with the German threat during both World Wwars (Mearsheimer 1990) and due to the Soviet threat during the Cold War (Farber and Gowa 1995; Henderson 2002; Rosato 2003). With military power centralized in the superpowers during the Cold War, their smaller allies did not need to build up their power capabilities and thus lacked the wherewithal to move from disputes to military conflict, freeing them to devote their attention to economic development and growth. But after the Cold War, democracy-democracy wars have returned to pre-Cold War levels (Gowa 2011).

Later studies have disputed the Cold War as the sole reason for the "democratic peace." Lars-Erik Cederman and Mohan Rao (2001), for example, note that the decline in democracy-democracy wars has continued over time, both before and after the Cold War. But Johann Park (2013) found that the "democratic peace" has thrived even since the end of the Cold War.

Military integration. Even beyond the Cold War, military integration may be a factor in limited wars. The American military has been integrated into the military forces of a wide range of democratic states, even beyond the North Atlantic Treaty Organization, such that war between democracies has appeared unthinkable. The United States maintains a staggering number of bilateral military arrangements, stationing ships and troops in about one hundred fifty countries today (Davis, Pettyjohn, Sisson, Worman, McNerney 2012). One basis for American hegemony, in other words, is presumed to be a set of pseudo-military alliances involving democracies and non-democracies. Most alliance partners have been less likely to initiate force, leaving that option for the major alliance partner (Ireland and Gartner 2001). But when two democratic alliance partners are negotiating to resolve a dispute, they are unlikely to make concessions (Huth and Allee 2002).

Power calculations. In the end, calculations based on power may determine policy choices, not vague notions about constitutional constraints, common culture, domestic conflict, or economic considerations. For example, democratic publics have resisted wars and made concessions to avoid wars with powerful adversaries (Huth and Allee 2002) but have not minded as much when the opponents were weak (Ostrom and Job 1986). Balance-of-power calculations have kept the peace but have also led to war (Kacowicz 1995). A military historian has asserted that wars arise "not from any irrational and emotive drives, but from almost a superabundance of analytic rationality" (Howard 1984:14-15,22). Indeed, Russett and Antholis (1992: 429) found that Greek democracies attacking Athens were seeking to increase their relative power position. Several scholars, however, have argued that democracies sometimes go to war without careful rational power calculations (e.g., Mearsheimer 1990; Huth and Allee

2002; Lipson 2003:74).

Democracies that seek to initiate foreign conflicts have been characterized as particularly sensitive to the need for allies to back them up (Krause 2004:139; Senese and Vasquez 2004). One example is the Gulf War, in which President George H. W. Bush collected allies before launching war to reverse Iraq's seizure of Kuwait. Two other examples are George W. Bush's entry into Afghanistan in 2001 and Iraq in 2003.

Another view is that democracies are satisfied with their role in the world polity, lacking irredentist impulses; as status quo powers, they are unlikely to want an adjustment in their power position through war (Kacowicz 1995; Hart and Reed 1998). But democracies will attack other democracies when the threat level is very high (Mintz, Geva, Redd, Carnes 1997), a vital interest is involved (Huth and Allee 2002), or there is someting tangible to be gained (Geva, deRouen, Mintz 1993).

The issues involved in power disputes are matters of national interest, such as land and maritime territorial boundaries. Such disputes have been found to be increasingly bloodless, shorter in duration, and less frequent among democracies than nondemocracies, presumably because democracies are more satisfied with the status quo and have fewer such unresolved problems (Mitchell and Prins 1999:175). Any two dissatisfied countries, regardless of regime type, are unlikely to challenge the status quo (Lemke and Reed 1996).

Bruce Bueno de Mesquita and David Lalman (1992), computing expected utilities, predict interstate escalation and violence from democracies. But, according to John Mueller (1989:217-18), there has been a learning process over the centuries to the effect that wars have been increasingly "repulsive, immoral, and uncivilized—and methodologically ineffective—futile," with the "world wars . . . as horrific learning experiences." Two studies have found that democracies have learned that lesson and are less likely to initiate conflicts than nondemocracies (Morgan and Campbell 1991:205-6; Partell and Palmer 1999). One form of calculation is that war is sometimes not worth the effort or expense (Layne 1994), but that explanation has also been disputed (Maoz 1998).

One conclusion can be drawn from an impressive study of leaders in 154 foreign policy crises: The nature of the external threat is more important in determining leadership responses than regime types (Keller 2005). Smaller countries are more realistic about their diminutive power status (Elman 1997a,b). The more severe the threat, regardless of regime type, the more likely war will result (James and Oneal 1991).

Power transition theory. Countries increasing in power, according to the theory of power transition, will go to war in order to advance toward major power status, whereas wars sometimes emerge to forestall a trend toward decrease in world power. In contrast, democracies have been characterized as status quo powers, content with their power position, and therefore unlikely to go to war (Kacowitz 1995; Lemke and Werner 1996). Schweller (1992) has showed that democracies declining from topdog status are more peaceful than nondemocracies under similar conditions, but more research is needed.

Deterrence strategies. Democracies and nondemocracies alike can use deterrence to lessen the probability of war. But democracies tend to win when they fight (Reiter and Stam 1998a,b; Bueno de Mesquita, Morrow, Siverson, Smith 1999; Gelpi and Griesdorf 2001; cf. Desch 2002) and thus are less likely to be attacked (Reiter and Stam 2002). The reason appears to be that they have better military and political leadership and fight with more resolve because they can mobilize enthusiastic soldiers more quickly (Ferejohn and Rosenbluth 2008). However, another study found that morale, technological superiority, and better military intelligence are unrelated (Reiter and Stam 1998b). David Lake (1992, 2003) has argued that democratic leaders are constrained from feathering their own nests, so they allocate taxes rationally to matters of defense; thus, they are better prepared to fight wars and win against profligate leaders of nondemocracies, who are thereby deterred.

On the other hand, democracies tend to win short wars; when a war drags out past 18 months, the advantage passes to autocracies (Bennett and Stam 1998). Yet geopolitical factors are more important than regime type: Democracies only win or deter wars when they have superior military capabilities (Rasler and Thompson 2005:155).

Democracies are said to engage in coercive diplomacy, selecting only winnable conflicts and escalate slowly (if at all) to show force, and are perceived as potential credible adversaries because of public support, with the result that democracies with which they are at odds will back down, realizing that they are not bluffing in a confrontation situation. But the same strategy could equally apply to nondemocracies (Huth and Allee 2002). The coercion will be seen as a bluff if a democracy manipulates the public (Potter and Baum 2010).

Another deterrence strategy is to form an alliance. Democracies tend to ally with other democracies, thus giving them the edge over nondemocracies, which have more difficulty finding allies (Choi 2004). According to Schweller (1992:252) democracies under threat are more likely to set up a defensive alliance with one another (cf. Siverson and Emmons 1991), especially if undergoing a decline in strength. But common membership in alliances, as noted above, is a most unreliable predictor of war avoidance.

Although Immanuel Kant (1795[1957]:12-13) suggested that democracies would avoid casualties and therefore rely on mechanized warfare more than large armies, the data do not bear out his theory of deterrence (Gartzke 2001). The technology of war has advanced for both democracies and nondemocracies.

Major powers. The strength of major powers, whether democracies or not, is more likely to tempt its leaders to enter war and engage in MIDs than minor powers (Gowa 1999:9; Kinsella and Russett 2002), though there is uncertainty whether pairs of countries with equal military capabilities are much more or less likely to fight than dyads with unequal capabilities. Bremer (1992:330) has discovered that pairs of highly militarized states are more likely to show off their power than dyads that include one less militarized state. For Raymond (1994:35), two major power democracies are more likely to use third-party conflict resolution than disputes involving countries with asymmetric power, but he did not compare major power nondemocracies. Major power rivalries between democracies or democratizing countries are likely to be short (Bennett 2007) and rarely escalate (Hewitt and Wilkenfeld 1996). For Ireland and Gartner (2001), countries with large populations are more likely to be involved in foreign conflicts.

Percentage of democracies. Is the world becoming more peaceful? Rummel (2002), for example, has constructed on the Internet a "democratic peace clock," which gets closer to world peace as the percentage of democracies in the world increases. The percentage of democracies in the world has increased since the end of the Cold War in what Huntington (1991) called the "third wave." The prediction is that as the world is increasingly filled with democracies, peace will spread (Mitchell 2002). However, there was an increase in wars after the Cold War (Brecher and Wilkenfeld 1997; Gowa 2011), especially with the disintegration of Yugoslavia.

Contiguity. In some studies, the proximity between two countries has been found to be the best predictor of war between two countries (Terrell 1977), although Nils Gleditsch (1995) calculated that the distance between democracies is no different from that between all other pairs of states. For Gibler and Tir (2014), if contiguous countries agree upon their mutual boundaries, they have removed the most contentious issue for war from their foreign policies; democracy washes out the relationship, as a country with settled borders is more likely to be democratic. Contrariwise, when two countries are very distant, the only likelihood that they will be involved in militarized conflict is when one is a major power. For that reason, many "democratic peace" samples exclude noncontiguous dyads unless one is a major power. Although some studies have reported that contiguity washes out as a factor when controlling for regime type, other studies have found that democracies, even new democracies, are much less likely to initiate conflicts in politically "mature" subregions (Enterline 1998; cf. Gibler and Braithwaite 2013). Yet "mature" democracies are prominent in a list of deadly wars (Götze 2006; see also the Appendix below).

In sum, if power capabilities or calculations explain why some countries are more peaceful than others, then the "democratic peace" is a spurious relationship. At least "power" is not a definitional element of "democracy," so there is no autocorrelation, as in some previous explanations.

Leadership

Thus far, the human element of decision making has been left out. The next set of theoretical explanations deals with leadership. Decisions have to be made to enter or avoid war by decision makers.

Wright (1942:847-48; cf. Merritt and Zinnes 1991:219) once suggested that leadership is the most important intervening variable between regime type and war (regime type→leadership→peace). Yet most "democratic peace" research blackboxes the role of those who make decisions for war and peace while pursuing statistical analyses. In other words, the "democratic peace" makes a crucial assumption that leaders are mere puppets of correlational findings, unable to resist statistical pressures! Careful studies of leaders encounter much more ambiguity (Table 5.5).

Table 5.5. Leadership Styles and the "Democratic Peace"

Leadership Style	Studies in Agreement	Refutations
diplomatic propensities	Dixon (1993, 1994); Raymond (1994:32-34, 1996); Eyerman & Hart (1996); Starr (1997); Mousseau (1998); Dixon & Senese (2002); Dorussen & Ward (2008:190)	Mitchell & Prins (1999) ; Huth & Allee (2002)
selectorate theory	Bueno de Mesquita & Lalman (1992); Lake (1992); Morgan & Schwebach (1992); Fearon (1994); Bueno de Mesquita & Siverson (1995, 1997); Hermann & Kegley (1995); Siverson (1995); Eyerman & Hart (1996); Stam (1996); Bennett & Stam (1998); Reiter & Stam (1998 a,b); Rioux (1998); Bueno de Mesquita, Siverson, Woller (1992); Bueno de Mesquita, Morrow, Siverson, Smith (2001:202); Gelpi & Griesdorf (2001); Bueno de Mesquita, Smith, Siverson, Morrow (2003); Bueno de Mesquita, Morrow, Siverson, Smith (2004); Downes & Lilley (2010)	Mearsheimer (1990:49); Ireland & Gartner (2001); Rosato (2003); Chiozza & Goemans (2004); Keller (2005); Rousseau (2005:344); Debs & Goemans (2010)
personal beliefs and traits	Hermann & Hermann (1989); Hermann & Kegley (1995); Bueno de Mesquita & Siverson (1997); Schafer & Walker (2006)	Elman (1997b); Layne (1997); Kacowicz (1997); Keller (2005)
perceptual images	Hagan (1993); Mintz & Geva (1993); Owen (1994a:95); Hermann & Kegley (1995)	Lipson (2003:74); Keller (2005); Geis (2006)
unpopularity	Russett (1990:133-34); Miller (1995); Smith (1998b)	Ostrom & Job (1986); James & Oneal (1991); Keller (2005)

Noting that most discussions on the "democratic peace" leave out the perceptions of leaders, Layne (1994) cited evidence that differing leadership qualities and styles are important for democracies during crisis situations that might result in violence. Many researchers agree (George 1980:47-49; Lebow 1981:69-79; Janis 1982; Lebow and Stein 1993; Hagan 1994; Weart 1994:311; Hermann and Kegley 1995; Oren 1995; Keller 2005).

Diplomatic propensities. The argument is that democracies in conflict with other democracies are more likely to use third-party methods to settle their differences. Dixon (1993, 1994) analyzed 264 interstate disputes in the Cold War era, found that democracies are more likely to accept third-party mediation efforts than nondemocracies, though the disputes may remain unsettled. Raymond (1994:32-34) discovered that pairs of democracies are more likely to choose arbitration than mediation, whereas other types of dyads chose mediation at a higher rate than democracies. However, having chosen arbitration, democracies do not necessarily resolve their disputes with that method (Raymond 1996).

In several studies, however, democracies worked out many conflicts bilaterally through diplomatic compromises, moreso than with nondemocracies (Mousseau 1998; Mitchell and Prins 1999; Dixon and Senese 2002). But there are many exceptions, according to Huth and Allee (2002): Concessions are less likely when the public would be upset, a stalemate has been reached, a vital interest in involved, the leader is weak, elections are approaching, or the opposing country is militarily weaker. However, Gowa (1999:41) reported that there was no relation between decisions for war and impending elections. One study found that democracies go through six stages in handling conflict situations, whereas nondemocracies went through fewer stages (Eyerman and Hart 1996), though there evidently is no difference in regime type on whether countries escalate disputes (Dixon and Senese 2002). But democratic leaders are not uniquely clever in negotiations, as any biography of Castlereagh, Metternich, and Talleyrand will demonstrate (Kissinger 1957). Final terms of settlement depend on initial war aims and the cost of continuing the conflict rather than regime type (Werner 1998). The literature on crisis decisionmaking contains much confusion and dissensus (Haas 1986; Huth and Allee 2002).

Selectorate theory. As developed by Bruce Bueno de Mesquita, selectorate theory views democratic leaders as wisely making decisions to maximize domestic support—that is, they only choose war when they estimate that they are likely to win vis-à-vis another country, and that is the case when those in power have domestic legitimacy (Bueno de Mesquita, Morrow, Siverson, Smith 2001:202; Krause 2004:134). Accordingly, democracies are more likely to enter disputes than nondemocracies (cf. Downes and Lilley 2010). (The "selectorate" is the sum of all persons who are empowered to chose leaders.) A common view is that democratic leaders are able to mobilize support for war because they often have the economic and military resources and are more likely to be viewed by their public as legitimate than nondemocratic leaders (Reiter and Stam 1998a,b, 2002). Responsiveness of leaders to their base of support as well as to the nature of a foreign threat is a critical element. Whether a leader will ignore or cater to the will of domestic validators is the factor left out of the view that democratic constraints predict peaceful responses to foreign conflicts. But, as noted above, sometimes the public demands war (Huth and Allee 2002), and sometimes leaders select war as a diversionary tactic to consolidate their power. Some ideologically militant or radical leaders drive forward into foreign conflict regardless of domestic constraints (Morgan and Schwebach 1992; Hagan 1993, 1994). Leaders propagandize the selectorate more than the reverse (Baker and Oneal 2001), so the key to obtaining public support is a compliant press (Downes and Lilley 2010). The main problem with selectorate theory is that perceptions of leaders are blackboxed and need case study validation.

Personal beliefs and traits. Personality can also determine leadership styles, as they comprise the identity of decision makers, and identities need reinforcement (Hermann and Kegley 1995). One hypothesis is that democracies tend to encourage leaders who are cautious, pragmatic and are sensitive to social-emotional orientations within groups, whereas autocratic rule seems to attract ideological, inner-directed, and task-oriented leaders who engage in risky behavior (Bueno de Mesquita and Siverson 1997; Gallaher and Allen 2014). Stereotypically, leaders in democracies are presumed to be conciliatory, whereas leaders in autocracies are presumably aggressive (Hermann and Hermann 1989).

Conciliatory autocratic leaders who deal with aggressive democratic leaders, thus, would be deviant cases to confound such insight. Several case studies prove that democratic leaders can be pigheaded and autocratic leaders quite reasonable (Elman 1997b; Freedman 1997; Layne 1997; Kacowicz 1997; Rock 1997; Brock 2006).

Even if more evidence establishes that certain leadership styles are more likely to be found in democracies, which in turn predispose them to prefer peaceful international behavior, the variability of personality types in terms of needs for power, interpersonal- versus task-orientation, tendencies to be suspicious or trusting, and other psychological elements is far too vast to expect definitive results until a large number of cases are analyzed. But what would be a representative sample?

Perceptual images. Leaders differ in how they process and respond to information. Hermann and Kegley (1995; cf. Weart 1998) identify one image that might guide leaders to simplify reality in making decisions—whether a country is part of an in- or out-group: In-groups of democracies can be trusted, out-groups cannot, according to a simulation of decision makers (Mintz and Geva 1993). However, "democracy" is a complicated concept, so leaders must somehow classify a variety of political systems into a "democratic" in-group. Statistically, democracies do tend to join alliances with other democracies (Siverson and Emmons 1991; Maoz and Russettt 1992; Dixon 1994), but those studies do not necessarily use the same classification rules as decision makers. Indeed, Polity II classified Spain as a democracy in 1898, but Russett (1993b:8) and Ray (1995) disagreed, based on evidence of perceptions of decision makers! Russett (1993b:17) claimed that the Philippines was a democracy in 1899, but noted that Washington did not, and the incipient Philippine democracy was attacked, occupied, and colonized. No such systematic evaluation of perceptual information has been applied to the thousands of cases that form the basis for the "democratic peace." Meanwhile, simplistic democratic leaders may view other countries in terms of a mere dichotomy or may be ideologically driven, whereas more clever leaders will perceive much more ambiguity (Druckman 1994). For Owen (1994a:95), as soon as a democracy identifies another state as a democracy, the likelihood of peaceful interaction increases, contrary to the history of the Yalta Conference of 1945.

Whereas some argue that leaders of democracies better understand one another because of similar regime types, such knowledge may also be exploited by democracies that go to war (Lipson 2003:74).

Unpopularity. Unpopular leaders may decide upon violent methods of solving conflict situations. The hope is that they will gain popularity through strong action, a diversionary strategy. But they also might prefer covert action (Forsythe 1992; Sørenson 1992; Van Evera 1992). Yet a popular democratic leader, such as President Lyndon Johnson, might also believe that the public consists of lemmings, ready to support almost anything (Ostrom and Job 1986). Alistair Smith (1998a,b) has found that very popular as well as very unpopular leaders, whether in democracies or nondemocracies, will opt for bold action to excite support, but he also reported that there is a hawk bias in democracies, since strong initiatives in foreign policy, especially during elections, give the impression of leadership competence. On the other hand, leaders recognized as doves will get out of war before elections to ensure reelection.

Racism

Yet another explanation for the contemporary peace among democracies alongside wars between the First and Third Worlds has been suggested by Forsythe (1992:393), who has noted that all the covert violent operations of the United States to topple democracies were in the Third World (cf. Shalom 1993:12-17; Cohen 1994; Koga 2011; Bell 2014). Russett, similarly, has admitted that European democracies practiced "racism" (1990:131) and were "ethnocentric" (1993b: 34-35) in pursuing colonialism. The inference is that when some peoples see others as inferior, they have fewer scruples about waging war against them.

Some scholars have found regional differences. That is, democracies sometimes fight democracies outside the West but not inside (Holsti 1996; Gangulu 1997; Rock 1997; Kacowicz 1998; Kivimaki 2001; Huth and Allee 2002; Lemke 2002; Goldsmith 2006; Henderson 2009; Haas 2013). Weart (1998:221) has expressed a similar judgment that racism is often involved in decisions of democracies to attack other democracies. Robert Johns and Graeme Davies (2012) found that in an experimental student sample there was more willingness to attack an Islamic state than a country with a predominantly Christian population

In other words, the "democratic peace" may simply be the "Caucasian peace." In trying to find explanations for anomalies, "democratic peace" researchers treat democracies outside Anglo-European countries with more skepticism than in those where white people predominate (see Appendix). The South Pacific, which consists of island democracies inhabited by nonwhite peoples, nevertheless, has been a zone of interstate peace ever since the Netherlands surrendered colonial control over West Papua to Indonesia in 1963 (Haas 2013).

Paradigms

Intervening variable approaches, mostly single-factor explanations, are thus far unsatisfactory. All other possible explanations have to be ruled out before a single factor can be elevated to a "cause." They are unnecessary if the "democratic peace" is rejected. Indeed, Errol Henderson (2002) decided to put several of the above explanations into a single study, controlling for economic interdependence, geographic contiguity, and political similarity. As a result, the "democratic peace" correlation disappeared, disputing an earlier study reporting that the "democratic peace" remained after controlling for a single variable—contiguity (Gleditsch 1995). Jervis (2002) suggested the conventional approach of explaining war as a function of several factors, but that is not a paradigm (cf. Rasler and Thompson 2005:234).

Three researchers, however, have made larger connections. Michael Doyle has articulated Kant's framework as a paradigm with three "definitive articles"—republican representation, interdependence, and human rights (Doyle 1983, 1997, 2005; cf. Cederman 2001). Having gone beyond the simplistic bivariate "democratic peace" formula in favor of the Kantian agenda, Doyle is making headway but on his own paradigmatic path while quantitative hypothesis testing continues unabated. But, despite evidence to the contrary summarized above, Doyle does not dispute the "democratic peace," suggesting that his quest is ideological. Moreover, Kant (1795 [1970]:101) was not in favor of "democracy," which he characterized as "necessarily a despotism." In a more recent study (Danilovic and Clare 2011), peace was related to Kantian liberalism (individual freedoms) and constitutionalism (rule of law and legal equality) but not representative government, which is usually equivalenced to mean "democracy."

Gordon Henderson (2006) has identified Kant within the larger conversation of social contract theory, involving Hobbes, Locke, Rousseau as well, and he found trade to be a fourth pillar within Kant (ibid., p. 214). But most studies believe that trade has no relationship to peace.

Michael Mousseau (2003, 2009, 2013a), meanwhile, has developed a very different paradigm in which both democracy and war are a result of the development of contract-intensive economies, domestic and worldwide. Based on the insights of Polanyi (1944), he refers to his paradigm as "economic norms theory," while others refer to a similar "capitalist peace" (Gartzke 2007; Weede 2003). One problem is that he has never counted the number of contracts for any country beyond insurance policies, and the Napoleonic Wars have been determined to based on economic competition between Britain and France (Bond 1979:1-2,8).

For some reason, "democratic peace" researchers have screened many paradigms on the causes of war out of their reading matter (cf. Haas 1992:ch7; 1997b:133-36). Even though a democratic leader must make a decision whether to go to war, they blackbox all the *decisionmaking* paradigms developed by Graham Allison, Sigmund Freud, Alexander George, Charles and Margaret Hermann, A. R. Luria, Robert North, and many others (Haas 1992:162-76).

Although the focus on regime type is of a societal factor, they do not draw upon even one of four major *societal* paradigms:

- Marxian theory (Kende 1971, 1978),
- lateral pressure theory (Choucri and North 1975,1989),
- mass society theory (Speier 1952), or
- national culture theory (Mead and Metraux 1965).

Moreover, many critics draw upon the following well-known *systemic* paradigms to refute their claims:

- action-reaction theory (Richardson 1960a),
- balance-of-power theory (Morgenthau 1948; Kaplan

1957),
* rank disequilibrium theory (Galtung 1964; Organski 1958), or
* hegemony theory (Wallerstein 1984).

Not having footnoted any of the above paradigms, "democratic peace" researchers are trapped at the level of hypothesis testing of ad hoc middle-range theories, unmindful of the need in any science to develop a covering law that links broadly to other related phenomena.

Contemporary paradigms should also be taken into account: The rational actor paradigm may indeed explain calculations between democratic and nondemocratic decision makers (Levi and Razin 2003). Human development theory (Sen 1999) and Marxian theory (Kende) could refocus economic explanations. The regime (Young 1989, 1999) paradigms address such issues as culture and leadership.

Conclusion

As long as "democratic peace" researchers focus on a simple correlation with only one possible intervening variable, they are really stuck in hypothesis testing and not engaging in theory building. Until they connect with paradigms, the term "democratic peace theory" is an oxymoron.

And until they realize that they are pushing a distasteful normative agenda, they are ignoring the fundamental basis of science—to improve life. The following chapter exposes the latter naïveté.

6

Normative Problems

What may seem baffling to many observers is the reason for all the attention to the alleged lawlike relationship between democracy and peace. Why are some scholars, primarily American, so keen on reaffirming a statistical regularity and ignoring various objections? As a Rorschach reading, my understanding of the literature is that various researchers are in favor of democracy and want the world to consist of more democracies, which they hope will mean a more peaceful world, even if they are fundamentally naïve about the implications of their research (cf. Xenias 2005:358-59). They do not seem interested in how various governments might transform themselves from nondemocracies into democracies, consistent with their views, but leave such an agenda as beyond the scope of their research.

Since a careful normative agenda is largely absent from their writings, we should take at face value the claim by various scholars that they are engaging in pure science without regard to normative implications other than an understandable ideological preference for democracies. Nonetheless, the findings of their research made their way to the highest echelons of power during the last decade of the twentieth century (Fukuyama 1992:280; Halperin 1993; James Baker and Bill Clinton, cited in Russett 1993b:10-11,129; Russett 2005: 395; Anthony Lake, cited in Layne 1994:46; cf. White House 1994: 19-20). Implicitly, the "law" was cited to bomb Serbia in 1999 so that Kosovo could be saved from genocide. Within Israel, opponents of the Arab-Israeli peace process have even cited the "democratic peace" literature to justify intransigence, including Prime Minister Benjamin Netanyahu (Cohen 1994:223; Ish-Shalom 2006, 2008a). President George W. Bush also expressed considerable enthusiasm:

> democracies don't go to war with each other. . . I've got great faith in de-
> mocracies to promote peace. And that's why I'm such a strong believer
> that the way forward in the Middle East, the broader Middle East, is to
> promote democracy (New York Times 2004).

In other words, promulgation of the "democratic peace" boomer-anged.

When the "law" was specifically cited as a reason to invade Iraq, my worst fears about "democratic peace" research were realized, and Bruce Russett (2005) felt compelled to comment with chagrin. Yet in his Nobel Peace Prize acceptance speech of 2009, Barack Obama gave support to the falsehood that "America has never fought a war against a democracy."

In 1995, when I first wrote my critique of the confused "demo-cratic peace" literature, I was very concerned that President Clinton or his successors would succumb to academic propaganda. The find-ings of social science are often subject to distortion outside the social sciences, so a constant barrage from social scientists about inherent peaceful qualities of democracies could be abused in matters of poli-cy. I submitted my critique to *The Journal of Conflict Resolution*, and Bruce Russett rejected the paper for publication. Although even-tually published in an edited collection during 1997, few saw or heeded the advice; among the two exceptions (Gates, Knutsen, Mo-ses 1996; Xenias 2005:361), the latter held onto the paper for ten years. At the time, I thought that the flaws were so obvious that other researchers would see the same problems and eschew that line of re-search. I never expected that hundreds of scholars would be seduced, that a mushrooming of imperfect studies would last nearly two dec-ades from the mid-1990s.

There are at least ten aspects of what I have deconstructed as a hidden agenda. "Democratic peace" researchers have been largely unaware of that agenda, preferring scholarly discourse. Readers can judge the wisdom of my deconstruction for themselves, which remains almost as originally submitted to *The Journal of Conflict Resolution*:

Countries should be encouraged to democratize.

"Democratic peace" researchers are in love with democracy, as they should be. Although Huntington (1968:23,27) once urged aid to democratic political parties in the Third World, later he became more cautious about external programs to hasten the transition of governments from nondemocratic to democratic forms (Huntington 1989). Naïve interpretations of social science research in support of efforts to favor one democratic faction over a less democratic faction, thereby making the latter more nationalistic and thus more popular, retard democracy in the long run. Democratizing states have been among the least peaceful over the last two centuries (Mansfield and Snyder 1995, 2005), though one study has indicated that the reason may be that the executives were weak (Braumoeller 2004) or that surrounding countries were not democratic (Ray 1993; Weede 2004). Countries just beginning to democratize are especially likely to become involved in war (Braumoeller 2004).

According to Anastasia Xenias (2005:365), "promoting democracy to promote peace is nearly futile." Her reason is that solid democracies are difficult to emerge, involving as they do complex attitudinal and institutional arrangements that must be agreed upon in a lengthy domestic conversation.

Democracy promotion is perilous. If the Arab Spring has not provided sufficient caution, research on the warlike propensities of transitional democracies should also give pause.

Democracies should join together.

One obvious policy stimulus is for democratic countries to get together in a common forum so that they can work out their differences and come together when nondemocracies emerge as threats to world peace. Such a laudable goal has actually come to pass, though never mentioned in the "democratic peace" literature.

Frustrated that the United Nations would not respond to Serbia's attempt to suppress Kosovars in Kosovo, American Secretary of State Madeline Albright brought about a new intergovernmental organization, the Community of Democracies, during 2000 after the goal of "democratic enlargement" was announced by President Bill Clinton (1996) as a successor American foreign policy to the Cold War. Although delegates to the organization from about 100 countries meet annually, the organization has been underutilized and needs practical research. "Democratic peace" researchers have not volunteered.

Democracies need not fear wars from other democracies.

The view that democracies can become undemocratic, and thus presumably more violent, is one basis for criticism of the complacency of the "democratic peace" by Layne (1994) and Mearsheimer (1990). As Alex Mintz and associates (1997) have demonstrated experimentally, democracies will fight other democracies if the level of threat is sufficiently high, confirming data studied by Gowa (1995:516). Huntington (1991) has documented the fact that waves of democratization have always been followed by eras of reversal. Iran, because of policies distasteful to Israel, has been threatened by the latter and the United States, but illiberal Iran fulfills several of the conditions of "democracy" accepted by "democratic peace" researchers (Table 3.1). Tehran has every reason to fear threats from Tel Aviv and Washington; their democracy was overthrown in 1953 with covert intervention by Britain and the United States.

Democracies may justifiably attack nondemocracies.

That nondemocracies are unworthy and should suffer accordingly at the hands of democracies is an unmistakable hidden agenda. The analysis of why the United States has repeatedly gone to war without provocation is absent from "democratic peace" research. Although Russett (1990:130) scolded democracies for fighting imperialist wars, he and his cohorts have excluded aggressive wars by the United States from their studies, thus implying that wars unleashed by democracies on nondemocracies are of lesser interest. On the same page, he falsely excused the United States for fighting Vietnamese who "could be identified as not self-governing."

Similarly, Russett (1993b:124-26) went to great length in showing that democratic processes slowed during the decision making of President George H. W. Bush to fight Iraq in 1991 in the name of democracy. But he failed to mention how American diplomats earlier appeared to have given Saddam Hussein a blank check to annex Kuwait (cf. Hallett 1991). And, rather than negotiating to bring peace to Cambodia, the United States secretly provided diplomatic and financial support to the Khmer Rouge in the 1980s (Haas 1991a,b).

Harald Müller (2004) has noted that democracies have fought wars that no other countries wanted to get involved, including the Gulf War in 1991, Somalia in 1993, and Kosovo in 1999. The Responsibility to Protect mandate of the United Nations has involved democracies is stopping mass killings, as in Libya during 2010.

The mission of the *Enola Gay* in 1945, which many researchers believe was mistaken, may have cost the lives of some 200,000 innocent civilians. Yet the secret American bombing of democratic Cambodia in 1969 and thereafter may have sacrificed as many persons (Haas 2012a:ch1) for the familiar rationale of shortening a war, this time with Vietnam. As Robert Jay Lifton and Greg Mitchell (1995) have argued, the American government needs to apologize for repeatedly participating in "pointless apocalypse."

Distinguishing "good" democracies from "bad" nondemocracies enables researchers to exculpate democracies for aggressively fighting nondemocracies, as has been discovered in experiments on foreign policy (Geva, deRouen, Mintz 1993; Mintz and Geva 1993). Which country will be attacked next for the sin of being a nondemocracy? In *Cool War* (2013), Noah Feldman suggests that there is a hidden motive within American foreign policy scenario creators, who appear to preparing for war with China because Beijing is a dictatorship that abuses human rights.

Democracies may justifiably subvert other countries.

The exclusion of covert operations from the sample of military conflicts serves subliminally to say that democracies will not be scrutinized by "democratic peace" researchers when they work to change democracies into dictatorships. The United States clearly acted to end democracy in democratic Chile, the Dominican Republic, Guatemala, Hawai'i, Iran, Nicaragua, and elsewhere (Mead 1987:263;

Emerson 1988; Chomsky 1991; Forsythe 1992; Ransom 1992; Snyder 1991:ch7; Smith 1994; Kegley and Hermann 1996a,b; Dudley and Agard 1990; Rosato 2003).

Russett (1993b:121) pointed to the U.S. government's "deep culpability" in fighting the democratic Sandinista government of Nicaragua, and he noted that the instability in Iran during 1953 was due to policies of Washington (ibid., p.22). But he excluded Washington's covert interventions in both countries from his sample because they were "justified by a cold war ideology and public belief that the government in question was allying itself with the major nondemocratic adversary" (ibid.,p.130).

"Democratic peace" researchers play shell games in determining samples, hiding instances when democratic governments frustrate democracy in other countries. Democratic forces in these countries resent the intrusion even more.

Democracies may justifiably attack other democracies.

When a democracy attacks another democracy, we are told not to worry: The scale will be small, the casualties will be light, and the duration will be short. Such wars are deleted from the sample under study, usually because they do not reach the 1,000 battle death threshold. In other words, "democratic peace" researchers have no concern over a few dead citizens in a democratic county. Starr (1997:158) has even congratulated democracies for intervening in other democracies, though such action has its critics (Forsythe 1992; Stedman 1993).

Meanwhile, the American government justifies drone attacks in Pakistan and Yemen (Bashir and Crews 2012); the number of civilian Pakistanis killed by drone attacks is estimated so far at from 411 to 884, including 197 children (Hamid 2013:23). One consequence of the attacks is an increase in jihadists, including the American of Pakistani origin who tried to set off a bomb in Times Square during 2010 precisely because of drone attacks on the land of his birth (Haas 2010a:ch46). "Democratic peace" researchers shamefully continue to look the other way while the national security of the United States and allies is used as a pretext to kill citizens in other democracies. What is the real reason for insisting on the "democratic peace" if not to provide cover to certain countries to claim that they are democracies while engaging in aggressive behavior?

Democracies may justifiably impose democracy.

The "white man's burden" was a common justification for European countries to subdue and "civilize," while the United States was even more crass in proclaiming its "manifest destiny" to clear North America of indigenous peoples by any means necessary. Napoléon, believing that the Declaration of the Rights of Man applied to the entire world, not just France, embarked on a war to depose monarchies. After World War II, the United States joined allies in restoring democracy to Germany and Japan, and after the Cold War the capitalist states encouraged Eastern Europe to reintroduce capitalist democracy. But restoration is different from creation and imposition. The new "white man's burden," according to some foolish interpreters of the "democratic peace," appears to be a new form of imperialism—to impose democracy. The "enemy," in other words, consists of non-democracies, especially "outlaw states" (Rawls 1999:14). In short, the "democratic peace" is not a theory but rather began and continues as an ideology, a guide to policy that defenders guard with rhetoric disguised as methodological.

The current agenda can be discerned from pleas "to spread freedom from one state to another" (Rummel 1983a:38), to "expand" the "sphere of democracy" (Fukuyama 1992:280), to export democracy as America's "manifest destiny" (Muravchik 1991:4; cf. Meernik 1990; Hermann and Kegley 1998), and to foster Wilsonianism (Russett 1993b:48, 2005:395). No matter that Woodrow Wilson embarked on military adventures in the Caribbean, México, and Central America (Levin 1968; Sweetman 1968; Cooper 1968). The ethnocentric belief that the United States played "a major role in persuading dictators in South Korea and the Philippines to surrender power" (Russett 2005:406), clearly at odds with the reality in both countries, where people's power demonstrations among the middle classes gained overwhelming support (Haas 2014a:ch4), says a lot about the motivations of "democratic peace" researchers. So do scholars who urge the United States to take cognizance of the "democratic peace" and project power abroad (Slaughter and Ikenberry 2006; McFaul 2010; Traub 2008). Although Russett (1993b:126; cf. Doyle 1983; Weart 1994:311) explicitly argued against a unilateral "crusade for democracy" during the late twentieth century, he was somehow converted to that very crusade at the beginning of the twenty-first century (Russett and Oneal 2001:272).

According to Paul Miller (2012), who served on the National Security Council staff during much of the last decade, the extension of democracies abroad has been the grand strategy of American in the four administrations since the end of the Cold War. The goal of Wilsonian foreign policy to encourage democracies caught the attention of neoconservatives (Smith 2007; Ish-Shalom 2008b:682). Thus, President Reagan supported an invasion of Grenada in 1983, and George W. Bush was eager to attack Panamá in 1999. President Clinton indicated that his foreign policy goal of democratization was "not a democratic crusade" (White House 1994:19) yet he favored "democratic enlargement" (Elman 1997d: 498).

Then came the Iraq War of 2003, the quintessential example of imposing democracy in accordance with the supposed "democratic peace" nostrum. Neoconservative pundit Max Boot (2003), seeking to explain the rationale to the general public, explicitly cited the "democratic peace" as justification, and even the Democratic Party establishment bought the concept (Progressive Policy Institute 2003). George W. Bush's second inaugural speech in 2005 extolled the goal of promoting democracy, congratulating himself for turning Afghanistan and Iraq into democracies, however perilous they were while he was in office. On September 18, 2008, Prime Minister Tony Blair, while interviewed on *The Daily Show with Jon Stewart*, professed the same belief. Economist David Cesarini (2011), commenting on developments in Egypt, showed that academics outside political science also have been duped. The "democratic peace" hypothesis has even delighted torture supporters Robert Delahunty and John Yoo (2010).

How did the "democratic peace" idea get from esoteric researcherly journals to the White House? Tony Smith (1997) has identified neoliberal academic Larry Diamond (1994, 2001) as the one with appropriate access to positions of power in Washington.

Small and Singer (1976:51) objected strenuously to such a "stimulus to war." Long before the Iraq War of 2003, several scholars expressed the fear that a "democratic peace" dogma might encourage American interventions for the purpose of democratizing a society (Doyle 1983:324; Rothstein 1991:48; Sørensen 1992:400; Vincent 1987a:104; Arat 1991:42; Shalom 1993; Stedman 1993; Haass 1994;

Layne 1994:46-47; Hendrickson 1994-1995), a concern pooh-poohed by Rummel (1987:113).

But what did "democratic peace" researchers do as the Bush administration stepped up propaganda for war with Iraq? There was no outcry, no petition, and not even a response to Boot's op-ed in the *New York Times* or *Washington Post*. In an academic journal, Russett (2005) professed to be "Bushwhacked." Although he has noted that he earlier said that he did not want "democratic peace" research to be misinterpreted as favoring wars to impose democracy (Russett and Oneal 2001:303), he was entirely unreceptive to publishing the warning that I presented to him in 1995, and he did not object to the same justification for the Kosovo War of 1999. Although I would not go so far as to accuse "democratic peace" researchers of collusion in promoting the Iraq War, as has Tony Smith (2007), their collective failure to sound the alarm is an example of ivory tower academic irresponsibility (cf. Ish-Shalom 2008b:689), an astonishing lack of commitment to the goal of peace that presumably sparked the flurry of excitement over "democratic peace" research in the first place.

Russett (2005) only later acknowledged the failure of American interventions to result in democracies (cf. Van Evera 1992:289; Peceny 1997, 1999:195; Tures 2005). Similarly, UN interventions have often failed to create full-fledged democracies in such places as Cambodia (Chandler 2010; Richmond 2011). The lesson that efforts to introduce democracy has often resulted in increased instability should have been learned from history, such as the Athenian wars (Bachteler 1997:317) and more than two dozen contemporary cases (Meernik 1990). Mark Peceny and Jeffrey Pickering (2006), studying dozens of interventions historically, found that most produced no change in regime type, though UN interventions were the most likely to result in democracy, American and French had more plusses than minuses, and British interventions have been more disastrous. Imposing democracy evidently works best when most nearby countries are already democracies (Enterline and Grieg 2006:155).

Often, unpopular puppets have been installed and supported, especially when Washington has been the intervening country (Bueno de Mesquita and Downs 1996). Today, the academic consensus is that imposition of democracy is unwise (cf. Ayers 2010; Talentino 2010), but very few had the good sense to broadcast scholarly alarm to stop the Iraq War. Meanwhile, several neoconservative pundits have called for an all-out war on Islamic fundamentalism (Berman 2003; Perle and From 2003).

Democracies may ignore the needs of nondemocracies.

By exclusion from "democratic peace" samples, nondemocracies are treated as second-rate citizens of the global polity. Instead of studying important problems faced by nondemocracies in the global economy and polity, "democratic peace" researchers look elsewhere. For example, "five U.S. administrations ignored the dismantling of Philippine democracy [by Ferdinand Marcos] because of strategic concerns over continued U.S. access to bases in the country" (Schraeder 1992b:401; Kessler 1992).

In an early work, Amitai Etzioni (1962:ch11) urged democracies to encourage democratization through foreign aid and to punish nondemocracies by withholding foreign aid. Morton Halperin (1993: 105) proposed aid to "fledgling democracies," but only at the invitation of the countries, and he recommended terminating such aid if "democratization is interrupted." Alternatively, aid is being withheld from states that violate human rights, hoping that they will improve, though there is scant empirical evidence that such a strategy has ever worked (Haas 1994:ch5, 2014a:ch8; Drury and Peksen 2010). Indeed, some researchers warn that democracy promotion can boomerang (Huntington 1991; Yom 2010).

The indifference agenda, which has long had strong adherents in Washington, was advocated by Max Singer and Aaron Wildawsky in *The Real World Order* (1993). Mueller (1989:251-53), though predicting that the less developed countries will follow the trend of the First World in avoiding war, failed to ask whether world inequality, so well defended by the First World, might be a reason for wars within and between less developed countries. The need to increase respect human rights is undeniably a major concern in the field of international relations, as millions are being persecuted and are starving in the world today (Haas 2014a).

But researchers are being hypocritical by not following the very logic of the "democratic peace" thesis: If they expect more democracies to bring about a more peaceful world, then they should be studying why more countries are not democracies and why others backslide from democracy. The focus should shift to how to promote democracy in individual cases, not endless statistical studies trying to improve the validity of the "democratic peace" thesis. For "democratic peace" researchers to ignore the needs of nondemocracies is an arrogant misuse of scholarly competence.

Democracies may continue undemocratic practices.

For Hannah Arendt (1951:pt2), colonialism by democracies produced less democracy within the metropole countries. But "democratic peace" researchers excuse Herrenvolk democracies, imperial democracies, and democracies that treat their minorities as internal colonies by including them in their samples of "peaceful democratic dyads." Eager to beancount as many "democracies" as possible, they study countries when minorities and women have been refused the right to vote yet baptize them as "democracies." Perhaps the most insidious of all the hidden agendas is that various countries coded as "democracies" are supposed to rest on their laurels for reaching the penultimate stage of history (Fukuyama 1992). Never mind the racism, the homeless who lie in the doorways of unoccupied office buildings, the decapitalization of "democracies" by corporations that relocate their factories elsewhere, efforts to depress voter turnout by insisting on hard-to-obtain identification cards, civil rights enforcement at a low ebb, and ample instances of undemocratic processes of foreign policy continuing unabated (Mead 1987:ch21; Chomsky 1991; Reisman and Baker 1992:144-152; Shalom 1993). "Democratic peace" theorists show no interest in perfecting democracy.

The agenda of "democratic peace" researchers also ignores cases where democracies make arrangements with nondemocracies in order to trample upon human rights by supporting coups. How can a country that supports dictatorships and other forms of authoritarian rule abroad be called a "democracy"? How can a country promote democracy while undermining the right to privacy in the counterterrorist surveillance state? Democracy is best promoted by example (Johnson 2010; Pillar 2010; Rieffer-Flanigan 2010).

When leaders permit a serious widening of the gap between rich and poor despite impressive economic growth, democracies are endangered and might even be overthrown. Alternatively, when the poor lose job security by a deliberate diminution in welfare state benefits by the rich, they may be more likely to favor external violence (Lees 2013), which will open up employment in the military sector. But social democracy has not been of much interest to "democratic peace" researchers.

Meanwhile, as Lifton and Mitchell (1995) have claimed, the ignorance of the American people about Hiroshima and similar misdeeds, combined with repeated cover-ups of covert action, has been linked to an alienation of citizens from the political process. Indeed, writings on "control of foreign policy," which once enjoyed popularity (Buck and Travis 1957; Millis and Murray 1958), have all but disappeared from mainstream international relations scholarship. Morgenthau (1958:chl7-19), for example, eschewed the mendacity and secrecy of American foreign policy, and described the American government as "not perfectly democratic" (ibid., p.295). While not without a tendency to overdramatize, efforts of Chomsky over the years to sound warnings about undemocratic practices in Washington have been ridiculed by prominent researchers in the field (cf. Holsti and Rosenau 1984:174). The fact that foreign policy decisions in democracies are made undemocratically is the supreme paradox not appreciated by "democratic peace" researchers.

"Democratic peace" research is fun in the ivory tower.

Clearly, the various studies say that the eleventh commandment is that democracies should rarely be tempted to go to war, especially against one another. That war is uncivilized, costly, and morally reprehensible rings through most of the scholarship.

The "democratic peace" concern arose during the Cold War, when the West was chiding Communist countries for having poor human rights records. But the Cold War is over, and pretensions to moral superiority are anachronistic in light of grotesque human rights violations at Abu Ghraib, Bagram Air Force Base prison in Afghanistan, Guantánamo, and elsewhere. Instead of the Cold War effort to perfect democracy by civil rights legislation, the United States is violating democratic norms by such obscenities as executing an American citizen without trial inside democratic Yemen, and pretending moral superiority over China's human rights record (Feldman 2013).

But are interstate wars really the problem in the post-Cold War era? The cost of war, according to Kalevi Holsti (1991), is such a deterrent to wars by democracies that less expensive low-level lethal violence is increasingly important on the world stage. Problems of human rights, internal conflict, international terrorism, and the world economy loom much larger in the foreign policy agenda today than studies that try to link regime type with external be. But endless statistical studies can be fun for those who never interview the people who make decisions for violence. And the treatment of the 15-year-old son of General Hamid Zabar at Abu Ghraib was certainly not fun: He was stripped, drenched with mud and water, driven around on the back of a truck on a cold winter night, and then his shivering presence was displayed to gain his father's confession (Haas 2009: 160).

Implications

Defenders of the "democratic peace" will object that they are pursuing a very important quest—to identify the causes of war and conditions of peace. But are they? Democracies and nondemocracies both cause wars. What the research has demonstrated is that the macro-causes of war and peace remain difficult to identify, while case studies also deviate from established theoretical foundations. If indeed their goal is to find ways to enhance peace prospects, who among them really employs such a research design?

7

Conclusion

The policy-relevant points are perhaps stated too harshly in the preceding chapter. But social science research has been misapplied so often that more than a word of caution is needed. My opinion is that the smug "democratic peace" thesis has become a dogma, requiring so many cases to be swept under the rug that normative imperatives attached to those discarded cases are ignored. Rather than defining naked aggression and other misdeeds by democracies out of the sample to be studied, they should be acknowledged and analyzed in depth. Deeds, not regime type, are ultimately the basis for international good citizenship. Many countries now classified as "democracies" fall very short of democratic ideals. Scales that rate current regimes as "democracies" should not encourage complacency but instead the need for vigilance to increase democratic control of foreign policy.

When democracies fight democracies, the scholarly penalty appears to be to deny retrospectively that one of the two countries was a democracy in the first place. Such an exercise can be applied as well to winnow the number of democracies to such a small number of countries that the "democratic peace" hypothesis applies to the current Belgium-Netherlands dyad and very few other cases.

According to Errol Henderson (2004), David Singer did not regard mere statistical findings sufficient to sing the praises of a "democratic peace." Instead, he wanted case study validation, and his requirements clearly have not been met. He was enthusiastic about my critique in 1997, when I had my first critique published, and I regret that he is no longer around to provide more perspective.

Nearly two decades ago, when I first critiqued "democratic peace" research in the manner indicated above, there was a time to take corrective action. But I pity the researchers who have painted themselves so far into a research agenda corner that they cannot repudiate the current morass for the sake of their own careers. The term "democracy" remains inadequately defined, the methods used have been too crude, the anomalies too numerous, and the results of the research have been mixed and hardly definitive. Attempts to explain the so-called "democratic peace" are so theoretically impoverished that they amount to sand castles that are being washed away by the tide of a new generation of researchers (cf. Geddes 2003). The attempt to promote a "democratic peace" has clearly boomeranged.

True, some democracies have not fought one another. But some of those very regimes have advanced nasty agendas, from imperialism to covert disruption of democratic yearnings to extraordinary rendition and war crimes, all to the acclaim of greedy war industrialists and power-hungry nationalists, while the poorest citizens in propagandized democracies have served as cannon fodder for democracies eager for regime changes that have been mired in blood. Most of all, the topic is of trivial importance, lacking meaningful policy relevance except for the very misadventures and misconduct that "democratic peace" researchers prefer to ignore.

Nevertheless, some technically excellent, empirically cumulative research has been taking place in a concerted manner over the past decade regarding a "democratic peace." Instead of confining their research to dialog inside ideological sects, research on the "democratic peace" has brought researchers of diverse opinions into a wide conversation. Miriam Elman (1997d:497) has referred to their quest as "romantic." Researchers who have ignored the normative and paradigmatic implications of their research should not be faulted for focusing entirely on empirical aspects of their studies. One way to develop a research agenda is to begin with an odd empirical finding.

But efforts to find a theoretical explanation have found that factors other than democracy may better account for the incidence of war and peace. As Gartzke (2000:210) has asserted, "there appears to be a gradual withering away of democracy's preeminence." Meanwhile, case study analysis, always needed to verify statistical analysis that operationalizes concepts, undermines not only the scientific basis of the findings but also the moral legitimacy of the research. Elman (1997d), surveying the import of several case studies, concluded that the results neither negated nor vindicated the effort of "democratic peace" reseachers to refute traditional international relations theories of realpolitik.

"Democratic peace" research began during the Cold War as a celebration of the unity of democracies that were allied and peaceful vis-à-vis the equally allied and peaceful Soviet bloc. But covert actions and military interventions were conveniently ignored for the sake of a rally-round-the-democratic-flag agenda. When the Cold War ended, the purpose for the research was lost, while the covert and interventionist behavior continued. What was a liberal agenda during the Cold War has become an illiberal agenda in the twenty-first century.

Meanwhile, the number of "democratic peace" research studies has greatly dwindled in recent years. We are now left with a reverse "baby thrown out with the bathwater" conundrum: How can the excellent research on the margins of the "democratic peace" be salvaged while the main thesis is abandoned? Various peripheral studies are a sort of humpty dumpty that cannot be repackaged until a new paradigm emerges. That must be the next step.

"Democratic peace" researchers should stop wasting their time trying to gild the lily of a discredited and worn-out research finding. They should instead work on issues of practical significance— human rights, problems of refugees and the poor around the world, terrorism and excesses of counterterrorism, violent internal conflicts, and world inequality. And they might even condescend to study how to build and perfect democracy, something in which they have thus far shown little interest. For example, why not seek to identify the specific components that will best accelerate the transition to democracy? Another research question is whether globalization, by facilitating the transfer of manufacturing from the First to the Third

Would, has irrevocably sacrificed the middle class hegemony that is necessary to preserve democracy (cf. Choi 2010a). Then there is the matter of recent American and British war crimes (Haas 2009).

Those who nonparadigmaticaly indulge the "democratic peace," in other words, divert attention from important policy questions, such as civil liberties violations and war crimes by democracies, issues that urgently need scholarly attention. Such inconsequential behavioralist numbercrunching studies as those focusing on the "democratic peace" are exactly what prompted the rise of postbehavioralism.

Research should ideally be put to humanistic ends. Those who pursue "democratic peace" have narrowed their attention to a very few well-behaved countries in a quite limited period of time. Yet wars have occupied a large set of countries over a longer period of time, historically and contemporaneously. What does research on the relationship between regime type and peace or war really provide for those who want to stop killing fields and to prevent future battlefield carnage? If the agenda is for imperfect democracies to congratulate one another, to ignore their own undemocratic behavior, and to carry on reckless crusades in the name of democracy, then the "democratic peace" is a betrayal of the basic needs of the human race. Scholars of international studies and political science can and will do better.

Appendix: Deviant Cases

The first column lists cases of militarized conflicts between democracies. The second column contains documentary sources of those conflicts. The reasons why "democratic peace" theorists believe that the conflict is not a deviant case appear in the third column, sometimes quoted word for word.

Deviant Cases	Sources	Attempted Refutations
Athens vs Elis 431 BCE	Weart (1994:315)	Elis' democracy status is uncertain.
Athens vs Megara 424 BCE	Russett & Antholis (1992:426)	"hardly a full-scale battle"
Athens vs Scione 423 BCE	Ray (1995:33)	Less than half were eligible to vote.
Athens vs Mende 423 BCE	Russett & Antholis (1992:426)	"revolt approved by the people"
Athens vs Amphipolis 422 BCE	Russett & Antholis (1992:426)	Amphipolis was allied with an oligarchy.
Athens vs Mantinea 418 BCE	Russett & Antholis (1992:425)	"less than fully free"
Athens vs Syracuse (Sicily) 415 BCE	Weart (1994: 303)	Syracuse's democracy status is ambiguous.
Athens v Miletus 412 BCE	Russett & Antholis (1992:426)	"switched sides"
Argos vs Miletus 411 BCE	Weart (1994:315)	Melitus was an oligarchy.
Athens vs Aetolia 411 BCE	Weart (1994:315)	Aetolia possibly was an anocracy.

Carthage vs Rome 265-146 BCE (Punic Wars)	Goldsworthy (2001)	nr ll
Aetolian League vs Rome 191-189 BCE	Weart (1994): 315)	The League was anocratic.
Florence vs Siena 1250-1270	Weart (1998:41)	nr ll
Florence vs Pisa and Venice 1356	Weart (1998:51)	nr ll
Perugia vs Siena 1358	Weart (1998:50)	nr ll
Genoa vs Venice 1397	Weart (1998:42)	nr
Florence vs Lucca 1431	Weart (1998:301)	nr ll
Bern vs Zürich 1443	Weart (1998:3017)	nr
Florence and Milan vs Venice 1447	Weart (1998:301)	nr ll
Appenzell vs Schwyz 1490	Weart (1998:304)	nr
Florence vs Pisa 1494-1510	Weart (1998:52)	nr ll
Florence vs Siena 1529	Weart (1998:303)	nr ll
Lucerne vs Zürich 1531	Weart (1998:97)	nr ll
Danzig vs Poland 1576	Weart (1998:303)	nr ll
Ukraine (Zaporozhian Cossacks) vs Poland 1625	Weart (1994): 315-16)	nr
England vs Netherlands 1652	Weart (1998:304)	nr ll
Bern vs Lucerne 1656	Weart (1998:97)	nr ll
Bern vs Lucerne 1712	Weart (1998:97)	nr ll
Britain vs USA 1775-1783	McCullough (2005)	nr ll
Anglo-Dutch War 1780-1884	Ray (1993, 1995: 106)	Few in England were eligible to vote.
Anglo-French War 1782	Ray (1993, 1995: 106)	Few in England were eligible to vote.
USA vs Native Americans 1783-1890	Stannard (1992)	nr ll
Pennamite-Yankee War 1784	Fisher (1896)	nr ll
Anglo-French War 1792-1802	Layne (1994:14-38)	nr ll
France vs USA 1797-1801 (quasi-War)	De Conde (1966)	nr ll
Britain vs USA 1807 (*Chesapeake* affair)	Thompson (1996)	same as the following case
Britain and Canada vs USA 1812-1815	Babst (1964,1972)	Parliament did not choose the prime minister until 1832.
Britain and Canada vs USA 1812-1815 (continued)	Small & Singer (1976:55,67)	Fewer than 10% of the British had the right to vote.

Belgium vs Netherlands 1830-1831	Ray (1993, 1995: 108)	Belgium was not independent.
France vs Netherlands 1831	Layne (1997)	nr ll
Canada vs USA 1837-1841 (*Caroline* incident)	Haas (2013:ch7)	nr ll
France vs México 1838-1839 (Pastry War)	Marley (1998)	nr ll
Georgia, USA vs Cherokee Nation 1838-1839	Weart (1998:306)	nr ll
Comanchería vs México and USA 1840-1875	DeLay (2008)	nr ll
Lucerne vs Bern and Zürich 1842	Weart (1998:309)	nr
USA vs México 1846	Gleditsch & Hegre (1992:296)	nr ll
Swiss Civil War 1847	Ray (1993, 1995: 108)	too few died
France vs Roman Republic 1849	Small & Singer (1976:55,67)	The Roman Republic was "ephemeral."
United States vs Mormon State of Utah	Oakes (2012:ch5)	nr
American Civil War 1861-1865	Weart (1994:316)	The Confederate States of America was an oligarchy.
Britain vs USA (*Trent* Affair) 1861	Layne (1994:14-38)	nr
Britain vs México 1861-1862 (Veracruz)	Cunningham (2001)	nr
Ecuador-Perú 1863	Doyle (1983:213)	Both democracies were less than 3 years old.
Canada vs USA 1866-1871	Vronsky (2011)	nr
Franco-Prussian War 1870-1871	Russett (1993b:16-19)	No legislative checks on executives.
Chile vs Perú 1879	Weart (1994:315, 1998:67)	Perú's democracy lasted only 11 months.
Britain vs Transvaal (First Boer War) 1880-1881	Babst (1964, 1972)	The Boer South Africa Republic was not independent.
Samoa (Germany v USA + Britain) 1887	Layne (1994:14-38)	nr ll
France vs Italy 1880s- 1890s	Layne (1994:14-38)	nr ll
France vs Italy 1891 (Tunis)	Cohen 1994:219	nr
France vs Britain 1893	Mousseau (1998:219)	nr
Hawai'i coup by USA 1893	Dudley & Agard (1990)	nr

Britain vs USA (Venezuela) 1895	Layne (1994:14-38)	nr
France vs Britain 1896	Mousseau (1998:219)	nr
Britain vs France (Fashoda Crisis) 1898	Doyle (1997:259)	Economic concerns prevented war.
UK vs USA 1897	Weart (1994:316)	There was inconsequential military activity.
Spanish-American War 1898	Russett (1993b:16-19)	Spanish elections were perceived as a farce.
Germany v Britain (Samoa) 1898-1899	Layne (1994:14-38)	nr ll
Germany v USA (Philippines) 1898-1899	Layne (1994:14-38)	nr
American-Philippine War 1898-1901	Russett (1993b:16-19)	The Republic held no election.
Britain vs Orange Free State + Transvaal Republic (2nd Boer War) 1899-1902	Babst (1964,1972) Russett (1993b:16-19)	Boers not independent. Only 5% of Boers eligible to vote.
Britain vs. USA 1902-1903 (Venezuela Crisis)	Mousseau (1998:219)	nr
Germany vs France and Britain (Morocco) 1905-1906	Layne (1994:14-38)	nr
Serbia vs Turkey 1912-1913 (First Balkan War)	Erickson (2003)	nr ll
Bulgaria vs Serbia 1913 (Second Balkan War)	Gleditsch & Hegre (1992:296)	nr ll
Austria-Hungary vs Serbia 1914	Babst (1964, 1972)	The emperor chose the prime minister.
Netherlands vs Britain 1914	Mousseau (1998:319)	nr
Norway vs Britain 1914	Mousseau (1998:319)	nr
Britain vs USA 1914	Mousseau (1998:319)	nr
Germany vs Britain 1914-1918	Babst (1964, 1972); Ray (1993, 1995)	The Kaiser chose the prime minister.
Germany vs France 1914-1918	Babst (1964, 1972); Ray (1993, 1995)	Executive power was unchecked.
Germany vs USA 1914-1918	Babst (1964, 1972); Ray (1993, 1995)	Executive power was unchecked.
Armenia vs Azerbaijan 1918-1920	Croissant (1998)	nr ll
Czechoslovakia vs Hungary 1919	Rousseau (2005:292-99)	nr ll
Czechoslovakia vs Poland 1919	Mousseau (1998:319)	nr ll
France vs Turkey 1919	Gleditsch & Hegbre (1992:296)	nr ll

Lithuania vs Poland 1919	Small & Singer (1983:338)	few casualties
Poland vs Ukraine 1919	Small & Singer (1983:337)	few casualties
Ireland vs Britain 1919-1921	Weart (1998:312)	nr ll
Britain vs Ireland 1921	Weart (1994:316)	Ireland anocratic
Germany vs France (Ruhr) 1923	Weart (1994:316)	Germany partly oligarchic
Cuna (Tule Republic) vs Panamá 1925	Howe (1998)	nr ll
Bolivia vs Paraguay 1932-1935	Weart (1994:316; 1998:69)	anocratic cultures
Germany in World War II 1939-1945	Ray (1993, 1995)	Executive power unchecked.
France vs Thailand 1940	Bremer (1992:329)	France = Vichy State.
Britain vs France 1940	Collier (1967)	nr ll
Britain vs Iceland 1940	Bittner (1983)	nr
Britain vs Sweden 1940	Mousseau (1998:219)	nr
Britain vs Finland 1941	Gleditsch (1995: 315); Gowa (1999)	Bombing on German forces was incidental.
Ecuador vs Perú 1942	Weart (1994:316)	anocratic cultures
India vs Pakistan 1947-1948 (First Kashmir War)	Ray (1995:120)	Pakistan was not yet demoratic.
Israel vs Egypt 1948	Gleditsch & Hegre (1992:296)	nr
Israel vs Lebanon 1948	Russett (1993b:16-19)	Israel had not yet held elections.
Israel vs Syria 1948	Gleditsch & Hegre (1992:288)	Syria was not a democracy.
Israel vs Jordan 1949	Kegley & Hermann (1997a)	nr ll
Israel vs Britain 1948-1949	Kegley & Hermann (1997a)	nr ll
Britain + USA vs Iran 1953	Forsythe (1992:386-88)	nr ll
Guyana vs USA 1953	Forsythe (1992:386)	nr
Israel vs Britain 1954	Gleditsch (1992:372)	nr
USA vs Guatemala 1954	Russett (1993b:122)	Guatemala was allying with USSR.
USA vs Switzerland 1954	Kegley & Hermann (1997a)	nr
Syria vs Israel 1954-1955	Kegley & Hermann (1997a)	nr ll
Costa Rica vs USA 1955	Forsythe (1992:391-92)	nr

Turkey vs Syria 1955-1956	Kegley & Hermann (1997a)	nr ll
India vs Pakistan 1956-1957	Kegley & Hermann (1997a)	nr ll
India vs. Burma 1957	Mousseau (1998:219)	nr
Indonesia vs USA 1957	Forsythe (1992:388-89)	nr ll
USA vs Syria 1957	Kegley & Hermann (1997a)	nr
Syria vs Turkey 1957	Kegley & Hermann (1997a)	nr ll
Greece vs Turkey 1958	Kegley and Hermann (1997a)	nr ll
Iceland vs Britain 1958	Storey (1992)	Nr
Egypt vs Israel 1958-1960	Kegley & Hermann (1997a)	nr ll
Switzerland vs USA 1959	Kegley & Hermann (1997a)	nr
Austria vs USA 1960	Kegley & Hermann (1997a)	nr
Austria vs Italy 1960	Kegley & Hermann (1997a)	nr
Ecuador vs USA 1960	Forsythe (1992:386)	nr
Iceland vs Britain 1960	Kegley & Hermann (1997a)	nr
Japan vs South Korea 1960	Kegley & Hermann (1997a)	nr
Brazil vs USA 1961	Forsythe (1992:386)	nr
Denmark vs Britain 1961	Kegley & Hermann (1997a)	nr
Cambodia vs Thailand 1962	Haas (2013:118)	nr
USA vs Egypt 1962	Kegley & Hermann (1997a)	nr
USA vs Perú 1962	Kegley & Hermann (1997a)	nr
India vs Pakistan 1962-1963	Kegley & Hermann (1997a)	nr ll
Greece vs Turkey 1964	Weart (314:316)	Cyprus democracy was only 4 years old. ll
Ecuador vs Perú 1964	Kegley & Hermann (1997a)	nr
Britain/Malaya vs Indonesia 1963-1965	Gordon (1966:ch3)	nr ll
Britain/Malaya vs Philippines 1963-1965 (Sabah)	Gordon (1966:ch3)	nr

India vs Pakistan 1964	Kegley & Hermann (1997a)	nr ll
USA vs Cambodia 1964-70	Kaplan (1999); Haas (1991; 2012:3-4)	nr ll
Second Kashmir War 1963-1965	Bremer (1992:329)	Pakistan was less democratic beforehand.
USA vs Dominican Republic 1965	Sørensen (1992:404)	nr ll
Israel attacks *USS Liberty* 1967	Rummel (1983b:213)	Israel was too socialist.
Israel v Lebanon 1967 (Six-Day War)	Russett (1993:16-19)	too few died.
Malaysia vs Philippines 1968 (Corregidor)	Haas (2013:121)	nr ll
El Salvador vs Honduras 1969	Ray (1998:38)	One country not a democracy.
Norway vs Denmark 1969	Kegley & Hermann (1997a)	nr
Botswana vs Zimbabwe 1969	Kegley & Hermann (1997a)	nr
India vs Pakistan 1971	Gleditsch & Hegre (1997a)	coup in Pakistan
India vs USA 1971	Widmaier (2005)	nr
Iceland vs Germany 1972-1973	Storey (1992)	nr
Iceland vs Britain 1972-1973	Weart (1994:316)	inconsequential military action
USA vs Chile 1973	Russett (1993b:122)	justified by the Cold War ideology
Iceland vs. West Germany 1974	Mousseau (1998:219)	nr
Iceland vs Britain 1974-1976	Storey (1992); Weart (1994:316)	inconsequential military action
Botswana vs Zimbabwe 1974	Kegley &d Hermann (1997a)	nr
Mali vs Upper Volta 1974	Kegley & Hermann (1995:94)	nr ll
Turkey v Cyprus 1974	Weart (1994:316)	Turkey's democracy was only 1 year old.
Iceland vs Germany 1974	Kegley & Hermann (1997a)	nr
USA vs Canada 1974-1975	Kegley & Hermann (1997a)	nr
Thailand vs Laos 1975	Kegley & Hermann (1995:94)	nr ll

Greece vs Turkey 1975-1976	Kegley & Hermann (1997a)	nr ll
Indonesia vs East Timor 1975-1980	Kiernan (2008)	nr ll
Botswana vs Zimbabwe 1975-1977	Kegley & Hermann (1997a)	nr ll
Botswana vs Zambia 1976	Kegley & Hermann (1995:94)	nr
El Salvador vs Honduras 1976	Kegley & Hermann (1997a)	nr ll
Israel vs Greece 1976	Kegley & Hermann (1997a)	nr
Israel vs Turkey 1976	Kegley & Hermann (1997a)	nr
Israel vs USA 1976	Kegley & Hermann (1997a)	nr
South Africa vs Botswana 1976	Kegley & Hermann (1995:94)	nr
South Africa vs Namibia 1976	Kegley & Hermann (1995:94)	nr ll
Morocco vs Zambia 1977	Kegley & Hermann (1995:94)	nr
Ecuador vs Perú 1978	Ray (1995:122)	premature democracies
Egypt vs Cyprus 1978	Kegley & Hermann (1995:94)	nr ll
Greece vs Turkey 1978	Mousseau (1998:219)	nr
Israel vs Lebanon 1978	Gabriel (1984)	nr
Nicaragua vs Costa Rica 1978	Kegley & Hermann (1995:94)	nr
Botswana vs Zimbabwe 1978-1979	Kegley & Hermann (1997a)	nr
Canada vs USA 1979	Kegley & Hermann (1997a)	nr
Ecuador vs USA 1980	Kegley & Hermann (1997a)	nr
Malaysia vs Philippines 1980	Haas (2013:121)	nr
Ecuador vs Perú 1981	Ray (1993,1995)	nonpeaceful transfer of power
Honduras vs El Salvador 1981	Kegley & Hermann (1995:94)	nr ll
Honduras vs Nicaragua 1981	Kegley & Hermann (1995:94)	nr ll
Norway vs Denmark 1981	Kegley & Hermann (1997)	nr

Sénégal vs Gambia 1981	Kegley & Hermann (1995:94)	nr ll
Norway vs Denmark 1981	Kegley & Hermann (1997a)	nr
USA vs Nicaragua 1981-1987	Russett (1993b:120-24)	Nicaragua was not fully democratic.
Argentina vs Britain 1982 (Falklans/Malvinas War)	Ray (1998:38)	Argentina had military rule.
Colombia vs Venezuela 1982	Kegley & Hermann (1997a)	nr ll
Guatemala vs México 1982	Kegley & Hermann (1995:94)	nr
Britain vs Venezuela 1982	Kegley & Hermann (1997a)	nr
Israel vs Lebanon 1982-1985	Elman (1997b); Maoz (2006)	nr ll
Honduras vs Costa Rica 1983	Kegley & Hermann (1995:94)	nr
Honduras vs Nicaragua 1983	Russett (1993b:120-24)	Nicaragua was not fully democratic.
Nicaragua vs Costa Rica 1983	Kegley & Hermann (1995:94)	nr ll
Rhodesia vs Botswana 1983	Kegley & Hermann (1995:94)	nr
USA vs Grenada 1983	Rousseau (2005:250-56)	nr ll
Ecuador vs Perú 1984	Gleditsch, Christiansen, Hegre (2005)	nr ll
France vs Spain 1984	Kegley & Hermann (1997a)	nr
Ireland vs Spain 1984-1985	Kegley & Hermann (1997a)	nr
Botswana vs South Africa 1984-1985	Kegley & Hermann (1997)	nr
Greece vs Turkey 1984-1987	Gleditsch, Christiansen, Hegre (2005)	nr ll
Egypt vs Malta 1985	Kegley &d Hermann (1995:94)	nr ll
France vs New Zealand 1985	Kegley & Hermann (1997a)	nr
Israel vs Tunisia 1985	Kegley & Hermann (1995:93)	nr ll
Malaysia vs Philippines 1985	Haas (2013:121)	nr ll

South Africa vs Botswana 1985	Kegley & Hermann (1995:94)	nr ll
Botswana vs South Africa 1986	Kegley & Hermann (1995:94)	nr ll
Cyprus vs Turkey 1986	Kegley & Hermann (1997a)	nr ll
Qatar vs Bahrain 1986	Kegley & Hermann (1995:95)	nr
Spain vs Britain 1986	Kegley & Hermann (1997a)	nr
Colombia vs Venezuela 1986-1987	Gleditsch, Christiansen, Hegre (2005)	nr
Argentina vs Japan 1987	Kegley & Hermann (1997a)	nr
Cyprus vs Israel 1987	Kegley & Hermann (1997a)	nr ll
India vs Sri Lanka 1987	Kegley & Hermann (1995:93)	nr ll
Canada vs France 1987-1988	Kegley & Hermann (1997a)	nr
Colombia vs Venezuela 1988	Kegley & Hermann (1997a)	nr
Cyprus and Turkey 1988	Kegley & Hermann (1997a)	nr ll
Japan vs Papua New Guinea 1988	Kegley & Hermann (1997a)	nr
Malaysia vs Philippines 1988	Haas (2013:121)	nr
South Africa vs Botswana 1988	Kegley and Hermann (1995:94,1997a)	nr
Armenia vs Azerbaijan 1988-1994	Ray (1995:122)	premature democracies
Mauritania vs Sénégal 1989-1992	Kacowicz (1997)	nr ll
Greece vs Turkey 1989	Kegley & Hermann (1997a)	nr
USA vs Canada 1989	Kegley & Hermann (1997a)	nr
USA vs Panamá 1989	Donnelly (1991)	nr ll
France vs Gabon 1990	Kegley & Hermann (1995:93)	nr
India vs Pakistan 1990	Gleditsch, Christiansen, Hegre (2005)	nr
Russia vs Moldova 1990-1992	Ray (1993)	nonpeaceful transfer of power

Egypt vs Iraq 1991	Kegley & Hermann (1995:94)	nr ll
France vs Iraq 1991	Kegley & Hermann (1995:93)	nr ll
Ecuador vs Perú 1991	Kegley & Hermann (1997a)	nr
Italy vs Iraq 1991	Kegley & Hermann (1997a)	nr ll
Nicaragua vs Honduras 1991	Kegley & Hermann (1997a)	nr
Nigeria vs Sierra Leone 1991	Kegley & Hermann (1995:94)	nr ll
Serbia vs Croatia 1991	Weart (1994:316)	Croatian government newborn
Serbia vs Slovenia 1991	Weart (1998:316)	nr ll
United Arab Emirates vs Kuwait 1991	Kegley & Hermann (1995:95)	nr ll
Britain vs Iraq 1991	Kegley & Hermann (1995:93)	nr ll
USA vs Canada 1991	Kegley & Hermann (1997a)	nr
India vs Papua New Guinea 1992	Kegley & Hermann (1997a)	nr
Malaysia vs Singapore 1992	Haas (2013:126)	nr
Russia vs Estonia 1992	Kegley & Hermann (1997a)	nr
Russia vs Sweden 1992	Kegley & Hermann (1997a)	nr
Russia vs Ukraine 1992	Kegley & Hermann (1997a)	nr
Serbia vs Bosnia 1992-1995	Ray (1995:122)	Serbia not democratic
South Yemen vs North Yemen 1994	Weart (199:318)	nr ll
Ecuador vs Perú 1995	Herz & Noguiera (2002)	nr ll
India vs Bangladesh 1996	Gleditsch, Christiansen, Hegre (2005)	nr
Serbia vs NATO countries 1998-1999 (Kosovo)	Ray (1993)	nonpeaceful transfer of power ll
India vs Pakistan (Kargil War) 1999	Singh (1999)	nr ll
India vs Bangladesh 2001	Roy (2007:55-57)	nr ll
USA vs Pakistan 2004-13	Bashir and Crewes (2012)	nr ll
Indonesia vs Malaysia 2005	Mak (2009)	nr

Israel vs Lebanon 2006	Hirst (2010)	nr ll
Turkey vs Iraq (Kurds) 2007	Hösebalaban (2011)	nr ll
Israel vs Gaza Strip 2008	Chomsky & Pappé (2010)	nr ll
Georgia v Russia 2008	Haas (2010b:ch6)	nr ll
Cambodia vs Thailand 2008	Haas (2013:118)	nr ll
Indonesia vs Malaysia 2009	Mak (2009)	nr
Israel vs Turkey (Flotilla Raid) 2010	Bayoumi (2010)	nr ll
Pakistan vs India 2011	Reuters (2011)	nr ll
Israel vs Gaza Strip 2012	Sapir (2012)	nr ll
Afghanistan vs Pakistan 2013	Salahuddin (2013)	nr ll
Malaysia vs Philippines 2013	Grant (2013)	nr ll
Pakistan vs India 2013	BBC (2013)	nr ll
Philippines vs Taiwan 2013	Demick (2013)	nr

Key: nr No refutation provided
        ll Loss of life, according to Maoz (2005) and other sources

References

Adelman, Irma, and Cynthia T. Morris (1967). *Society, Politics, and Economic Development*. Baltimore, MD: Johns Hopkins Press

Alker, Hayward R., and Frank L. Sherman (1986). *International Conflict Episodes, 1945-1979*. Ann Arbor, MI: Inter-University Consortium for Political and Social Research

Almond, Gabriel A., and Sidney Verba (1963). *The Civic Culture: Political Attitudes and Democracy in Five Nations*. Englewood Cliffs, NJ: Prentice-Hall

Alvarez, Michael, José Antonio Cheibub, Fernando Limongi, and Adam Przeworski (1996). "Classifying Political Regimes," *Studies in Comparative International Development*, 31 (2): 1-37

Anderson, Charles H., and John R. Carter (2003). "Does War Disrupt Trade?" In *Globalization and Armed Conflict*, eds. Gerald Schneider, Katherine Barbieri, and Nils Petter Gleditsch, Chap. 15. Lanham, MD: Rowman and Littlefield

Angell, Norman (1910). *The Great Illusion: A Study of the Relation of Military Power in Nations to Their Economic and Social Advantage*. New York: Putnam's Sons

Arat, Zehra F. (1991). *Democracy and Human Rights in Developing Countries*. Boulder, CO: Rienner

Archibugi, Danielle (2008). *The Global Commonwealth of Citizens: Toward Cosmopolitan Democracy*. Princeton, NJ: Princeton

University Press

Arendt, Hannah (1951). *The Origins of Totalitarianism.* New York: Harcourt, Brace.

Ayers, R. William (2010). "Competing Values in U.S. Democratization Policy." In *Democratic Peace in Theory and Practice*, ed. Steven W. Hook, Chap. 7. Kent, OH: Kent State University Press

Azar, Edward E. (1980). *Codebook of the Conflict and Peace Data Bank (COPDAB).* Ann Arbor, MI: Inter-University Consortium for Political and Social Research.

Babst, Dean V. (1964). "Elective Governments—A Force for Peace," *Wisconsin Sociologist*, 3 (1): 9-14

Babst, Dean V. (1972). "A Force for Peace," *Industrial Research*, 14 (4): 55-58

Bachrach, Peter (1969). *The Theory of Democratic Elitism: A Critique.* London: University of London Press

Bachteler, Tobias (1997). "Explaining the Democratic Peace: The Evidence from Ancient Greece Reviewed," *Journal of Conflict Resolution*, 34 (3): 315-323

Baker, William P., and John Oneal (2001). "Patriotism or Opinion Leadership: The Nature and Origins of the 'Rally 'Round the Flag' Effect," *Journal of Conflict Resolution*, 45 (5): 661-687

Banks, Arthur S. (1972). "Correlates of Democratic Performance," *Comparative Politics,* 4 (2): 217-230

Barbieri, Katherine (1996). "Economic Interdependence: A Path to Peace or a Source of Conflict?," *Journal of Peace Research*, 33 (1): 29-49

Barbieri, Katherine (1997). "Risky Business: The Impact of Trade Linkages on Interstate Conflict, 1870-1985." In *Enforcing Cooperation: "Risky" States and the Intergovernmental Management of Conflict*, eds. Gerald Schneider and Patricia A. Weitsman, pp. 202-231. New York: St. Martin's Press

Barbieri, Katherine, and Jack S. Levy (1999). "Sleeping with the Enemy: The Impact of War on Trade," *Journal of Peace Research*, 36 (4): 443-462

Barbieri, Katherine, and Jack S. Levy (2003). "The Trade-Disruption Hypothesis and the Liberal Economic Theory of Peace." In *Globalization and Armed Conflict*, eds. Gerald Schneider, Katherine Barbieri, and Nils Petter Gleditsch, Chap. 14. Lanham, MD:

Rowman and Littlefield

Barkawi, Tarak, and Mark Laffey, eds. (2001) *Democracy, Liberalism, and War: Rethinking the Democratic Peace Debate*. Boulder, CO: Rienner

Bashir, Shabzad, and Robert D. Crews, eds. (2012). *Under the Drones: Modern Lives in the Afghanistan-Pakistan Borderlands*. Cambridge, MA: Harvard University Press

Bateson, Gregory (1958). *Naven: A Survey of the Problems Suggested by a Composite Picture of the Culture of a New Guinea Tribe Drawn from Three Points of View*, 2nd edn. Stanford, CA: Stanford University Press

Bayoumi, Moustafa, ed. (2010). *Midnight on the Mavi Marmara: The Attack on the Gaza Freedom Flotilla and How It Changed the Course of the Israeli/Palestine Conflict*. New York: Haymarket Books

BBC (2013). "Kashmir: Five Indian Soldiers Killed in Shooting," *bbc.com*, August 6

Bearce, David H. (2003). "Grasping the Commercial Institutional Peace," *International Studies Quarterly,* 47 (3): 347-370

Bearce, David H., and Sawa Omori (2005). "How Do Commercial Institutions Promote Peace?," *Journal of Peace Research,* 42 (6): 659-678

Beck, Nathaniel (2003). "Modeling Dynamics in the Study of Conflict." In *Globalization and Armed Conflict*, eds. Gerald Schneider, Katherine Barbieri, Nils Petter Gleditsch, Chap 8. Lanham, MD: Rowman and Littlefield

Beck, Nathaniel, and Simon Jackman (1998). "Beyond Linearity by Default: Generalized Additive Models," *American Journal of Political Science,* 42 (2): 596-627

Beck, Nathaniel, and Jonathan N. Katz (2001). "Throwing out the Baby with the Bath Water: A Comment on Green, Kim, and Yoon," *International Organization,* 55 (2): 487-495

Beck, Nathaniel, Jonathan N. Katz, and Richard Tucker (1998). "Taking Time Seriously: Time-Series Cross Section Analysis with a Binary Dependent Variable," *American Journal of Political Science*, 43 (4): 1260-1288

Beck, Nathaniel, Gary King, and Langche Zeng (2004). "Theory and Evidence in International Conflict: A Response to de Marchi, Gelpi, and Grynaviski," *American Political Science Review,* 98

(2): 379-389

Bell, Duncan (2014). "Before the Democratic Peace: Racial Utopianism, Empire, and the Abolition of War," *European Journal of International Relations*, 20 (1): forthcoming

Bennett, Scott D. (2006). "Toward a Continuous Specification of the Democracy-Autocracy Connection," *International Studies Quarterly*, 50 (2): 313-338

Bennett, Scott D. (2007). "Democracy, Regime Change, and Rivalry Termination," *International Interactions*, 22 (4): 369-397

Bennett, Scott D., and Alan C. Stam III (1998). "The Declining Advantages of Democracy: A Combined Model of War Outcomes and Duration," *Journal of Conflict Resolution*, 42 (3): 344-366

Bennett, Scott D., and Alan C. Stam III (2000). "Research Design and Estimator Choices in the Analysis of Interstate Dyads: When Decisions Matter," *Journal of Conflict Resolution*, 44 (5): 653-683

Benoit, Kenneth (1996). "Democracies Really Are More Pacific (in General)," *Journal of Conflict Resolution*, 40 (4): 636-657

Bercovitch, Jacob J., Theodore Anagnoson, and Donnette L. Wille (1991). "Some Conceptual Issues and Empirical Trends in the Study of Successful Mediation in International Relations," *Journal of Peace Research*, 28 (1): 7-17

Berman, Paul (2003). *Terror and Liberalism*. New York: Norton

Bittner, Donald F. (1983). *The Lion and the White Falcon: Britain and Iceland in the World War II Era*. Hamdon, CT: Archon Books

Blechman, Barry M., and Stephen S. Kaplan (1978). *Force Without War: U.S. Armed Forces as a Political Instrument*. Washington, DC: Brookings

Bliss, Harry, and Bruce M. Russett (1998). "Democratic Trading Partners: The Liberal Connection," *Journal of Politics*, 60 (4): 1126-1147

Boehmer, Charles, Erik Gartzke, and Timothy Nordstrom (2004). "Do Intergovernmental Organizations Promote Peace?," *World Politics*, 57 (1): 1-38

Boix, Carles, Michael Miller, and Sebastian Rosato (2013). "A Complete Data Set of Political Regimes, 1800–2007," *Comparative Political Studies*, 46 (12): 1523-1554

Bollen, Kenneth A. (1980). "Issues in the Comparative Measurement of Political Democracy," *American Sociological Review*, 45 (2): 370-390

Bollen, Kenneth A. (1991). "Political Democracy: Conceptual and Measurement Traps." In *On Measuring Democracy: Its Consequences and Concomitants*, ed. Alex Inkeles, Chap. 1. New Brunswick, NJ: Transaction

Bollen, Kenneth A. (1993). "Liberal Democracy: Validity and Method Factors in Cross-National Measures," *American Journal of Political Science*, 37 (4): 1207-1230

Bond, Gordon C. (1979). *The Grand Expedition*. Athens: University of Georgia Press

Boot, Max (2003). "What Next? The Bush Foreign Policy Agenda after Iraq," *Weekly Standard*, May 5:27-33

Braumoeller, Bear F. (1997). "Deadly Doves: Liberal Nationalism and the Democratic Peace in the Soviet Successor States," *International Studies Quarterly*, 41 (3): 375-402

Braumoeller, Bear F. (2004). "Hypothesis Testing and Multiplicative Interaction Terms," *International Organization*, 58 (4): 807-820

Brawley, Mark R. (1993). "Regime Types, Markets and War: The Importance of Pervasive Rents in Foreign Policy," *Comparative Political Studies*, 26 (2): 178-197

Brecher, Michael, and Jonathan Wilkenfeld (1997). *A Study of Crisis*. Ann Arbor: University of Michigan Press

Brecher, Michael, Jonathan Wilkenfeld, and Sheila Moser (1988). *Handbook of International Crises in the Twentieth Century*, vol. 1. New York: Pergamon

Bremer, Stuart A. (1992). "Dangerous Dyads: Conditions Affecting the Likelihood of Interstate War, 1816-1965," *Journal of Conflict Resolution*, 36 (3): 309-341

Bremer, Stuart A. (1993). "Democracy and Militarized Interstate Conflict, 1816-1965," *International Interactions*, 18 (3): 231-249

Brock, Lothar (2006). "Triangulating War: The Use of Force by Democracies as a Variant of the Democratic Peace." In *Democratic Wars: Looking at the Dark Side of the Democratic Peace*, eds. Anna Geis, Lothar Brock, and Harald Müller, Chap. 2. New York: Palgrave Macmillan

Brown, Dee (1971). *Bury My Heart at Wounded Knee: An Indian History of the American West*. New York: Holt, Rinehart, Winston

Buck, Philip W., and Martin B., Travis, Jr., eds. (1957). *Control of Foreign Relations in Modern Nations.* New York: Norton

Bueno de Mesquita, Bruce (1990). "Big Wars, Little Wars: Avoiding Selection Bias," *International Interactions,* 16 (3): 159-169

Bueno de Mesquita, Bruce, and George W. Downs (1996). "Intervention and Democracy," *International Organization,* 60 (3): 627-649

Bueno de Mesquita, Bruce, and David Lalman (1986). "Reason and War," *American Political Science Review,* 80 (4): 1113-1129

Bueno de Mesquita, Bruce, and David Lalman (1990). "Dyadic Power, Expectations, and War." In *Prisoners of War? Nation-States in the Modern Era,* eds. Charles S. Gochman and Alan Ned Sabrosky, Chap. 11. Lexington, MA: Lexington

Bueno de Mesquita, Bruce, and David Lalman (1992). *War and Reason.* New Haven, CT: Yale University Press

Bueno de Mesquita, Bruce, and James Lee Ray (2004). 'The National Interest Versus Individual Political Ambition: Democracy, Autocracy, and the Reciprocation of Force and Violence in Militarized Interstate Disputes." In *The Scourge of War: New Extensions on an Old Problem,* ed., Paul Diehl, pp. 94-119. Ann Arbor: University of Michigan Press

Bueno de Mesquita, Bruce, James D. Morrow, Randolph M. Siverson, and Alastair Smith (1999). "An Institutional Explanation of the Democratic Peace," *American Political Science Review,* 93 (4): 791-807

Bueno de Mesquita, Bruce, James D. Morrow, Randolph M. Siverson, and Alastair Smith (2001). "Political Survival and International Conflict." In *War in a Changing World,* eds. Zeev Maoz and Azar Gat, pp 183-206. Ann Arbor: University of Michigan Press

Bueno de Mesquita, Bruce, James D. Morrow, Randolph M. Siverson, and Alastair Smith (2004). "Testing Implications from the Selectorate Theory of War," *World Politics,* 56 (3): 363-388

Bueno de Mesquita, Bruce, and Randolph M. Siverson (1995). "War and the Survival of Political Leaders: A Comparative Study of Regime Types and Political Accountability," *American Political Science Review,* 89 (4): 841-855

Bueno de Mesquita, Bruce, and Randolph M. Siverson (1997). "Nasty or Nice? Political Systems, Endogenous Norms, and the Treatment of Adversaries," *Journal of Conflict Resolution*, 41 (1): 175-199

Bueno de Mesquita, Bruce, Randolph M. Siverson, and Gary Woller (1992). "War and the Fate of Regimes: A Comparative Analysis," *American Political Science Review*, 86 (3): 638-646

Bueno de Mesquita, Bruce, Alastair Smith, Randolph M. Siverson, and James D. Morrow (2003). *The Logic of Political Survival.* Cambridge, MA: MIT Press

Buhaug, Halvard (2005). "Dangerous Dyads Revisited: Democracies May Not Be That Peaceful after All," *Conflict Management and Peace Science*, 22 (2): 95-111

Burkhart, Rosse E., and Michael S. Lewis-Beck (1994). "Comparative Democracy: The Economic Development Thesis," *American Political Science Review,* 88 (4): 903-910

Burley, Anne-Marie S. (1994). "Liberal International Relations Theory." In *International Law Anthology,* ed. Anthony D'Amato, pp. 381-384. Cincinnati, OH: Anderson

Butterworth, Robert L. (1976). *Managing Interstate Conflict, 1945-74: Data with Synopses.* Pittsburgh, PA: University Center for International Studies

Buzan, Barry (1984). "Economic Structure and International Security: The Limits of the Liberal Case," *International Organization,* 38 (4): 597-624

Caprioli, Mary, and Peter F. Trumbore (2006). "Human Rights Rogues in Interstate Disputes, 1980-2001," *Journal of Peace Research*, 43 (2): 131-145

Carment, David, and Patrick James (1995). "Internal Constraints and Interstate Ethnic Conflict: Toward a Crisis-Based Assessment of Irredentism," *Journal of Conflict Resolution*, 39 (1): 82-109

Carpenter, Ted Galen (1992). "Direct Military Intervention." In *Intervention into the 1990s: U.S. Foreign Policy in the Third World,* ed. Peter J. Schraeder, Chap. 9. Boulder, CO: Rienner

Casper, Gretchen (1995). *Fragile Democracies: The Legacies of Authoritarian Rule.* Pittsbugh, PA: University of Pittsburgh Press

Casper, Gretchen, and Michelle M. Taylor (1996). *Negotiating Democracy: Transitions from Authoritarian Rule.* Pittsburgh, PA: University of Pittsburgh Press

Casper, Gretchen, and Claudiu Tufis (2003). "Correlation Versus Interchangeability: The Limited Robustness of Empirical Findings on Democracy Using Highly Correlated Data Sets," *Political Analysis*, 11 (2): 196-203

Cederman, Lars-Erik (2001). "Back to Kant: Reinterpreting the Democratic Peace as a Macrohistorical Learning Process," *American Political Science Review*, 95 (1): 15-31

Cederman, Lars-Erik, and Mohan Penubarti Rao (2001). "Exploring the Dynamics of the Democratic Peace," *Journal of Conflict Resolution*, 45 (6): 818-833

Cesarini, David (2011). "Egypt Protests: The Hypocrisy of the West Must Be Deplored," *The Telegraph*, February 9

Chan, Steve (1984). "Mirror, Mirror on the Wall. . . : Are Freer Countries More Pacific?," *Journal of Conflict Resolution*, 28 (4): 617-648

Chan, Steve (1993). "Some Thoughts on the Future Research Agenda," *International Interactions*, 28 (2): 205-213

Chan, Steve (1997). "In Search of Democratic Peace: Problems and Promise," *Mershon International Studies Review*, 41:59-91

Chandler, David, ed. (2010). *International Statebuilding: The Rise of Post-Liberal Governance*. London: Routledge

Cheibub, José, and Jennifer Gandhi (2004). "A Six Fold Measure of Democracies and Dictatorship." Paper presented at the Annual Meeting of the American Political Science Association

Chernoff, Fred (2004). "The Study of Democratic Peace and Progress in International Relations," *International Studies Review*, 6 (1): 49-77

Chernoff, Fred (2008). "International Relations, Paleontology, and Scientific Progress: Parallels Between Democratic Peace Studies and the Meteor Impact Extinction Hypothesis," *International Studies Perspectives*, 9 (1): 49-78

Chiozza, Giacomo, and H. E. Goemans (2004). "International Conflict and the Tenure of Leaders: Is War Still 'Ex Post' Inefficient?," *American Journal of Political Science*, 48 (3): 604-619

Choi, Ajin (2004). "Democratic Synergy and Victory in War, 1816-1992," *International Studies Quarterly*, 48 (3): 663-682

Choi Seung-Wham (2010a). "Beyond Kantian Liberalism: Peace Through Globalization?," *Conflict Management and Peace Science*, 27 (3): 272–295

Choi Seung-Whan (2010b). "Fighting Terrorism Through the Rule of Law?," *Journal of Conflict Resolution*, 54 (6): 940-966

Choi, Seung-Whan (2011). "Re-Evaluating Capitalist and Democratic Peace Models, *International Studies Quarterly*, 55 (3): 759-769

Choi Seung-Whan, and Patrick James (2005). *Civil-Military Dynamics, Democracy, and International Conflict: A New Quest for International Peace.* New York: Palgrave Macmillan

Choi, Seung-Whan, and Patrick James (2006). "Media Openness and Militarized Interstate Disputes," *British Journal of Political Science*, 37 (1): 23-46

Choi, Seung-Whan, and Patrick James (2008). "Civil Military Structure, Political Communication and the Democratic Peace," *Journal of Peace Research*, 45 (1): 37-53

Choi, Seung-Whan, and Yiagadeesen Sam (2008). "Reexamining the Effect of Democratic Institutions on Inflows of Foreign Direct Investment in Developing Countries," *Foreign Policy Analysis*, 4 (1): 83-103

Chojnacki, Sven (2006). "Democratic Wars and Military Interventions, 1946-2002: The Monadic Level Reconsidered." In *Democratic Wars: Looking at the Dark Side of the Democratic Peace*, eds. Anna Geis, Lothar Brock, and Harald Müller, Chap. 2. New York: Palgrave Macmillan

Chomsky, Noam (1991). *Deterring Democracy.* New York: Hill and Wang

Chomsky, Noam, and Ilan Pappé (2010). *Gaza in Crisis: Reflections on Israel's War Against the Palestinians.* Chicago, IL: Haymarket Books

Choucri, Nazli, and Robert C. North (1975). *Nations in Conflict: National Growth and International Violence.* San Francisco: Freeman

Choucri, Nazli, and Robert C. North (1989). "Lateral Pressure in International Relations: Concept and Theory." In *Handbook of War Studies*, ed. Manus I. Midlarsky, Chap. 12. Boston: Unwin Hyman

Clare, Joe (2013). "The Deterrent Value of Democratic Allies," *International Studies Quarterly*, 57 (3): 545-555

Clark, David H., and Timothy Nordstrom (2003). "Risky Inference: Unobserved Treatment Effects in Conflict Studies," *International Studies Quarterly*, 47 (3): 417-429

Clinton, Bill (1996). *A National Security Strategy of Engagement and Enlargement*. Washington, DC: Government Printing Office

Cohen, Raymond (1994). "Pacific Unions: A Reappraisal of the Theory That Democracies Do Not Go to War with Each Other," *Review of International Studies*, 20 (3): 207-233

Cohen, Raymond (1995). "Needed: A Disaggregate Approach to the Democratic-Peace Theory," *Review of International Studies*, 21 (3): 323-325

Collier, Basil (1967). *The Second World War: A Military History; From Munich to Hiroshima*. New York: Morrow

Cooper, John Milton, ed. (1968). *Reconsidering Woodrow Wilson: Progressivism, Internationalism, War, and Peace*. Baltimore, MD: Johns Hopkins University Press

Cooper, Richard V. L. (1982). "Military Manpower and Recruitment: Equity, Efficiency, and National Security." In *Registration and the Draft*, ed. Martin Anderson, pp. 343-376. Stanford, CA: Hoover Institution

Copeland, Dale C. (1996). "Economic Interdependence and War: A Theory of Trade Expectations," *International Security*, 20 (1): 5-41

Copeland, Dale C. (2000). "Trade Expectations and the Outbreak of Peace: Détente, 1970-74 and the End of the Cold War, 1985-91." In *Power and the Purse: Economic Statecraft, Interdependence, and National Security*, eds. Jean-Marc F. Blanchard, Edward D. Mansfield, and Norrin M. Ripsman, pp. 15-58. London: Cass

Coppedge, Michael (1997). "Modernization and Thresholds of Democracy: Evidence for a Common Path and Progress," *Inequality, Democracy, and Economic Development*, ed. Manus I. Midlarsky, pp. 177-201. New York: Cambridge University Press

Coppedge, Michael, and Reinecke, Wolfgang H. (1991). "Measuring Polyarchy." In *On Measuring Democracy: Its Consequences and Concomitants*, ed. Alex Inkeles, Chap. 3. New Brunswick, NJ: Transaction

Crescenzi, Mark J. C., and Andrew Enterline (1999). "Ripples from the Waves? A Systemic, Time-Series Analysis of Democracy, Democratization, and Interstate War," *Journal of Peace Research*, 36 (1): 75-94

Crescenzi, Mark J. C., and Andrew Enterline (2001). "Time Remembered: A Dynamic Model of Interstate Interaction," *Interna-*

tional Studies Quarterly, 45 (3): 409-431

Crescenzi, Mark J. C., Kelly M. Kadera, Sara McLaughlin Mitchell, and Clayton L. Thyne (2011). "A Supply Side Theory of Mediation," *International Studies Quarterly*, 55 (4): 1069-1095

Croco, Sarah E., and Tze Kwang Teo (2005). "Assessing the Dyadic Approach to Interstate Conflict Processes: A.k.a. 'Dangerous' Dyad-Years," *Conflict Management and Peace Science*, 22 (1): 5-18

Croissant, Michael P. (1998). *Armenia-Azerbaijan Conflict: Causes and Implications*. Westport, CT: Praeger

Crozier, Michel, Samuel P. Huntington, and Joji Watanuki (1975). *The Crisis of Democracy: Report on the Governability of Democracies to the Trilateral Commission*. New York: New York University Press

Cunningham, Michelle (2001). *Mexico and the Foreign Policy of Napoleon III*. New York: Palgrave Macmillan

Cutright, Phillips (1963). "National Political Development: Its Measurement and Social Correlates," *American Sociological Review*, 28 (2): 253-264

Daase, Christopher (2006). "Democratic Peace—Democratic War: Three Reasons Why Democracies Are War-Prone." In *Democratic Wars: Looking at the Dark Side of the Democratic Peace*, eds. Anna Geis, Lothar Brock, and Harald Müller, Chap. 4. New York: Palgrave Macmillan

Dafoe, Allan (2011). "Statistical Critiques of the Democratic Peace: Caveat Emptor," *American Journal of Political Science*, 55 (2): 247-262

Dafoe, Allan, John R. Oneal, and Bruce Russett (2013). "The Democratic Peace: Weighing the Evidence and Cautious Inference," *International Studies Quarterly*, 57 (1): 201-214

Dafoe, Allan, and Bruce M. Russett (2013). "Does Capitalism Account for the Democratic Peace? The Evidence Says No." In *The Capitalist Peace: The Origin and Prospects of a Liberal Idea*, eds. Gerald Schneider and Nils P. Gleditsch, Chap 5. London: Routledge

Dahl, Robert A. (1956). *A Preface to Democratic Theory*. Chicago: University of Chicago Press

Dahl, Robert A. (1971). *Polyarchy, Participation, and Opposition*. New Haven, CT: Yale University Press

Dahl, Robert A. (1985). *A Preface to Economic Democracy*. Berkeley: University of California Press

Danilovic, Vesna, and Joe Clare (2007) "The Kantian Liberal Peace (Revisited)," *American Journal of Political Science*, 51 (2): 397–414

Darby, W. Evans (1904). *International Tribunals*, 4th edn. London: Dent

Davenport, Christian (2004). "Democracy and the Violation of Human Rights: A Statistical Analysis from 1976 to 1996," *American Journal of Political Science*, 48 (3): 538–554

Davenport, Christian (2007). *State Repression and the Domestic Democratic Peace*. New York: Cambridge University Press

David, Stephen R. (1991). "Explaining Third World Realignment," *World Politics*, 43 (2): 233-256

Davies, Graeme A. M. (2002). "Domestic Strife and the Initiation of International Conflict," *Journal of Conflict Resolution*, 46 (5): 672-692

Davis, Lynn E., Stacie L. Pettyjohn, Melanie W. Sisson, Stephen M. Worman, and Michael J. McNerney (2012). *U.S. Overseas Military Presence: What Are the Strategic Choices?* Santa Monica, CA: RAND Corporation

De Conde, Alexander (1966). *The Quasi-War: The Politics and Diplomacy of the Undeclared War with France 1797–1801*. New York: Scribner's

de Toqueville, Alexis (1835). *Democracy in America*. New York: Knopf, 1945

de Vries, Michiel S. (1990). "Interdependence, Cooperation and Conflict: An Empirical Analysis." *Journal of Peace Research*, 27 (4): 429-444

Delahunty, Robert J., and John Choon Yoo (2010). "Kant, Habermas, and the Democratic Peace," *Chicago Journal of International Law*, 10 (2): 1-37

DeLay, Brian (2008). *The War of a Thousand Deserts*. New Haven, CT: Yale University Press

Dembinsky, Matthias, Andreas Hasenclever, and Wolfgang Wagner (2004). "Towards an Executive Peace? The Ambivalent Efforts of International Democratic Institutions on Democracy, Peace, and War," *International Politics*, 41 (4): 543-564

Demick, Barbara (2013). "China, Taiwan Protest Fatal Shooting of

Fisherman by Philippines," *Los Angeles Times*, May 10

deRouen, Karl, Jr. (2000). "Presidents and the Diversionary Use of Force: A Research Note," *International Studies Quarterly*, 44 (3): 317-328

Debs, Alexandre, and H. E. Goemans (2010). "Regime Type, the Fate of Leaders, and War," *American Political Science Review*, 104 (2): 430-445

Desch, Michael C. (1996). "War and Strong States, Peace and Weak States," *International Organization*, 30 (2): 237-268

Desch, Michael C. (2002). "Democracy and Victory," *International Security*, 27 (1): 4-47

Deutsch, Karl W., Sidney A. Burrell, Robert A. Kann, Maurice Lee, Jr., Martin Lichterman, Raymond E. Lindgren, Frances L. Loewenheim, and Richard W. Van Wagenen (1957). *Political Community and the North Atlantic Area: International Organization in the Light of Historical Experience*. Princeton, NJ: Princeton University Press

Diamond, Larry (1994). "The Global Imperative: Building a Democratic World Order," *Current History*, 93 (1): 1-7

Diamond, Larry (2001). "Building a World of Liberal Democracies." In *Foreign Policy for America in the Twenty-First Century*, ed. Thomas H. Hendriksen, Chap. 3. Stanford, CA: Hoover Institution Press

Dick, G. William (1974). "Authoritarian Versus Nonauthoritarian Approaches to Economic Development," *Journal of Political Economy*, 82 (4): 817-827

Dixon, William J. (1993). "Democracy and the Management of International Conflict," *Journal of Conflict Resolution*, 37 (1): 42-68

Dixon, William J. (1994). "Democracy and the Peaceful Settlement of International Conflict," *American Political Science Review*, 88 (1): 14-32

Dixon, William J., and Bruce E. Moon (1993). "Political Similarity and American Foreign Trade Patterns," *Political Research Quarterly*, 46 (1): 5-25

Dixon, William J., and Patrick Senese (2002). "Democracy, Disputes, and Negotiated Settlements," *Journal of Conflict Resolution*, 46 (4): 547-571

Domke, William K. (1988). *War and the Changing Global System*.

New Haven, CT: Yale University Press

Dorussen, Han, and Hugh Ward (2008). "Intergovernmental Organizations and the Kantian Peace: A Network Perspective," *Journal of Conflict Resolution*, 52 (2): 189-212

Downes, Alexander B., and Mary Lauren Lilley (2010). "Overt Peace, Covert War?: Covert Intervention and the Democratic Peace," *Security Studies*, 19 (2): 266–306

Doyle, Michael W. (1983). "Kant, Liberal Legacies, and Foreign Affairs," *Philosophy and Public Affairs,* 12 (3-4): 205-235, 323-353

Doyle, Michael W. (1986). "Liberalism and World Politics," *American Political Science Review,* 80 (4): 1151-1169

Doyle, Michael W. (1995). "Reflections on the Liberal Peace and Its Critics," *International Security*, 19 (4): 180-184

Doyle, Michael W. (1996). "Michael Doyle on the Democratic Peace—Again." In *Debating the Democratic Peace*, eds. Michael E. Brown, Sean M. Lynn-Jones, and Steven E. Miller, pp. 364-377. Cambridge, MA: MIT Press

Doyle, Michael W. (1997). *Ways of War and Peace.* New York: Norton

Doyle, Michael W. (2005). "Three Pillars of the Democratic Peace," *American Political Science Review*, 99 (3): 463-466

Druckman, Daniel (1994). "Nationalism, Patriotism, and Group Loyalty," *Mershon International Studies Review*, 38 (1): 43-68

Drury, A. Cooper, and Dursen Peksen (2010). "Sanctioning for Democracy." In *Democratic Peace in Theory and Practice*, ed. Steven W. Hook, Chap. 9. Kent, OH: Kent State University Press

Dudley, Michael Keoni, and Keoni Kealoha Agard (1990). *A Call for Hawaiian Sovereignty.* Honolulu: Na Kane o Ka Malo Press

Dupuy, R. Ernest, and Trevor N. Dupuy (1977). *The Encyclopedia of Military History: From 3500 BC to the Present.* New York: Harper & Row

Dussel, Kurt (1997). "Domestic Instability, the Military, and Foreign Policy: Indonesia, 1956-71." In *Paths to Peace: Is Democracy the Answer?*, ed. Miriam Fedius Elman, Chap 10. Cambridge, MA: MIT Press

Duvall, Raymond (1976). "An Appraisal of the Methodological and Statistical Procedures of the Correlates of War Project." In *Quantitative International Politics: An Appraisal*, eds. Francis

W. Hoole and Dina A. Zinnes, Chap. 4. New York: Praeger

East, Maurice A., and Gregg, Phillip M. (1967). "Factors Influencing Cooperation and Conflict in the International System," *International Studies Quarterly*, 11 (3): 244-269

East, Maurice A., and Charles F. Hermann (1974). "Do Nation-Types Account for Foreign Policy Behavior?" In *Comparing Foreign Policies: Theories, Findings, and Methods*, ed. James N. Rosenau, pp. 269-303. New York: Wiley

Egan, David (2010). "Democracy, the State, and Global Capitalism." In *Democratic Peace in Theory and Practice*, ed. Steven W. Hook, Chap. 4. Kent, OH: Kent State University Press

Eilstrup-Sangiovanni, Mette, and Daniel Verdier (2005). "European Integration as a Solution to War," *European Journal of International Relations*, 11 (1): 99-135

Ellis, Glynn, Sara McLaughlin Mitchell, and Brandon C. Prins (2010). "How Democracies Keep the Peace: Contextual Factors That Influence Conflict Management Strategies," *Foreign Policy Analysis*, 6 (4): 373-398

Elman, Miriam Fedius (1997a). "Finland in World War II: Alliances, Small States, and the Democratic Peace." In *Paths to Peace: Is Democracy the Answer?*, ed. Miriam Fedius Elman, Chap 4. Cambridge, MA: MIT Press

Elman, Miriam Fedius (1997b). "Israel's Invasion of Lebanon: Regime Change and War Decisions." In *Paths to Peace: Is Democracy the Answer?*, ed. Miriam Fedius Elman, Chap 7. Cambridge, MA: MIT Press

Elman, Miriam Fedius, ed. (1997c). *Paths to Peace: Is Democracy the Answer?* Cambridge, MA: MIT Press

Elman, Miriam Fedius (1997d). "Testing the Democratic Peace Theory." In *Paths to Peace: Is Democracy the Answer?*, ed. Miriam Fedius Elman, pp. 473-506. Cambridge, MA: MIT Press

Ember, Carol R., and Melvin Ember (1992). "Resource Unpredictability, Mistrust, and War: A Cross-Cultural *Study*," *Journal of Conflict Resolution*, 36 (2) :242-262

Ember, Carol R., Melvin Ember, and Bruce M. Russett (1992). "Peace Between Participatory Polities: A Cross-Cultural Test of the 'Democracies Rarely Fight Each Other' Hypothesis," *World Politics*, 44 (4): 573-599

Emerson, Steven (1988). *Secret Warriors: Inside the Covert Military*

Operations of the Reagan Era. New York: Putnam

Enterline, Andrew J. (1996). "Driving While Democratizing," *International Security*, 20 (2): 183-196

Enterline, Andrew J. (1998). "Regime Changes, Neighborhoods, and Interstate Conflict, 1862-1992," *Journal of Conflict Resolution*, 42 (6): 804-829

Enterline, Andrew J., and Michael Greig (2006). "Just the Good, No Bad and Ugly? The Regional Impact of Externally Imposed Democracy." In *Conflict Prevention and Peacebuilding in Post-War Societies: Sustaining the Peace*, eds., James Meernik and T. David Mason, Chap. 7. New York: Routledge

Erickson, Edward J. (2003). *Defeat in Detail: The Ottoman Army in the Balkans, 1912-1913.* Westport, CT: Greenwood

Etzioni, Amitai (1962). *The Hard Way to Peace: A New Strategy.* New York: Collier

Eyerman, Joe, and Robert A. Hart, Jr. (1996). "An Empirical Test of the Audience Cost Proposition: Democracy Speaks Louder than Words," *Journal of Conflict Resolution*, 40 (4): 597-616

Farber, Henry S., and Joanne Gowa (1995). "Polities and Peace," *International Security*, 20 (2): 123-146

Farber, Henry S., and Joanne Gowa (1997). "Common Interests or Common Polities? Reinterpreting the Democratic Peace," *Journal of Politics*, 59 (2): 393-417

Farnham, Barbara (2003). "The Theory of Democratic Peace and Threat Perception," *International Studies Quarterly*, 47 (3): 395-415

Fearon, James D. (1994). "Domestic Political Audiences and the Escalation of International Disputes," *American Political Science Review*, 88 (3): 577-592

Fearon, James D. (1995). "Rationalist Explanations for War," *International Organization*, 49 (3): 379-414

Feierabend, Ivo K., and Feierabend, Rosalind L. (1972). "Systematic Conditions of Political Aggression: An Application of Frustration-Aggression Theory." *In Anger, Violence, and Politics: Theories and Research,* eds. Ivo K. Feierabend, Rosalind L. Feierabend, and Ted Robert Gurr, pp. 136-183. Englewood Cliffs, NJ: Prentice-Hall

Feldman, Noah (2013). *Cool War: The Future of Global Competition.* New York: Random House

Ferejohn, John, and Frances McCall Rosenbluth (2008). "Warlike Democracies," *Journal of Conflict Resolution*, 52 (1): 3-38

Ferris, Wayne H. (1973). *The Power Capabilities of Nation-States: International Conflict and War*. Lexington, MA: Heath

Finel, Bernard L., and Kristin M. Lord, eds. (2000). *Power and Conflict in the Age of Transparency*. New York: Palgrave Macmillan

Fisher, Sydney George (1896). *The Making of Pennsylvania*. Philadelphia, PA: Lippincott

Flanigan, William, and Edwin Fogelman (1971). "Patterns of Democratic Development: An Historical Comparative Analysis." In *Macro-Quantitative Analysis: Conflict, Development, and Democratization*, eds. John V. Gillespie and Betty A. Nesvold, Chap. 21. Beverly Hill, CA: Sage

Fordham, Benjamin O. (2002). "Domestic Politics, International Pressure, and the Allocation of American Cold War Military Spending," *Journal of Politics*, 64 (1): 63-88

Fordham, Benjamin O., and Christopher C. Sarver (2002). "Militarized Interstate Disputes and United States Uses of Force," *International Studies Quarterly*, 45 (3): 455-466

Fordham, Benjamin O., and Thomas C. Walker (2005). "Kantian Liberalism, Regime Type, and Military Resource Allocation: Do Democracies Spend Less?," *International Studies Quarterly*, 49 (1): 141-157

Forsythe, David P. (1992). "Democracy, War, and Covert Action," *Journal of Peace Research*, 29 (4): 385-395

Foyle, Douglas C. (1999). *Counting the Public In: Presidents, Public Opinion, and Foreign Policy*. New York: Columbia University Press

Frakt, Phyllis, M. (1977). "Democracy, Political Activity, Economic Development, and Governmental Responsiveness: The Case of Labor Policy," *Comparative Political Studies*, 10 (1): 177-212

Frank, André Gunder (1967). *Capitalism and Underdevelopment in Latin America: Historical Studies of Chile and Brazil*. New York: Monthly Review Press

Fraser, Cary (2013). "Decolonization and the Cold War." In *The Oxford Handbook of the Cold War*, eds. Richard Immerman and Petra Goedde, Ch 26. New York: Oxford University Press

Freedman, Lawrence (1997). "How Did the Democratic Process Affect Britain's Decision to Reoccupy the Falkland Islands?" In

Paths to Peace: Is Democracy the Answer?, ed. Miriam Fedius Elman, Chap 5. Cambridge, MA: MIT Press

Freedom House (1978-). *Freedom in the World: Political Rights and Civil Li*berties. Lanham, MD: Freedom House, annual

Friedman, Gil (2008). "Identifying the Place of Democratic Norms in Democratic Peace," *International Studies Review*, 10 (3): 548-570

Frost, Robert I. (2000). *The Northern Wars: War, State and Society in Northeastern Europe, 1559-1721.* New York: Longman

Fukuyama, Francis (1992). *The End of History and the Last Man.* New York: Free Press

Gabriel, Richard A. (1984). *Operation Peace for Galilee: The Israeli-PLO War in Lebanon.* New York: Hill & Wang

Gallagher, Maryann E., and Susan H. Allen (20140. "Presidential Personality: Not Just a Nuisance," *Foreign Policy Analysis*, 10 (1): 1-21

Galtung, Johan (1964). "A Structural Theory of Aggression," *Journal of Peace Research*, 1 (1): 95-119

Gangulu, Sumit (1997). "War and Conflict Behavior Between India and Pakistan: Revisiting the Pacifying Power of Democracy." In *Paths to Peace: Is Democracy the Answer?*, ed. Miriam F. Elman, Chap. 6. Cambridge, MA: MIT Press

Gartzke, Erik (1998). "Kant We All Just Get Along? Opportunity, Willingness, and the Origins of the Democratic Peace," *American Journal of Political Science*, 42 (1): 1-27

Gartzke, Erik (2000). "Preferences and the Democratic Peace," *International Studies Quarterly*, 44 (2): 191-212

Gartzke, Erik (2001). "Democracy and the Preparation for War: Does Regime Type Affect States' Anticipation of Casualties?," *International Studies Quarterly*, 45 (3): 467-484

Gartzke, Erik (2007). "The Capitalist Peace," *American Journal of Political Science*, 51 (1): 166-191

Gartzke, Eric, and J. Joseph Hewitt (2010). "International Crises and the Capitalist Peace," *International Interactions*, 36 (1): 115-145

Gartzke, Erik, and Quan Li (2003). "How Globalization Can Reduce International Conflict." In *Globalization and Armed Conflict*, eds. Gerald Schneider, Katherine Barbieri, and Nils Petter Gleditsch, Chap. 6. Lanham, MD: Rowman and Littlefield

Gartzke, Erik, Quan Li, and Charles Boehmer (2001). "Investing in

Peace: Economic Interdependence and International Conflict," *International Organization*, 55 (2): 391-438

Gartzke, Erik, and Alex Weisiger (2013). "Permanent Friends? Dynamic Difference and the Democratic Peace," *International Studies Quarterly*, 57 (1): 171-185

Gasiorowski, Mark J. (1986). "Economic Interdependence and International Conflict: Some Cross-National Evidence," *International Studies Quarterly*, 30 (l): 23-38

Gasiorowski, Mark J. (1991). "The Political Regimes Project." In *On Measuring Democracy: Its Consequences and Concomitants*, ed. Alex Inkeles, Chap. 5. New Brunswick, NJ: Transaction

Gasiorowsky, Mark J. (1996). "An Overview of the Political Regime Change Dataset," *Comparative Political Studies*, 29 (4): 469-483

Gasiorowski, Mark J., and Solomon W. Polachek (1982). "Conflict and Interdependence: East-West Trade and Linkages in the Era of Detente," *Journal of Conflict Resolution*, 26 (4): 709-729

Gat, Azar (2005). "The Democratic Peace Theory Reframed: The Impact of Modernity," *World Politics*, 58 (1): 73-100

Gat, Azar (2006). *War in Human Civilization*. New York: Oxford University Press

Gates, Scott, Torejohn L. Knutsen, and Jonathan W. Moses (1996). "Democracy and Peace: A More Skeptical View," *Journal of Peace Research*, 33 (1): 1-10

Gaubatz, Kurt Taylor (1991). "Election Cycles and War," *Journal of Conflict Resolution*, 35 (2): 212-244

Gaubatz, Kurt Taylor (1999). *Elections and War: The Electoral Incentive in the Democratic Politics of Peace*. Stanford, CA: Stanford University Press

Geddes, Barbara (2003). *Paradigms and Sand Castles: Theory Building and Research Design in Comparative Politics*. Ann Arbor: University of Michigan Press

Geis, Anna (2006). "Spotting the 'Enemy'? Democracies and the Challenge of the 'Other'." In *Democratic Wars: Looking at the Dark Side of the Democratic Peace*, eds. Anna Geis, Lothar Brock, and Harald Müller, Chap. 7. New York: Palgrave Macmillan

Geller, Daniel S. (1985). *Domestic Factors in Foreign Policy: A Cross-National Statistical Analysis*. Cambridge, MA: Schenkman

Gelpi, Christopher F. (1997). "Democratic Diversions, Governmental Structures and the Externalization of Domestic Conflict," *Journal of Conflict Resolution*, 41 (2): 255-282

Gelpi, Christopher F., and Michael Griesdorf (2001). "Winners or Losers? Democracies in International Crisis, 1918-94," *American Political Science Review*, 95 (3): 633-647

George, Alexander L. (1980). *Presidential Decision Making in Foreign Policy: The Effective Use of Information and Advice*. Boulder, CO: Westview

Geva, Nehemia, Karl deRouen, and Alex Mintz (1993). "The Political Incentive Explanation of the 'Democratic Peace' Phenomenon: Evidence from Experimental Research," *International Interactions*, 18 (3): 215-229

Gibler, Douglas M. (2007). "Bordering on Peace: Democracy, Territorial Issues, and Conflict," *International Studies Quarterly*, 51 (3): 509-532

Gibler, Douglas, M. (2010). "Outside-In: The Effects of External Threat on State Centralization," *Journal of Conflict Resolution*, 54 (4): 519-542

Gibler, Douglas M. (2012). *The Territorial Peace: Borders, State Development, and International Conflict*. New York: Cambridge University Press

Gibler, Douglas M., and Alex Braithwaite (2013). "Dangerous Neighbours, Regional Territorial Conflict and the Democratic Peace," *British Journal of Political Science*, 43 (4): 877-887

Gibler, Douglas, M., and Jaroslav Tir (2010). "Settled Borders and Regime Type: Democratic Transitions as Consequences of Peaceful Territorial Transfers," *American Journal of Political Science*, 54 (4): 961-968

Gibler, Douglas, M., and Jaroslav Tir (2014). "Territorial Peace and Democratic Clustering," *Journal of Politics*, 76 (1): 27-40

Gilpin, Robert (1981). *War and Change in World Politics*. Cambridge, UK: Cambridge University Press

Gleditsch, Kristian S., and Michael D. Ward (1997). "Double Take: A Re-Examination of Democracy and Autocracy," *Journal of Conflict Resolution*, 41 (3): 361-383

Gleditsch, Kristian S., and Michael D. Ward (2000). "War and Peace in Space and Time: The Role of Democratization," *International Studies Quarterly*, 44 (10: 1-29

Gleditsch, Kristian S., and Michael D. Ward (2006). "Diffusion and the International Content of Democratization," *International Organization*, 60 (4): 911-933

Gleditsch, Nils Petter (1992). "Focus on Democracy and Peace," *Journal of Peace Research*, 29 (4): 369-376

Gleditsch, Nils Petter (1995). "Geography, Democracy and Peace," *International Interactions*, 20 (4): 297–314

Gleditsch, Nils Petter, Lene Siljeholm Christiansen, and Hårvard Hegre (2007). *Democratic Jihad?* Washington, DC: World Bank

Gleditsch, Nils Petter, and Hårvard Hegre (1997). "Peace and Democracy: Three Levels of Analysis," *Journal of Conflict Resolution*, 41 (2): 283-310

Gleditsch, Nils Petter, Hilde Ravlo, and Hans Dorussen (2003). "Colonial War and the Democratic Peace," *Journal of Conflict Resolution*, 47 (4): 520-548

Gleditsch, Nils Petter, and Michael D. Ward (1997). "Double Take: A Reexamination of Democracy and Autocracy in Modern Polities," *Journal of Conflict Resolution*, 41 (3): 361-383

Gochman, Charles (1996). "Correspondence: Democracies and Peace," *International Security*, 32 (3): 177-186

Gochman, Charles, and Zeev Maoz (1984). "Militarized Interstate Disputes, 1916-1976: Procedures, Patterns, and Insights," *Journal of Conflict Resolution,* 28 (4): 585-616

Goemans, Cullen F. (2004). "Uncertainty of the Liberal Peace, *Journal of Peace Research*, 41 (5): 589-605

Goenner, Cullen F. (2004). "Uncertainty of the Liberal Peace," Journal of Peace Research, 41 (5): 589-605

Goldsmith, Benjamin E. (2006). "A Universal Proposition? Region, Conflict, War and the Robustness of the Kantian Peace," *European Journal of International Relations*, 12 (4): 533-563

Goldsmith, Benjamin E. (2007) "Defense Effort and Institutional Theories of Democratic Peace and Victory: Why Try Harder?," *Security Stu*dies, 16 (2): 189–222

Goldsworthy, Adriam (2001). *The Punic Wars*. London: Cassell

Gordon, Bernard K. (1966). *The Dimensions of Conflict in Southeast Asia.* Englewood Cliffs, NJ: Prentice-Hall

Götze, Catherine (2006). "Sameness and Distinction: Understanding Democratic Peace in a Bourdieusian Perspective." In *Democratic Wars: Looking at the Dark Side of the Democratic Peace*, eds.

Anna Geis, Lothar Brock, and Harald Müller, Chap. 8. New York: Palgrave Macmillan

Gowa, Joanne (1994). *Allies, Adversaries, and International Trade*. Princeton, NJ: Princeton University Press

Gowa, Joanne (1995). "Democratic States and International Disputes," *International Organization*, 49 (3): 511-522

Gowa, Joanne (1999). *Ballots and Bullets—The Elusive Democratic Peace*. Princeton, NJ: Princeton University Press

Gowa, Joanne (2011). "The Democratic Peace after the Cold War," *Economics & Politics*, 23 (2): 153-171

Gowa, Joanne, and Edward D. Mansfield (1993). "Power Politics and International Trade," *American Political Science Review*, 37 (2): 408-420

Grant, Jeremy (2013). "'Sultan of Sulu' Invasion of Borneo Creates Problems in Malaysia, Philippines," *Financial Times*, March 4

Green, Donald P., Soon Yeon Kim, and David H. Yoon (2001). "Dirty Pool," *International Organization*, 55 (2): 441-468

Gregg, Phillip M., and Arthur S. Banks (1965). "Dimensions of Political Systems: Factor Analysis of a Cross-Polity Survey," *American Political Science Review,* 59 (3): 602-613

Gurr, Ted Robert (1978). *Polity Data Handbook.* Ann Arbor, MI: Inter-University Consortium for Political and Social Research

Gurr, Ted Robert, Keith Jaggers, and Will Moore (1989). *Polity II Handbook.* Boulder, CO: Westview

Guttman, Louis (1951). "A Structural Theory for Intergroup Beliefs and Action," *American Sociological Review,* 24 (2): 318-328

Haas, Michael (1965). "Societal Approaches to the Study of War," *Journal of Peace Research,* 2 (4): 307-323

Haas, Michael (1968). "Social Change and National Aggressiveness, 1900-1960." In *Quantitative International Politics: Insights and Evidence*, ed. J. David Singer, pp. 215-244. New York: Free Press

Haas, Michael (1970). "International Subsystems: Stability and Polarity," *American Political Science Review*, 49 (1): 98-123

Haas, Michael (1974). *International Conflict.* Indianapolis, IN: Bobbs-Merrill

Haas, Michael (1986). "Research on International Crisis: Obsolescence of an Approach?," *International Interactions,* 13 (1): 23-58

Haas, Michael (1989). *The Asian Way to Peace: A Story of Regional*

Cooperation. New York: Praeger

Haas, Michael (1991a). *Cambodia, Pol Pot, and the United States*. New York: Praeger

Haas, Michael (1991b). *Genocide by Proxy: Cambodian Pawn on a Superpower Chessboard*. New York: Praeger

Haas, Michael (1992). *Polity and Society: Philosophical Underpinnings of Social Science Paradigms*. New York: Praeger

Haas, Michael (1994). *Improving Human Rights*. Westport, CT: Praeger

Haas, Michael (1995). "When Democracies Fight One Another, Just What Is the Punishment for Breaking the Law?" Paper presented at the annual convention of the American Political Science Association

Haas, Michael (1997a). "Deconstructing the 'Democratic Peace'." In *Deconstructing International Relations Theory*, ed. Michael Haas, pp. 127-148. New York: Norton

Haas, Michael (1997b). "International Communitarianism: The New Agenda of World Politics." In *Deconstructing International Relations Theory*, ed. Michael Haas, pp. 127-148. New York: Norton

Haas, Michael, ed. (1999). *The Singapore Puzzle*. New York: Praeger

Haas, Michael (2009). *George W. Bush, War Criminal? The Bush Administration's Liability for 269 War Crimes*. Westport, CA: Praeger

Haas, Michael (2010a). *America's War Crimes Quagmire: From Bush to Obama*. Los Angeles, CA: Publishinghouse for Scholars

Haas, Michael (2012a). *Mr. Calm and Effective: Evaluating the Presidency of Barack Obama*. Los Angeles, CA: Publishinghouse for Scholars

Haas, Michael (2012b). *Modern Cambodia's Emergence from the Killing Fields: What Happened in the Critical Years?* Los Angeles, CA: Publishinghouse for Scholars

Haas, Michael (2013). *Asian and Pacific Cooperation: Turning Arenas of Conflict into Zones of Peace*. New York: Palgrave Macmillan

Haas, Michael (2014a). *International Human Rights: A Comprehensive Introduction*, 2nd edn. London: Routledge

Haas, Michael, ed. (2014b). *The Singapore Puzzle*, 2nd edn. Los Angeles: Publishinghouse for Scholars

Haass, Richard (1994). *Intervention: The Use of American Military Force in the Post-Cold War World.* Washington, DC: Carnegie Endowment for International Peace

Hadenius, Axel (1992). *Democracy and Development.* New York: Cambridge University Press

Hafner-Burton, Emilie M., and Alexander Montgomery (2008). "Power or Plenty: International Organizations, Social Networks, and Conflict," *Journal of Conflict Resolution*, 52 (2): 213-242

Hagan, Joe D. (1993). *Political Opposition and Foreign Policy in Comparative Perspective.* Boulder, CO: Rienner

Hagan, Joe D. (1994). "Democratic Political Systems and War Proneness," *Mershon International Studies Review*, 38:183-207

Hall, D. G. E. (1964). *A History of South-East Asia*, 3rd edn. London: Macmillan

Hallett, Brien, ed. (1991). *Engulfed in War: Just War and the Persian Gulf.* Honolulu: Matsunaga Institute for Peace, University of Hawai'i

Halperin, Morton H. (1993). "Guaranteeing Democracy," *Foreign Policy,* 91 (Summer): 105-122

Hamid, Mohsin (2013). "Pakistan: Why Drones Don't Help," *New York Review of Books*, 60 (9): 23-25

Hardt, Michael, and Antonio Negri (2000). *Empire.* Cambridge, MA: Harvard University Press

Harff, Barbara (2003). "No Lessons Learned from the Holocaust? Assessing Risks of Genocide and Political Mass Murder Since 1955," *American Political Science Review*, 97 (1): 57-73

Harrison, Ewan (2004). "State Socialization, International Norm Dynamics and the Liberal Peace," *International Politics*, 41 (4): 521-542

Harrison, Ewan (2010). "The Democratic Peace Research Program and System-Level Analysis," *Journal of Peace Research*, 47 (2): 155-165

Hart, Robert A., Jr., and William Reed (1998). "Selection Effects and Dispute Escalation: Democracy and Status Quo Evaluations," *International Interactions*, 25 (3): 243-263

Hayes, Jerrod (2011). "The Democratic Peace and the New Evolution of an Old Idea," *European Journal of International Relations*, 17 (1): 1-25

Heagerty, Patrick, Michael D. Ward, and Kristian S. Gleditsch (2002). "Windows of Opportunity: Window Subseries Empirical Variance Estimator in International Relations," *Political Analysis*, 10 (3): 304-317

Hegre, Hårvard (2000). "Development and the Liberal Peace: What Does It Take to Be a Trading State?," *Journal of Peace Research*, 37 (1): 5-30

Hegre, Hårvard, Ranveig Gissinger, and Nils Petter Gleditsch (2003). "Globalization and Internal Conflict." In *Globalization and Armed Conflict*, eds. Gerald Schneider, Katherine Barbieri, and Nils Petter Gleditsch, Chap. 13. Lanham, MD: Rowman and Littlefield

Held, David (1987). *Models of Democracy*. Oxford, UK: Polity Press

Henderson, Errol A. (1999). "Neoidealism and the Democratic Peace," *Journal of Peace Research*, 36 (2): 203-231

Henderson, Errol A. (2002). *Democracy and War: The End of an Illusion?* Boulder, CO: Rienner

Henderson, Errol A. (2004). "The Slow Roasting of Sacred Cows: J. David Singer and the Democratic Peace." In *The Scourge of War: New Extension on an Old Problem*, ed. Paul F. Diehl, pp. 169-188. Ann Arbor: University of Michigan Press

Henderson, Errol A. (2009). "Disturbing the Peace: African Warfare, Political Inversion and the Universality of the Democratic Peace Thesis," *British Journal of Political Science*, 39 (1): 25-58

Henderson, Gordon F. (2006). "The Public and Peace: The Consequences for Citizenship of the Democratic Peace Literature," *International Studies Review*, 8 (2): 199-224

Hendrickson, David C. (1994-1995). "The Democratic Crusade: Intervention, Economic Sanctions, and Engagement," *World Policy Journal*, 11 (4): 18-30

Hensel, Paul R. (2001). "Contentious Issues and World Politics: The Management of Territorial Claims in the Americas, 1816-1992," *International Studies Quarterly*, 45 (1): 81-109

Hensel, Paul R., Gary Goertz, and Paul F. Diehl (2000). "The Democratic Pace and Rivalries," *Journal of Politics*, 64 (4): 1173-1188

Hensel, Paul R., Sara McLaughlin Mitchell, Thomas E. Sowers II, and Clayton L. Thyne (2008). "Bones of Contention: Comparing Territorial, Maritime, and River Issues," *Journal of Conflict Resolution*, 52 (1): 117-143

Herman, Frank L. (1994). "SHERFACS: A Cross Paradigm, Hierarchical and Contextually Sensitive, Conflict Management Dataset," *International Interactions*, 20 (1): 79-100

Hermann, Margaret G., and Charles F. Hermann (1989). "Who Makes Foreign Policy Decisions and How: An Empirical Inquiry," *International Studies Quarterly,* 33 (4): 361-387

Hermann, Margaret G., and Charles W. Kegley, Jr. (1995). "Rethinking Democracy and International Peace: Perspectives from Political Psychology," *International Studies Quarterly*, 39 (5): 511-5333

Hermann, Margaret G., and Charles W. Kegley, Jr. (1996). "Ballots, a Barrier Against the Use of Bullets and Bombs: Democratization and Military Intervention," *Journal of Conflict Resolution*, 40 (3): 436-460

Hermann, Margaret G., and Charles W. Kegley, Jr. (1997). "Putting Military Intervention into the Democratic Peace: A Research Note," *Comparative Political Studies*, 30 (1): 78-107

Hermann, Margaret G., and Charles W. Kegley, Jr. (1998). "The U.S. Use of Military Intervention to Promote Democracy: Evaluating the Record," *International Interactions*, 24 (2): 91-114

Hermann, Margaret G., Charles W. Kegley, Jr., and Gregory A. Raymond (1998). "The Rise and Fall of the Nonintervention Norm: Some Correlates and Potential Consequences," *Fletcher Forum of World Affairs*, 22 (1): 81-101

Herold, Marc W. (2012). "The Matrix of Death." *warand law.-homestead.com*

Herz, Monica, and João Nogueira (2002). *Ecuador vs. Peru: Peacemaking amid Rivalry*. Boulder, CO: Rienner

Hess, Gregory D., and Athanasios Orphanides (2001). "War and Democracy," *Journal of Political Economy*, 109 (4): 776-810

Hewitt, Christopher (1977). "The Effect of Political Democracy and Social Democracy on Equality in Industrial Societies," *American Sociological Review*, 42 (1):450-464

Hewitt, J. Joseph, and Jonathan Wilkenfeld (1996). "Democracies in International Crisis," *International Interactions*, 22 (2): 123-142

Hintze, Otto (1906). "Military Organization and State Organization." In *The Historical Essays of Otto Hintze*, ed. Felix Gilbert, pp. 178-215. New York: Oxford University Press, 1975

Hirst, David (2010). *Beware of Small States: Lebanon, Battleground of the Middle East*. New York: Nation Books

Hoebel, E. Adamson (1940). *The Political Organization and Law-Ways of the Comanche Indians*. Menasha, WI: American Anthropological Association

Holsti, Kalevi J. (1991). *Peace and War: Armed Conflicts and International Order, 1648-1989*. Cambridge, UK: Cambridge University Press

Holsti, Kalevi J. (1996). *The State, War, and the State of War*. Cambridge, UK: Cambridge University Press

Holsti, Ole R., and James N. Rosenau (1984). *American Leadership in World Affairs: Vietnam, and the Breakdown of Consensus*. Boston: Allen and Unwin

Hook, Steven W. (1995). *National Interest and Foreign Aid*. Boulder, CO: Rienner

Hook, Steven W., Charles W. Kegley, Jr., and Margaret G. Hermann (1995). "Dollar Diplomacy: Foreign Aid and the Promotion of Democracy." Paper presented at the annual convention of the International Studies Association

Hösebalaban, Hasan (2011). *Turkish Foreign Policy: Islam, Nationalism, and Globalization*. New York: Palgrave Macmillan

Howard, Michael (1984). *The Causes of War and Other Essays*, 2nd edn. Cambridge, MA: Harvard University Press

Howe, James (1998). *A People Who Would Not Kneel: Panama, the United States, and the San Blas Kuna*. Washington, DC: Smithsonian Institution Press

Hudson, William (1995). *American Democracy in Peril*. Chatham, NJ: Chatham House

Huntington, Samuel P. (1968). *Political Order in Changing Societies*. New Haven, CT: Yale University Press

Huntington, Samuel P. (1989). "No Exit: The Errors of Endism," *The National Interest*, 17 (1): 3-11

Huntington, Samuel P. (1991). *The Third Wave: Democratization in the Late Twentieth Century*. Norman: University of Oklahoma Press

Huntington, Samuel P. (2000). "Try Again: A Reply to Russett, Oneal & Cox," *Journal of Peace Research*, 37 (5): 609-610

Huth, Paul K., and Todd L. Allee (2002). "Domestic Political Accountability and the Escalation and Settlement of International Disputes," *Journal of Conflict Resolution*, 46 (6): 754-790

Inglehart, Ronald, and Christian Welzel (1995). *Modernization, Cultural Change, and Democracy: The Human Development Sequence*. New York: Cambridge University Press

Inkeles, Alex, ed. (1991). *On Measuring Democracy: Its Consequences and Concomitants*. New Brunswick, NJ: Transaction

Ireland, Michael J., and Scott Sigmund Gartner (2001). "Time to Fight: Government Type and Conflict Initiation in Parliamentary Systems," *Journal of Conflict Resolution*, 45 (5): 547-568

Ish-Shalom, Piki (2006). "Theory as a Hermeneutical Mechanism: The Democratic-Peace Thesis and the Politics of Democratization," *European Journal of International Relations*, 12 (4): 565-598

Ish-Shalom, Piki (2008a). "The Rhetorical Capital of Theories: The Democratic Peace and the Road to the Roadmap," *International Political Science Review*, 29 (3):281-301

Ish-Shalom, Piki (2008b). "Theorization, Harm, and the Democratic Imperative: Lessons from the Politicization of the Democratic Peace," *International Studies Review*, 10 (4): 680-692

Ish-Shalom, Piki (2013). *Democratic Peace: A Political Biography*. Ann Arbor: University of Michigan Press

Jackman, Robert W. (1975). *Politics and Social Equality*. New York: Wiley

Jaggers, Keith, and Ted Robert Gurr (1995). "Tracking Democracy's Third Wave with the Polity III Data," *Journal of Peace Research*, 32 (4): 469-482

James, Patrick (1988). *Crisis and War*. Kingston, ON: McGill-Queen's University Press

James, Patrick, and Glenn E. Mitchell II (1995). "Targets of Covert Pressure: The Hidden Victims of the Democratic Peace," *International Interactions*, 21 (1): 85-107

James, Patrick, and John R. Oneal (1991). "The Influence of Domestic and International Politics on the President's Use of Force," *Journal of Conflict Resolution*, 35 (2): 307-332

James, Patrick, Johann Park, and Choi Seung-Whan (2006). "Democracy and Conflict Management: Territorial Claims in the Western Hemisphere Revisited," *International Studies Quarterly*, 50 (4): 803-817

James, Patrick, and Jean Sebastien Rioux (1998). "International Crises and Linkage Politics: The Experience of the United States,

1953-1994," *Political Research Quarterly*, 51 (4): 781-812

James, Patrick, Eric Solberg, and Murray Wolfson (1999). "An Identified Systemic Model of the Democracy-Peace Nexus," *Defence and Peace Economics*, 10 (1): 1-37

Janis, Irving L. (1982). *Groupthink: Psychological Studies of Policy Decisions and Fiascoes*, 2nd edn. Boston: Houghton Mifflin

Jentleson, Bruce W., and Rebecca L. Britton (1998). "Still Pretty Prudent: Post-Cold War American Public Opinion on the Use of Military Force," *Journal of Conflict Resolution*, 42 (4): 395-417

Jervis, Robert (1976). *Perception and Misperception in International Politics*. Princeton, NJ: Princeton University Press

Jervis, Robert (2002). "Theories of War in an Era of Leading-Power Peace," *American Political Science Review*, 96 (1): 1-14

Johns, Robert, and Graeme Davies (2012) "Democratic Peace or Clash of Civilizations? Target States and Support for War in Britain and the United States," *Journal of Politics* 74 (4): 1038-1052

Johnson, Loch K. (2010). "Promoting Democracy by Example." In *Democratic Peace in Theory and Practice*, ed. Steven W. Hook, Chap. 11. Kent, OH: Kent State University Press

Jones, Daniel, Stuart Bremer, and J. David Singer (1996). "Militarized Interstate Disputes, 1816–1992: Rationale, Coding Rules, and Empirical Patterns," *Conflict Management and Peace Science*, 15 (2): 163–213

Kacowicz, Arie M. (1995). "Explaining Zones of Peace: Democracies as Satisfied Powers," *Journal of Peace Research*, 32 (3): 265-276

Kacowicz, Arie M. (1997). "Peru vs. Colombia and Senegal vs. Mauritania: Mixed Dyads and 'Negative Peace'." In *Paths to Peace: Is Democracy the Answer?*, ed. Miriam Fedius Elman, Chap 8. Cambridge, MA: MIT Press

Kacowicz, Arie M. (1998). *Zones of Peace in the Third World: South America and West Africa in Comparative Perspective*. Albany, NY: SUNY Press

Kahin, George McT. (1986). *Intervention: How America Became Involved in Vietnam*. New York: Knopf

Kahler, Miles (1979-1980). "Rumors of War: The 1914 Analogy," *Foreign Affairs*, 58 (2): 374-396

Kant, Immanuel (1795). *Perpetual Peace*. New York: Liberal Arts

Press, 1957

Kaplan, Morton A. (1957). *System and Process in International Relations.* New York: Wiley

Kaplan, Fred (1999). "Bombs Killing More Civilians than Expected," *Boston Globe,* May 30

Kegley, Charles W., and Margaret G. Hermann (1995a). "Military Intervention and the Democratic Peace," *International Interactions,* 21 (1): 1-21

Kegley, Charles W., and Margaret G. Hermann (1995b). "The Political Psychology of 'Peace Through Democratization'," *Cooperation and Conflict,* 30 (1): 5-30

Kegley, Charles W., and Margaret G. Hermann (1996a). "Ballots, a Barrier Against the Use of Bullets and Bombs: Democratization and Military Intervention," *Journal of Conflict Resolution,* 40 (3): 436-460

Kegley, Charles W., and Margaret G. Hermann (1996b). "How Democracies Use Intervention: A Neglected Dimension in Studies of the Democratic Peace," *Journal of Peace Research,* 33 (3): 309-322

Kegley, Charles W., and Margaret G. Hermann (1997a). "A Peace Dividend? Democracies' Military Interventions and Their External Affairs," *Cooperation and Conflict,* 32 (4): 339–369

Kegley, Charles W., and Margaret G. Hermann (1997b). "Putting Military Intervention into the Democratic Peace: A Research Note," *Comparative Political Studies,* 30 (1): 78-107

Keller, Jonathan W. (2005). "Leadership Style, Regime Type, and Foreign Policy Crisis Behavior: A Contingent Monadic Peace?," *International Studies Quarterly,* 49 (2): 205-231

Kende, Istvan (1971). "Twenty-Five Years of Local Wars," *Journal of Peace Research,* 8 (1): 5-22

Kende, Istvan (1978). "Wars of Ten Years," *Journal of Peace Research,* 13 (3): 227-242

Kende, Istvan (1982). *Über die Kriege seit 1945.* Bonn: Deutsche Gesellschaft für Friedensund Konflikforschung

Kessler, Richard J. (1992). "The Philippines." In *Intervention into the 1990s: U.S. Foreign Policy in the Third World,* ed. Peter J. Schraeder, Chap. 15. Boulder, CO: Rienner

Kiernan, Ben (2008). "The Demography of Genocide in Southeast Asia: The Death Tolls in Cambodia, 1975-1979, and East Timor,

1975-1980," *Critical Asian Studies*, 35 (4): 585-597

Kim, Hyung Min, and David L. Rousseau (2005). The Classical Liberals Were Half Right (or Half Wrong): New Tests of the 'Liberal Peace', 1960-88," *Journal of Peace Research*, 42 (5): 523-543

Kim, Soo Yeon, and Bruce M. Russett (1996). "The New Politics of Voting Alignment in the United Nations General Assembly," *International Organization*, 50 (4): 629-652

Kim, Woosang (1989). "Power, Alliance, and Major Wars, 1816-1975," *Journal of Conflict Resolution*, 33 (2): 255-273

King, Gary, and Longche Zeng (2001a). "Explaining Rare Events in International Relations," *International Organization*, 55 (3): 693-715

King, Gary, and Longche Zeng (2001b). "Proper Nouns and Methodological Propriety: Pooling Dyads in International Relations Dyads," *International Organization*, 55 (2): 497-507

Kinsella, David (2005). "No Rest for the Democratic Peace," *American Political Science Review*, 99 (3): 453-457

Kinsella, David, and Bruce M. Russett (2002). "Conflict Emergence and Escalation in Interactive International Dyads," *Journal of Politics*, 64 (4): 1045-1068

Kiser, Edgar, Kriss A. Drass, and William Brustein (1995). "Ruler Autonomy and War in Early Modern Western Europe," *International Studies Quarterly*, 39 (1): 109-138

Kissinger, Henry (1957). *A World Restored: Metternich, Castlereagh and the Problems of the Peace, 1812–1822*. London: Weidenfeld and Nicolson

Kivimaki, Timo (2001). "The Long Peace of ASEAN," *Journal of Peace Research*, 38 (1): 5-25

Koga, Jun (2011). "Where Do Third Parties Intervene? Third Parties' Domestic Institutions, and Military Interventions in Civil Conflicts," *International Studies Quarterly*, 55 (4): 1143-1166

Kohn, George Childs (1987). *Dictionary of Wars*. Garden City, NY: Anchor

Krause, Volker (2004). "Arms, Alliances, and Success in Militarized International Disputes and Wars, 1916-1992." In *The Scourge of War: New Extensions on an Old Problem*, ed., Paul F. Diehl, pp. 120-142. Ann Arbor: University of Michigan Press

Kugler, Jacek (1990). "The War Phenomenon: A Working Distraction," *International Interactions*, 16 (3): 201-213

Kull, Steven, and I. M. Dustler (1999). *Misreading the Public: The Myth of a New Isolationism*. Washington, DC: Brookings

Lagazio, Monica, and Bruce Russett (2004). "A Neural Network Analysis of Militarized Disputes, 1885-1992: Temporal Stability and Causal Complexity." In *The Scourge of War: New Extensions on an Old Problem*, ed., Paul F. Diehl, pp. 28-62. Ann Arbor: University of Michigan Press

Lai, Brian, and Dan Reiter (2000). "Democracy, Political Similarity, and International Alliances, 1810-1992," *Journal of Conflict Resolution*, 44 (2): 205-227

Lai, Brian, and Dan Slater (2006). "Institutions of the Offensive: Domestic Sources of Dispute Initiation in Authoritarian Regimes, 1950-1992," *American Journal of Political Science*, 50 (1): 113-136

Lake, David A. (1992). "Powerful Pacifists: Democratic States and War," *American Political Science Review,* 86 (l): 24-37

Lake David A. (2003) "Fair Fights? Evaluating Theories of Democracy and Victory," *International Security*, 28 (1): 154–167

Lange, Peter, and Geoffrey Garrett (1985). "The Politics of Growth: Strategic Interaction and Economic Performance n the Advanced Inustrial Countires, 1974-1980," *Journal of Politics*, 47 (3): 792-827

Lange, Peter, and Geoffrey Garrett (1987). "The Politics of Growth Reconsidered," *Journal of Politics*, 49 (1): 257-274

Layne, Christopher (1994). "Kant or Cant: The Myth of the Democratic Peace," *International Security,* 19 (2): 5-49

Layne, Christopher (1997). "Lord Palmerston and the Triumph of Realism: Anglo-French Relations, 1930-48." In *Paths to Peace: Is Democracy the Answer?*, ed. Miriam Fedius Elman, Chap 1. Cambridge, MA: MIT Press

Leblang, David, and Steve Chan (2003). "Explaining Wars Fought by Established Democracies: Do Institutional Constraints Matter?," *Political Research Quarterly*, 56 (4): 385-400

Lebow, Richard Ned (1981). *Between Peace and War: The Nature of International Crisis*. Baltimore, MD: Johns Hopkins University Press

Lebow, Richard Ned, and Janice Gross Stein (1993). "Afghanistan, Carter, and Foreign Policy Change: The Limits of Cognitive Models." In *Force, Diplomacy, and Statecraft: Essays in Honor of*

Alexander L. George, Chap. 5. Boulder, CO: Westview

Leeds, Brett Ashley, and David R. Davis (1999). "Beneath the Surface: Regime Type and International Interaction, 1953-78," *Journal of Peace Research*, 36 (1): 5-21

Lees, Nicholas (2013). "Structural Inequality, Quasi-Rents and the Democratic Peace: A Neo-Ricardian Analysis of International Order," *Millennium: Journal of International Studies*, 41 (3): 491-515

Legro, Jeffrey (1997). "Which Norms Matter? Revisiting the 'Failure' of Internationalism," *International Organization*, 51 (1): 31-63

Lemke, Douglas (2002). *Regions of War and Peace*. New York: Cambridge University Press

Lemke, Douglas, and William Reed (1996). "Regime Types and Status Quo Evaluations: Power Transition Theory and the Democratic Peace," *International Interactions*, 22 (2): 143-164

Lemke, Douglas, and Patrick M. Regan (2004). "Interventions as Influence." In *The Scourge of War: New Extensions on an Old Problem*, ed., Paul F. Diehl, pp. 145-168. Ann Arbor: University of Michigan Press

Lemke, Douglas, and Suzanne Werner (1996). "Power Parity, Commitment to Change, and War," *International Studies Quarterly*, 40 (2): 235-260

Leng, Russell J. (1993). "Reciprocating Influence Strategies and Success in Interstate Crisis Bargaining," *Journal of Conflict Resolution,* 37 (1): 3-41

Lerner, Daniel, ed. (1960). *Evidence and Inference*. New York: Free Press

Lektzian, David, and Mark Souva (2009). "A Comparative Theory Test of Democratic Peace Arguments, 1946–2000," *Journal of Peace Research*, 46 (1): 17-37

Levin, N. Gordon, Jr. (1968). *Woodrow Wilson and World Politics: America's Response to War and Revolution*. New York: Oxford University Press

Levine, Edward P. (1971). "Mediation in International Politics," *Peace Research Society, Papers,* 17: 23-43

Levy, Gilat, and Ronny Razin (2003). "It Takes Two: An Explanation of the Democratic Peace," *Journal of the European Economic Association*, 2 (1): 1-29

Levy, Jack S. (1983). "Misperceptions and the Causes of War," *World Politics*, 36 (1): 76-99

Levy, Jack S. (1989). "The Diversionary Theory of War: A Critique." In *Handbook of War Studies,* ed. Manus Midlarsky, pp. 259-288. Ann Arbor: University of Michigan Press

Levy, Jack S. (1990). Big Wars, Little Wars, and Theory Construction," *International Interactions*, 16 (3): 215-224

Lifton, Robert Jay, and Greg Mitchell (1995). *Hiroshima in America: Fifty Years of Denial.* New York: Grosset/Putnam

Lijphart, Arend (1984). *Democracies: Patterns of Majoritarian and Consensus Government in Twenty-One Countries.* New Haven, CT: Yale University Press

Lind, Michael (2006). *The American Way of Strategy.* New York: Oxford University Press

Lipset, Seymour Martin (1959). "Some Social Requisites of Democracy: Economic Development and Political Legitimacy," *American Political Science Review*, 53 (1): 69-105

Lipson, Charles (2003). *Reliable Partners: How Democracies Have Made a Separate Peace.* Princeton, NJ: Princeton University Press

Machiavelli, Niccolò (1715). *Discourses on Livy.* New York: Oxford University Press, 2008

MacKuen, Michael B. (1983). "Political Drama, Economic Conditions, and the Dynamics of Presidential Popularity," *American Journal of Political Science*, 27 (2): 165-192

MacMillan, John (1998). *On Liberal Peace.* London: Tauris

MacMillan, John (2003). "Beyond the Separate Peace," *Journal of Peace Research*, 40 (2): 233-243

Macpherson, C. B. (1963). *The Real World of Democracy.* Oxford, UK: Clarendon

Mak, J. N. (2008). "Sovereignty and the Problems of Maritime Cooperation in the South China Sea." In *Security and International Politics in the South China Sea: Towards a Cooperative Management Region*, eds. Sam Bateman and Emmers Ralf, pp. 110-127. London: Routledge

Malin, Martin (1997). "Is Autocracy an Obstacle to Peace? Iran and Iraq, 1975-1980." In *Paths to Peace: Is Democracy the Answer?*, ed. Miriam Fedius Elman, Chap 9. Cambridge, MA: MIT Press

Manicas, Peter T. (1989). *War and Democracy.* Oxford: Basil Blackwell

Mansfield, Edward D. (1988). "The Distribution of Wars over Time," *World Politics*, 41 (1): 21-51

Mansfield, Edward D. (1994). *Power, Trade and War*. Princeton, NJ: Princeton University Press

Mansfield, Edward D., Helen V. Milner, and B. Peter Rosendorff (2000). "Free to Trade: Democracies, Autocracies, and International Trade," *American Political Science Review*, 94 (2): 305-321

Mansfield, Edward D., and John C. Pevehouse (2000). "Trade Blocs, Trade Flows, and International Conflict," *International Organization*, 54 (4): 775-808

Mansfield, Edward D., and John C. Pevehouse (2003). "Institutions, Interdependence, and International Conflict." In *Globalization and Armed Conflict*, eds. Gerald Schneider, Katherine Barbieri, and Nils Petter Gleditsch, Chap. 12. Boulder, CO: Rowman and Littlefield

Mansfield, Edward D., John C. Pevehouse, and David H. Bearce (1999/2000). "Preferential Trading Arrangements and Military Disputes," *Security Studies*, 9 (1): 92-118

Mansfield, Edward D., and Brian Pollins, eds. (2003). *Economic Interdependence and International Conflict: New Perspectives on an Enduring Debate*. Ann Arbor: University of Michigan Press

Mansfield, Edward D., and Jack Snyder (1995). "Democratization and the Danger of War," *International Security*, 20 (1): 5-38

Mansfield, Edward D., and Jack Snyder (1996). "The Effects of Democratization on War," *International Security*, 20 (2): 196-207

Mansfield, Edward D., and Jack Snyder (2002). "Democratic Transitions, Institutional Strength, and War," *International Organization*, 56 (2): 297-337

Mansfield, Edward D., and Jack Snyder (2005). *Electing to Fight: Why Emerging Democracies Go to War*. Cambridge, MA: MIT Press

Maoz, Zeev (1982). *Paths to Conflict: International Dispute Initiation, 1816-1976*. Boulder, CO: Westview

Maoz, Zeev (1997). "The Controversy over the Democratic Peace: Rearguard Action or Cracks in the Wall?," *International Security*, 22 (1): 162-198

Maoz, Zeev (1998). "Realist and Cultural Critiques of the Democratic Peace: A Theoretical and Empirical Re-Assessment," *International Interactions*, 24 (1): 3-89

Maoz, Zeev (2001). Democratic Networks: Connecting National, Dyadic, and Systemic Levels of Analysis in the Study of Democracy and War." In *War in a Changing World*, eds. Zeev Maoz and Azar Gat, pp 143-182. Ann Arbor: University of Michigan Press

Maoz, Zeev (2005). Dyadic MID Dataset Version 2.0. *pfsfaculty.-ucdavis.edu/zmaoz/dyadmid.htr*

Maoz, Zeev, and Nasrin Abdolali (1989). "Regimes Types and International Conflict," *Journal of Conflict Resolution*, 33 (1): 199-231

Maoz, Zeev, and Bruce M. Russett (1992). "Alliances, Wealth, Contiguity and Political Stability: Is the Lack of Conflict Between Democracies a Statistical Artifact?," *International Interactions*, 17 (3): 245-267

Maoz, Zeev, and Bruce M. Russett (1993). "Normative and Structural Causes of Democratic Peace, *1946-1986*," *American Political Science Review*, 87 (3): 624-638

Marley, David (1998). *Wars of the Americas: A Chronology of Armed Conflict in the New World, 1492 to the Present.* Santa Barbara, CA: ABC-CLIO

Marshall, Monty, and Keith Jaggers (2000). *Polity IV: Political Regime Characteristics and Transitions, 1800-1999.* College Park, MD: Integrated Network for Societal Conflict (The data are updated from time to time.)

Matthews, John C., III (1997). "Turkish and Hungarian Foreign Policy During the Interwar Period: Domestic Institutions and the Democratic Peace." In *Paths to Peace: Is Democracy the Answer?*, ed. Miriam Fendius Elman, Chap. 11. Cambridge, MA: MIT Press

McClelland, Charles A., and Gary D. Hoggard (1969). "Conflict Patterns in the Interactions Among Nations." In *International Politics and Foreign Policy*, ed. James N. Rosenau, pp. 711-724. New York: Free Press

McCullough, David (2005). *1776.* New York: Simon & Schuster

McDonald, Patrick J. (2010). "Capitalism, Commitment, and Peace," *International Interactions*, 36 (2): 146-168

McFaul, Michael (2010). *Advancing Democracy Abroad: Why We*

Should and How We Can. Lanham, MD: Rowman & Littlefield

McLaughlin, Sara, Scott Gates, Hårvard Hegre, Ranvieg Gissinger, and Nils Petter Gleditsch (1998). "Timing the Changes in Political Structures: A New Polity Database," *Journal of Conflict Resolution* 42 (2): 231-242

Mead, Walter R. (1987). *Mortal Splendor: The American Empire in Transition.* Boston: Houghton Mifflin

Mearsheimer, John J. (1990). "Back to the Future: Instability in Europe after the Cold War," *International Security,* 15 (1): 5-57

Meehan, Eugene J. (1968). *Explanation in Social Science: A System Paradigm.* Homewood, IL: Dorsey

Meernik, James (1990). "United States Military Intervention and the Promotion of Democracy," *Journal of Peace Research,* 33 (4): 391-402

Meernik, James, and Peter Waterman (1996). "The Myth of the Diversionary Use of Force," *Political Science Quarterly,* 49 (3): 573-590

Merritt, Richard L., and Dina A. Zinnes (1991). "Democracies and War." In *On Measuring Democracy: Its Consequences and Concomitants,* ed. Alex Inkeles, Chap. 9. New Brunswick, NJ: Transaction

Midlarsky, Manus (1990). "Systemic Wars and Dyadic Wars: No Theory in Sight," *International Interactions,* 16 (3): 171-181

Midlarsky, Manus (1995). "Environmental Influences on Democracy: Acidity, Warfare, and the Reversal of the Causal Arrow," *Journal of Conflict Resolution,* 39 (2): 224-262

Miller, Paul (2012). "American Grand Strategy and the Democratic Peace," *Survival,* 54 (2): 49-76

Miller, Ross A. (1995). "Domestic Structures and the Diversionary Use of Force," *American Journal of Political Science,* 39 (3): 760-785

Miller, Ross A. (1999). "Regime Type, Strategic Interaction, and the Diversionary Use of Force," *Journal of Conflict Resolution,* 43 (3): 388-402

Millis, Walter, and John Courtney Murray (1958). *Foreign Policy and the Free Society.* Dobbs Ferry, NY: Oceana

Mintz, Alex, and Nehemia Geva (1993). "Why Don't Democracies Fight Each Other? An Experimental Assessment of the 'Political Assessment' Explanation," *Journal of Conflict Resolution,*

37 (3): 484-503

Mintz, Alex, Nehemia Geva, Steven B. Redd, and Amy Carnes (1997). "The Effect of Dynamic and Static Choice Sets on Political Decision Making: An Analysis Utilizing the Decision Board Platform," *American Political Science Review*, 92 (3): 553-566

Mintz, Alex, and Bruce M. Russett (1992). "The Dual Economy and Israeli Use of Force." In *Defense, Welfare, and Growth,* eds. Steve Chan and Alex Mintz, pp. 179-197. London: Routledge

Mitchell, Sara McLaughlin (2002). "A Kantian System? Democracy and Third-Party Conflict Resolution," *American Journal of Poliical Science*, 46 (4): 749-759

Mitchell, Sara McLaughlin, Scott Gates, and Hårvard Hegre (1999). "Evolution in Democratic Peace Dynamics," *Journal of Conflict Resolution*, 43 (6): 771-792

Mitchell, Sara McLaughlin, Kelly M. Kadera, and Mark J. C. Crescenzi (2009). "Practicing Democratic Community Norms: Third-Party Conflict Management and Successful Settlements." In *International Conflict Mediation: New Approaches and Findings*, eds. Jacob Bercovitch and Scott Sigmund Gartner, pp. 243-264. London: Routledge

Mitchell, Sara McLauglin, and Brandon C. Prins (1999). "Beyond Territorial Contiguity: Issues at Stake in Democratic Militarized Interstate Disputes," *International Studies Quarterly*, 43 (1): 169-183

Morgan, T. Clifton, and Christopher J. Anderson (1999). "Domestic Support and Diversionary External Conflict in Great Britain, 1950-1999," *Journal of Politics*, 61 (3): 376-396

Morgan, T. Clifton, and Kenneth N. Bickers (1992). "Domestic Discontent and the External Use of Force," *Journal of Conflict Resolution,* 36 (l): 25-52

Morgan, T. Clifton, and Sally Howard Campbell (1991). "Domestic Structure, Decisional Constraints, and War: So Why Kant Democracies Fight?," *Journal of Conflict Resolution,* 35 (2): 187-211

Morgan, T. Clifton, and Valerie L. Schwebach (1992). "Take Two Democracies and Call Me in the Morning: A Prescription for Peace?," *International Interactions,* 17 (4): 305-320

Morgenthau, Hans J. (1948). *Politics Among Nations: The Struggle for Power and Peace*. New York: Knopf, 1985

Morgenthau, Hans J. (1958). *Dilemmas of Politics.* Chicago, IL: University of Chicago Press

Morrow, James D. (2003). "When Do Relative Gains Impede Trade"? In *Globalization and Armed Conflict*, eds. Gerald Schneider, Katherine Barbieri, and Nils Petter Gleditsch, Chap. 3. Lanham, MD: Rowman and Littlefield

Morrow, James D., Randolph M. Siverson, and Tressa E. Taberes (1998). "The Political Determinants of International Trade: The Major Powers, 1907-1990," *American Political Science Review,* 92 (3): 649-661

Most, Benjamin A., and Harvey Starr (1983). "Conceptualizing 'War'," *Journal of Conflict Resolution,* 27 (1): 137-159

Mousseau, Michael (1997). "Democracy and Militarized Interstate Collaboration," *Journal of Peace Research,* 34 (1): 73-87

Mousseau, Michael (1998). "Democracy and Compromise in Militarized Interstate Conflicts, 1816-1992," *Journal of Conflict Resolution,* 42 (2): 210-230

Mousseau, Michael (2000). "Market Prosperity, Democratic Consolidation, and Democratic Peace," *Journal of Conflict Resolution,* 44 (4): 472-507

Mousseau, Michael (2002). "An Economic Limitation to the Zone of Democratic Peace and Cooperation," *International Interactions,* 28 (1): 137-164

Mousseau, Michael (2003). "The Nexus of Market Society, Liberal Preferences, and Democratic Peace: Interdisciplinary Theory and Evidence," *International Studies Quarterly,* 47 (4): 483-510

Mousseau, Michael (2005). "Comparing New Theory with Prior Beliefs: Market Civilization and the Democratic Peace," *Conflict Management and Peace Science,* 22 (1): 63-77

Mousseau, Michael (2009). "The Social Market Roots of Democratic Peace," *International Security,* 57 (1): 186-197

Mousseau, Michael (2013a). "The Democratic Peace Unraveled: It's the Economy," *International Studies Quarterly,* 57 (1): 186-197

Mousseau, Michael (2013b). Personal communication.

Mousseau, Michael, Hårvard Hegre, and John R. Oneal (2003). "How the Wealth of Nations Conditions Liberal Peace," *European Journal of International Relations,* 9 (2): 277-314

Mousseau, Michael, Omer F. Orsun, and Jameson Lee Ungerer (2013). "The Progress of Knowledge: The Market-Capitalist

Peace; Does the Market-Capitalist Peace Supersede the Democratic Peace? The Evidence Still Says Yes." In *The Capitalist Peace: The Origins and Prospects of a Liberal Idea*, eds. Gerald Schneider and Nils Petter Gleditsch, Chap 5. New York: Routledge

Mousseau, Michael, Omer F. Orsun, Jameson Lee Ungerer, and Demet Yalcin Mousseau (2013). "Capitalism and Peace: It's Keynes, Not Hayek." In *The Capitalist Peace: The Origins and Prospects of a Liberal Idea*, eds. Gerald Schneider and Nils Petter Gleditsch, Chap 5. New York: Routledge

Mousseau, Michael, and Yuhand Shi (1999). "A Test for Reverse Causality in the Demoratic Peace Relationship," *Journal of Peace Research*, 36 (6): 639-663

Mueller, John E. (1973). *War, Presidents, and Public Opinion*. New York: Wiley.

Mueller, John E. (1989). *Retreat from Doomsday: The Obsolescence of Major War*. New York: Basic Books

Muller, Edward N. (1988). "Democracy, Economic Development, and Income Inequality," *American Sociological Review*, 53 (1): 50-68

Muller, Edward N., and Mitchell A. Seligman (1994). "Civil Culture and Democracy: The Quest of Causal Relationships," *American Political Science Review*, 88 (3): 635-652

Müller, Harald (2004). "The Antimony of the Democratic Peace," *International Politics*, 41 (4): 494-520

Müller, Harald, and Jonas Wolff (2006). "Democratic Peace: Many Data, Little Explanation?" In *Democratic Wars. Looking at the Dark Side of Democratic Peace*, eds. Anna Geis, Lothar Brock, and Harald Müller, pp. 41-73. New York: Palgrave Macmillan

Munch, Gerardo L., and Jay Verkuilen (2002). "Conceptualizing and Measuring Democracy: Evaluating Alternative Indices," *Comparative Political Studies*, 35 (1): 5-34

Muravchik, Joshua (1991). *Exporting Democracy: Fulfilling America's Destiny*. Washington, DC: American Enterprise Institute

Neubauer, Deane E. (1967). "Some Conditions of Democracy," *American Political Science Review*, 41 (4): 1002-1009

New York Times (2004). "Bush and Blair Discuss the Middle East," *New York Times*, November 12

Nincic, Miroslav, and Bruce M. Russett (1979). "The Effect of Similarity and Interest on Attitudes Toward Foreign Countries," *Public Opinion Quarterly,* 33 (2): 68-78

Nye, Joseph S., Jr. (1993). *Understanding International Conflicts.* New York: Harper Collins

Nye, Joseph S., Jr. (2004). *Soft Power: The Means to Success in World Politics.* New York: Public Affairs

O'Donnell, Guillermo A. (1978). "Reflections on the Pattern of Change in the Bureaucratic Authoritarian State," *Latin American Research Review,* 13 (1): 23-38

Oakes, Amy (2012). *Diversionary War: Domestic Unrest and International Conflict.* Stanford, CA: Stanford University Press

Oneal, John R., Frances H. Oneal, Zeev Maoz, and Bruce M. Russett (1996). "The Liberal Peace: Interdependence, Democracy, and International Conflict, 1950-85," *Journal of Peace Research,* 33, (1): 11-28

Oneal, John R., and James Lee Ray (1997). "New Tests of the Democratic Peace Controlling for Economic Interdependence, 1950-85," *Political Research Quarterly,* 50 (4): 751-776

Oneal, John R., and Bruce M. Russett (1997). "The Classical Liberals Were Right: Democracy, Interdependence, and Conflict, 1950-85," *International Studies Quarterly,* 41 (2): 267-294

Oneal, John R., and Bruce M. Russett (1999a). "Assessing the Liberal Peace with Alternative Specifications: Trade Still Reduces Conflict," *Journal of Peace Research,* 36 (4): 423-442

Oneal, John R., and Bruce M. Russett (1999b). "Is the Liberal Peace Just an Artifact of Cold War Interests?," *International Interactions,* 25 (3): 213-241

Oneal, John R., and Bruce M. Russett (1999c). "The Kantian Peace: The Pacific Benefits of Democracy, Interdependence, and International Organizations, 1885-1992," *World Politics,* 52 (1): 1-37

Oneal, John R., and Bruce M. Russett (2000a). "A Response to Huntington," *Journal of Peace Research,* 37 (5): 611-612

Oneal, John R., and Bruce M. Russett (2000b). "Why 'An Identified Systemic Analysis of the Democracy-Peace Nexus' Does Not Persuade," *Peace and Defense Economics,* 11 (2): 197-214

Oneal, John R., and Bruce M. Russett (2001). "Clear and Clean: The Fixed Effects of Democracy and Economic Interdependence," *International Organization,* 55 (2): 469-485

Oneal, John R., and Bruce M. Russett (2003a). "Assessing the Liberal Peace with Alternative Specifications: Trade Still Reduces Conflict." In *Globalization and Armed Conflict*, eds. Gerald Schneider, Katherine Barbieri, and Nils Petter Gleditsch, Chap. 7. Lanham, MD: Rowman and Littlefield

Oneal, John R., and Bruce M. Russett (2003b). "Modeling Conflict While Studying Dynamics: A Response to Nathaniel Beck." In *Globalization and Armed Conflict*, eds. Gerald Schneider, Katherine Barbieri, and Nils Petter Gleditsch, Chap. 9. Lanham, MD: Rowman and Littlefield

Oneal, John R., and Bruce M. Russett (2005). "Rule of Three, Let It Be? When More Really Is Better," *Conflict Management and Peace Science*, 22 (2): 293–310

Oneal, John R., Bruce M. Russett, and Michael L. Berbaum (2003). "Causes of Peace: Democracy, Interdependence, and International Organizations, 1885-1992," *International Studies Quarterly*, 47 (3): 371-393

Oren, Udo (1995). "The Subjectivity of the 'Democratic Peace': Changing US Perceptions of Imperial Germany," *International Security*, 20 (1): 147-184

Oren, Udo, and Jude Hays (1997). "Democracies May Rarely Fight One Another, But Developed Socialist States Rarely Fight at All," *Alternatives*, 22 (4): 493-521

Organski, A. F. K. (1958). *World Politics*. New York: Knopf

Ostrom, Charles W., Jr., and Brian L. Job (1986). "The President and the Political Use of Force," *American Political Science Review*, 80 (2): 541-566

Owen, John M. (1993). *Testing the Democratic Peace: American Diplomatic Crises, 1794-1917*. Cambridge, MA: Ph.D. dissertation, Harvard University

Owen, John M. (1994a). "Democratic Peace Research: Whence and Whither?," *International Politics*, 41 (4): 605-617

Owen, John M. (1994b). "How Liberalism Produces Democratic Peace," *International Security,* 19 (2): 87-125

Owen, John M. (1997a). *Liberal Peace or Liberal War: American Politics and International Security*. Ithaca, NY: Cornell University Press

Owen, John M. (1997b). "Perceptions and the Limits of Liberal Peace: The Mexican-American and Spanish-American Wars." In *Paths to Peace: Is Democracy the Answer?*, ed. Miriam Fedius

Elman, Chap 3. Cambridge, MA: MIT Press

Paine, Thomas (1776). *The Complete Writings of Thomas Paine*, ed. Philip S. Foner. New York: Citadel, 1945

Papayoanou, Paul (1996). "Interdependence, Institutions, and the Balance of Power: Britain, Germany, and World War I," *International Security*, 20 (4): 42-76

Park, Johann (2013). "Forward to the Future? The Democratic Peace After the Cold War," *Conflict Management and Peace Science*, 30 (2): 178-194

Partell, Peter J., and Glenn Palmer (1999). "Audience Costs and Interstate Crises: An Empirical Assessment of Fearon's Model of Dispute Outcomes," *International Studies Quarterly*, 43 (2): 389-405

Pateman, Carole (1994). "Three Questions about Womanhood Suffrage." In *Suffrage and Beyond: International Feminist Perspectives*, eds. Caroline Daley and Melanie Nolan, Chap. 17. Auckland, NZ: Auckland University Press

Pearson, Frederic S., and Robert A. Baumann (1993-1994). *International Military Intervention, 1946-1988*. Ann Arbor, MI: Inter-University Consortium for Political Research

Peceny, Mark (1997). "A Constructivist Interpretation of the Liberal Peace: The Ambiguous Case of the Spanish-American War," *Journal of Peace Research*, 34 (4): 415-430

Peceny, Mark (1999). *Democracy at the Point of Bayonets*. University Park: Pennsylvania State University Press

Peceny, Mark, Caroline C. Beer, and Shannon Sanchez-Terry (2002). "Dictatorial Peace?," *American Political Science Review*, 96 (1): 15-26

Peceny, Mark, and Jeffrey Pickering (2006). "Can Liberal Intervention Build Liberal Democracy?" In *Conflict Prevention and Peacebuilding in Post-War Societies: Sustaining the Peace*, eds., James Meernik and T. David Mason, Chap. 6. New York: Routledge

Pennock, J. Roland (1979). *Democratic Political Theory*. Princeton, NJ: Princeton University Press

Perle, Richard, and David From (2003). *An End to Evil: How to Win the War on Terror*. New York: Random House

Pevehouse, Jon, and Bruce M. Russett (2006). "Democratic International Governmental Organizations Promote Peace," *Interna-*

tional Organization, 60 (4): 969-1000

Pickering, Jeffrey (2002). "Give Me Shelter," *International Inter-actions,* 28 (4): 293–324

Pickering, Jeffrey, and Emizet F. Kisangani (2005). "Democracy and Diversionary Military Intervention: Reassessing Regime Type and the Diversionary Hypothesis," *International Studies Quarterly*, 49 (1): 23-43

Pickles, Dorothy (1970). *Democracy.* New York: Basic Books

Pillar, Paul R. (2010). "Democracy and Counterterrorism: Multiple Issues, Varied Effects." In *Democratic Peace in Theory and Practice,* ed. Steven W. Hook, Chap. 12. Kent, OH: Kent State University Press

Polachek, Solomon W. (1980). "Conflict and Trade," *Journal of Conflict Resolution,* 24 (l): 55-78

Polachek, Solomon W. (1992). "Conflict and Trade: An Economics Approach to Political International Interactions." In *Economics of Arms Reduction and the Peace Process*, eds. Walter Isard and Charles H. Anderton, pp. 89-120. Amsterdam: North-Holland

Polachek, Solomon W. (1997). "Why Democracies Cooperate More and Fight Less: The Relationship Between International Trade and Cooperation," *Review of International Economics*, 5 (3): 295-309

Polachek, Solomon W. (2003). "Multilateral Interactions in the Trade-Conflict Model." In *Globalization and Armed Conflict*, eds. Gerald Schneider, Katherine Barbieri, and Nils Petter Gleditsch, Chap. 2. Lanham, MD: Rowman and Littlefield

Polachek, Solomon W., and Judith McDonald (1992). "Strategic Trade and Incentives for Cooperation." In *Disarmament, Economic Conversion and the Management of Peace*, eds. Manas Chattergi and Linda Renney Forcey, pp. 273-284. New York: Praeger

Polachek, Solomon W., John Robst, and Yuan-Ching Chang (1999). "Liberalism and Interdependence: Extending the Trade-Conflict Model," *Journal of Peace Research*, 36 (4): 405-422

Polanyi, Karl (1944). *The Great Transformation.* New York: Farrar & Rinehart.

Pollins, Brian (1989a). "Conflict, Cooperation, and Commerce: The Effect of International Political Interactions on Bilateral Trade Flows," *American Journal of Political Science*, 33 (3): 737-761

Pollins, Brian (1989b). "Does Trade Follow the Flag?," *American Political Science Review*, 93 (4): 465-480

Potter, Philip B. K., and Matthew A. Baum (2010). "Democratic Peace, Domestic Audience Costs, and Political Communication," *Political Communication*, 27 (4): 453-470

Powell, G. Bingham (1982). *Contemporary Democracies: Participation, Stability, and Violence.* Cambridge, MA: Harvard University Press

Prins, Brandon C. (2003). "Institutional Instability and the Credibility of Audience Costs: Political Participation and Interstate Crisis Bargaining, 1816-1992," *Journal of Peace Research*, 40 (1): 67-84

Prins, Brandon C., and Christopher Sprecher (1999). "Institutional Constraints, Political Opposition, and Interstate Dispute Escalation: Evidence from Parliamentary Systems," *Journal of Peace Research*, 36 (3): 271-287

Progressive Policy Institute (2003). *Progressive Internationalism: A Democratic National Security Strategy.* Washington, DC: Progressive Policy Institute

Przeworski, Adam (1991). *Democracy and the Market: Political and Economic Reforms in Eastern Europe and Latin America.* New York: Cambridge University Press

Quackenbush, Stephen L., and Michael Rudy (2009). "Evaluating the Monadic Democratic Peace," *Conflict Management and Peace Science*, 26 (3): 268-285

Rakenrud, Arvid, and Hårvard Hegre (1997). "The Hazard of War: Reassessing the Evidence for the Democratic Peace," *Journal of Peace Research*, 34 (4): 385-404

Ralston, Jackson H. (1929). *International Arbitration from Athens to Locarno.* Stanford, CA: Stanford University Press

Ransom, Harry Howe (1992). "Covert Intervention." In *Intervention into the 1990s: U.S. Foreign Policy in the Third World,* ed. Peter J. Schraeder, Chap. 7. Boulder, CO: Rienner

Rasler, Karen, and William R. Thompson (2005). *Puzzles of the Democratic Peace: Theory, Geopolitics, and the Transformation of World Politics.* New York: Palgrave Macmillan

Rathbun, Brian (2012). "Politics and Paradigm Preferences: The Implicit Ideology of International Relations Scholars," *International Studies Quarterly*, 56 (3): 607-622

Rawls, John (1999). *The Law of Peoples*. Cambridge, MA: Harvard University Press

Ray, James Lee (1990). "Friends as Foes: International Conflict and Wars Between Formal Allies." In *Prisoners of War? Nation-States in the Modem Era*, eds. Charles Gochman and Alien Ned Sabrosky, Chap. 6. Lexington, MA: Heath

Ray, James Lee (1992). *Global Politics*, 5th edn. Boston: Houghton Mifflin

Ray, James Lee (1993). "Wars Between Democracies: Rare or Nonexistent?," *International Interactions*, 18 (3): 251 -276

Ray, James Lee (1994). *Democracies in Confict*. Columbia: University of South Carolina Press

Ray, James Lee (1995). *Democracy and International Conflict: An Evaluation of the Democratic Peace Proposition*. Columbia: University of South Carolina Press

Ray, James Lee (1998). "Does Democracy Cause Peace?," *Annual Review of Political Science*, 1: 27-46

Ray, James Lee (2000). "On the Level(s), Does Democracy Correlate with Peace?" In *What Do We Know about War?*, ed. John Vasquez, pp. 299–316. Lanham, MD: Rowman and Littlefield.

Ray, James Lee (2003). "A Lakatosian View of the Democratic Peace Research Program." In *Progress in International Relations Theory*, eds. Colin Elman and Miriam Fendius Elman, Chap. 6. Cambridge, MA: MIT Press

Ray, James Lee (2005). "Constructing Multivariate Analysis (of Dangerous Dyads)," *Conflict Management and Peace Science*, 22 (2): 277-292

Ray, James Lee (2013). "War on Democratic Peace," *International Studies Quarterly*, 57 (1): 198-200

Ray, James Lee, and Kevin Wang (1995). "Democracy, Disputes and Crises: The Impact of Regime Type on Conflict Escalation." Paper presented at the annual convention of the American Political Science Association

Raymond, Gregory A. (1994). "Democracies, Disputes, and Third-Party Intermediaries," *Journal of Conflict Resolution*, 38 (1): 24-42

Raymond, Gregory A. (1996). "Demosthenes and Democracies: Regime-Types and Arbitration Outcomes," *International Interactions*, 22 (1): 1-20

Regens, James L., Ronald Keith Gaddie, and Brad Lockerbie (1995). "The Electoral Consequences of Voting to Declare War," *Journal of Conflict Resolution*, 39 (1): 168-182

Reisman, W. Michael, and James E. Baker (1992). *Regulating Covert Action: Practices, Contexts, and Policies of Covert Coercion Abroad in International and American Law*. New Haven, CT: Yale University Press

Reiter, Dan (1995). "Political Structure and Foreign Policy Learning: Are Democracies More Likely to Act on the Lessons of History?," *International Interactions*, 21 (1): 39-62

Reiter, Dan (2001). "Does Peace Nurture Democracy"," *Journal of Politics*, 63 (3): 935-948

Reiter, Dan, and Allan C. Stam III (1998a). "Democracy, War Initiation, and Victory." *American Political Science Review*, 92 (2): 377-389

Reiter, Dan, and Allan C. Stam III (1998b). "Democracy and Battlefield Military Effectiveness," *Journal of Conflict Resolution*, 42 (3): 258-277

Reiter, Dan, and Allan C. Stam III (2002). *Democracies at War*. Princeton, NJ: Princeton University Press

Reiter, Dan, and Allan C. Stam III (2003). "Identifying the Culprit: Democracy, Dictatorship, and Dispute Initiation," *American Political Science Review*, 97 (2): 333-337

Reiter, Dan, and Erik Tillman (2002). "Public, Legislative, and Executive Constraints on the Democratic Initiation of Conflict," *Journal of Politics*, 64 (3): 810-826

Rendell, Matthew (2004). "'The Sparta and the Athens of Our Age at Daggers Drawn': Politics, *Perceptions*, and Peace," *International Politics*, 41 (4): 582-604

Rengger, Nicholas (2006). "On Democratic War Theory." In *Democratic Wars: Looking at the Dark Side of the Democratic Peace*, eds. Anna Geis, Lothar Brock, and Harald Müller, Chap. 7. New York: Palgrave Macmillan

Reuters (2011). "3 Pakistani Troops Killed by Indian Soldiers: Army," *Express Tribune*, September 1

Reuveny, Rafael, and Quan Li (2003). "The Joint Democracy-Dyadic Nexus: A Simultaneous Equations Model," *Journal of Politics*, 47 (2): 325-346

Richardson, Lewis F. (1960a). *Arms and Insecurity*. Pittsburgh, PA:

Boxwood

Richardson, Lewis F. (1960b). *Statistics of Deadly Quarrels*. Pittsburgh, PA: Boxwood

Richmond, Oliver P., ed. (2011). *A Post-Liberal Peace*. London: Routledge

Rieffer-Flanigan, Barbara Ann J. (2010). "Encouraging Democracy or Terrorism?" In *Democratic Peace in Theory and Practice*, ed. Steven W. Hook, Chap. 13. Kent, OH: Kent State University Press

Rioux, Jean Sebastien (1998). "A Crisis-Based Evaluation of the Democratic Peace Proposition," *Canadian Journal of Political Science*, 31 (2): 263-283

Risse-Kappen, Thomas (1991). "Public Opinion, Domestic Structure, and Foreign Policy," *World Politics,* 43 (4): 479-512

Risse-Kappen, Thomas (1995a). *Cooperation Among Democracies: The European Influence on U.S. Foreign Policy*. Princeton, NJ: Princeton University Press

Rock, Stephen R. (1997). "Anglo-US Relations, 1845-1930: Did Shared Liberal Values and Democratic Institutions Keep the Peace?" In *Paths to Peace: Is Democracy the Answer?*, ed. Miriam Fedius Elman, Chap 2. Cambridge, MA: MIT Press

Rosas, Allan (1994). "Focus on the Case for Intervention: Towards Some International Law and Order," *Journal of Peace Research*, 31 (1): 129-135

Rosato, Sebastian (2003). "The Flawed Logic of Democratic Peace Theory," *American Political Science Review*, 97 (3): 585-602

Rosato, Sebastian (2005). "Explaining the Democratic Peace," *American Political Science Review*, 99 (3): 467-472

Rothstein, Robert L. (1991). "Democracy, Conflict, and Development in the Third World," *The Washington Quarterly,* 14 (2): 43-63

Rousseau, David L. (2005). *Democracy and War: Institutions, Norms and the Evolution of International Conflict*. Stanford, CA: Stanford University Press

Rousseau, David L, Christopher Gelpi, Dan Reiter, and Paul K. Huth (1996). "Assessing the Dyadic Nature of the Democratic Peace, 1918-88," *American Political Science Review*, 90 (3): 512-533

Roy, Srirupa (2007). *Violence and Democracy in India*. Calcutta: Seagull Books

Rummel, R. J. (1963). "Dimensions of Conflict Behavior Within and Between Nations," *Yearbook for the Society for General Systems*, 8:1-50

Rummel, R. J. (1972). *Dimensions of Nations*. Beverly Hills, CA: Sage

Rummel, R. J. (1975-1981). *Understanding Conflict and War*. Beverly Hills, CA: Sage, 5 vols.

Rummel, R. J. (1983a). "The Freedom Factor," *Reason*, 15 (3): 32-36, 38

Rummel, R. J. (1983b). "Libertarianism and International Violence," *Journal of Conflict Resolution*, 27 (1): 27-71

Rummel, R. J. (1985). "Libertarian Propositions on Violence Within and Between Nations: A Test Against Published Results," *Journal of Conflict Resolution*, 29 (3): 419-455

Rummel, R. J. (1987). "On Vincent's View of Freedom and International Conflict," *Journal of Conflict Resolution*, 31 (1): 113-117

Rummel, R. J. (1995). "Democracies ARE Less Warlike than Other Regimes," *European Journal of International Relations*, 1 (4): 457-479

Rummel, R. J. (1997). *Power Kills: Democracy as a Method of Nonviolence*. New Brunswick, NJ: Transaction

Rummel, R. J. (2002). "Democratic Peace Clock." *www.hawaii.edu/powerkills/DP.CLOCK.HTM*

Russett, Bruce M. (1967). *International Regions and the International System: A Study in Political Ecology*. Chicago: Rand McNally

Russett, Bruce M. (1970). "Case Studies and Cumulation." In *Approaches to the Study of Political Science,* eds. Michael Haas and Henry S. Kariel, Chap. 14. San Francisco: Chandler

Russett, Bruce M. (1989). "Democracy and Peace." *In Choices in World Politics: Sovereignty and Interdependence,* eds. Bruce M. Russett, Harvey Starr, and Richard J. Stoll, pp. 245-261. New York: Free Press

Russett, Bruce M. (1990). "Economic Decline, Electoral Pressure, and the Initiation of Interstate Conflict." In *Prisoners of War? Nation-States in the Modem Era,* eds. Charles Gochman and Allen Ned Sabrosky, Chap. 9. Lexington, MA: Heath

Russett, Bruce M. (1993a). "Can a Democratic Peace Be Built?," *International Interactions*, 18 (3): 277-282

Russett, Bruce M., ed. (1993b). *Grasping the Democratic Peace: Principles for a Post-Cold War World*. Princeton, NJ: Princeton University Press

Russett, Bruce M. (1994). "And Yet It Moves," *International Security*, 19 (4): 164-175

Russett, Bruce M. (1995). "The Democratic *Peace*," *International Security*, 19 (4): 164-175

Russett, Bruce M. (1996). "Counterfactuals About War and Its Absence." In *Counterfactual Thought Experiments in World Politics: Logical, Methodological, and Psychological Perspectives*, eds. Philip E. Tetlock and Aaron Belkin, pp. 171-186. Princeton, NJ: Princeton University Press

Russett, Bruce M. (1997). "A Rejoinder," *Journal of Peace Research*, 34 (3): 223-224

Russett, Bruce M. (1998). "A Neo-Kantian Perspective: Democracy, Interdependence and International Organization in Building Security Communities." In *Security Communities*, eds. Emanuel Adler and Michael Barnett, Chap. 11. New York: Cambridge University Press.

Russett, Bruce M. (2005). "Bushwhacking the Democratic Peace," *International Studies Perspectives*, 6 (4): 395-408

Russett, Bruce M. (2010). "Capitalism or Democracy? Not So Fast," *International Interactions*, 36 (2): 185-205

Russett, Bruce M. (2011). *Hegemony and Democracy*. New York: Routledge

Russett, Bruce M., and Antholis, William (1992). "Do Democracies Fight Each Other? Evidence from the Peloponnesian War," *Journal of Peace Research,* 29 (4): 415-434

Russett, Bruce M., Carol R. Ember, and Melvin Ember (1993). "The Democratic Peace in Nonindustrial Societies." In Bruce M. Russett, *Grasping the Democratic Peace*, Chap. 5. Princeton, NJ: Princeton University Press.

Russett, Bruce, M., and Zeev Maoz (1993). "The Democratic Peace Since World War II." In Bruce M. Russett, *Grasping the Democratic Peace*, Chap. 4. Princeton, NJ: Princeton University Press

Russett, Bruce M., and R. Joseph Momsen (1975). "Bureaucracy and Polyarchy as Predictors of Performance: A Cross-National Examination," *Comparative Political Studies*, 8 (1): 5-31

Russett, Bruce M., and John R. Oneal (2001). *Triangulating Peace:*

Democracy, Interdependence, and International Organizations. New York: Norton

Russett, Bruce M., John R. Oneal, and Michaelene Cox (2000). "Clash of Civilizations, or Realism and Liberalism Déjà Vu? Some Evidence," *Journal of Peace Research*, 37 (5): 583-608

Russett, Bruce M., John R. Oneal, and David R. Davis (1998). "The Third Leg of the Kantian Tripod for Peace: International Organizations and Militarized Disputes, 1950-1985," *International Organization*, 52 (3): 441-467

Russett, Bruce M., and David Lee Ray (1995). "Raymond Cohen on Pacific Unions: A Response and a Reply," *Review of International Studies*, 21 (3): 319-325

Russett, Bruce, and Harvey Starr (2000). "From Democratic Peace to Kantian Peace: Democracy and Conflict in the International System." In *Handbook of War Studies*, 2nd edn., ed. Manus Midlarsky, pp. 93-128. Ann Arbor: University of Michigan Press

Rustow, Dankwart A. (1967). *World of Nations: Problems of Political Modernization*. Washington, DC: Brookings

Salahuddin, Sayed (2013). "Afghan, Pakistani Forces Again Clash on Disputed Border; NATO Troops Broker Truce," *Washington Post*, May 7

Sapir, Leor (2012). "Iron Dome's Crucial Gaza Test," *Commentary*, March 27

Salmore, Stephen A., and Charles F. Hermann (1970). "The Effect of Size, Development and Accountability on Foreign Policy," *Peace Research Society (International), Papers*, 14:15-30

Sartori, Giovanni (1962). *Democratic Theory*. Detroit, MI: Wayne State University Press

Schafer Mark, and Stephen G. Walker (2006). "Democratic Leaders and the Democratic Peace: The Operational Codes of Tony Blair and Bill Clinton," *International Studies Quarterly*, 50 (3): 561–583

Schneider, Gerald, and Gunther G. Schulze (2003). "The Domestic Roots of Commercial Liberalism: A Sector-Specific Approach." In *Globalization and Armed Conflict*, eds. Gerald Schneider, Katherine Barbieri, and Nils Petter Gleditsch, Chap. 5. Lanham, MD: Rowman and Littlefield

Schoultz, Lars (1981a). "U.S. Foreign Policy and Human Rights Violations in Latin America," *Comparative Politics*, 13 (1): 149-

170

Schoultz, Lars (1981b). "U.S. Policy Toward Human Rights in Latin America: A Comparative Analysis of Two Administrations." In *Global Human Rights: Public Policies, Comparative Measures, and NGO Strategies*, eds. Ved P. Nanda, James R. Scarritt, and George Shepherd, Jr., Chap. 6. Boulder, CO: Westview

Schraeder, Peter J. (1992a). "Paramilitary Intervention." *In Intervention into the 1990s: U.S. Foreign Policy in the Third World*, ed. Peter J. Schraeder, Chap. 8. Boulder, CO: Rienner

Schraeder, Peter J. (1992b). "U.S. Intervention in Perspective." In *Intervention into the 1990s: U.S. Foreign Policy in the Third World*, ed. Peter J. Schraeder, Chap. 21. Boulder, CO: Rienner

Schoultz, Lars (2001). *Democracy and Coercive Diplomacy*. Cambridge, UK: Cambridge University Press

Schultz, Kenneth A. (1998). "Domestic Opposition and Signaling in International Crises," *American Political Science Review*, 92 (4): 829-840

Schultz, Kenneth A. (1999). "Do Democratic Political Institutions Constrain or Inform? Contrasting Two Institutional Perspectives on the Democracy and War," *International Organization*, 53 (2): 233-266

Schultz, Kenneth A. (2001). *Democracy and Coercive Diplomacy*. New York: Cambridge University Press

Schumpeter, Joseph A. (1919). *Imperialism and Social Classes*. New York: Kelly, 1951

Schumpeter, Joseph A. (1943). *Capitalism, Socialism, and Democracy*. New York: Routledge 2003

Schwartz, Thomas, and Kiron K. Skinner (2002). "The Myth of the Democratic Peace," *Orbis*, 46 (1): 159-172

Schweller, Randall L. (1992). "Domestic Structure and Preventive War: Are Democracies More Pacific?," *World Politics*, 44 (2): 235-269

Seawright, Jason, and David Collier (2014). "Rival Strategies of Validation: Tools for Evaluating Measures of Democracy," *Comparative Political Studies*, 47 (1): 111-138

Sen, Amartya (1999b). *Development as Freedom*. New York: Knopf

Senese, Paul (1997a). "Between Dispute and War: The Effect of Joint Democracy on Interstate Conflict Escalation," *Journal of Politics*, 59 (1): 1-27

Senese, Paul (1997b). "Costs and Demands: International Sources of Dispute Challenges and Reciprocation," *Journal of Conflict Resolution*, 41 (3): 407-427

Senese, Paul (1999). "Democracy and Maturity: Deciphering Conditional Effects on Levels of Dispute Intensity," *International Studies Quarterly*, 43 (3): 483-502

Senese, Paul (2005). "Territory, Contiguity, and International Conflict: Assessing a New Joint Explanation," *American Journal of Political Science*, 49 (4): 769-779

Senese, Paul, and John A. Vasquez (2004). "Alliances, Territorial Disputes, and the Probability of War: Testing for Interactions." In *The Scourge of War: New Extensions on an Old Problem*, ed. Paul F. Diehl, pp. 189-221. Ann Arbor: University of Michigan Press

Shalom, Stephen Rosskamm (1993). *Imperial Alibis: Rationalizing U.S. Intervention After the Cold War*. Boston: South End Press

Simon, Michael, and Erik Gartzke (1996). "Political System Similarity and the Choice of Allies: Do Democracies Flock Together; or Do Opposites Attract?," *Journal of Conflict Resolution*, 40 (4): 617-635

Singh, Jasjit (1999). *Kargil 1999: Pakistan's Fourth War for Kashmir*. Columbia, MO: South Asia Books

Singer, Max, and Aaron Wildawsky (1993). *The Real World Order: Zones of Peace/Zones of Turmoil*. Chatham, NJ: Chatham House

Siverson, Randolph M. (1995). "Democracies and War Participation: In Defense of the Institutional Constraints Argument," *European Journal of International Relations*, 1 (4): 481-490

Siverson, Randolph M., and Juliann Emmons (1991). "Birds of a Feather: Democratic Political Systems and Alliance Choices," *Journal of Conflict Resolution*, 35 (2): 285-306

Siverson, Randolph M., and Harvey Starr (1990) "Opportunity, Willingness, and the Diffusion of War," *American Political Science Review*, 84 (1): 47-67

Siverson, Randolph M., and Harvey Starr (1991). *The Diffusion of War: A Study of Opportunity and Willingness*. Ann Arbor: University of Michigan Press

Slantchev, Branislav L., Anna Alexandrova, and Erik Gartzke (2005). "Probabilistic Causality, Selection Bias, and the Logic of the Democratic Peace," *American Political Science Review*, 99

(1): 459-462

Slaughter, Anne-Marie, and G. John Ikenberry (2006). *Forging a World of Liberty Under Law: U.S. National Security in the 21st Century*. Princeton, NJ: Woodrow Wilson School of International Relations, Princeton University

Small, Melvin, and J. David Singer (1976). "The War-Proneness of Democratic Regimes," *Jerusalem Journal of International Relations*, 1 (2): 50-69

Small, Melvin, and J. David Singer (1982). *Resort to Arms: International and Civil Wars, 1816-1980*. Beverly Hills, CA: Sage

Smith, Alistair (1998a). "Fighting Battles, Winning Wars," *Journal of Conflict Resolution*, 42 (3): 301-320

Smith, Alistair (1998b). "International Crises and Domestic Politics," *American Political Science Review*, 92 (3): 623-638

Smith, Arthur K., Jr. (1969). "Socio-Economic Development and Political Democracy: A Causal Analysis," *American Journal of Political Science*, 13 (1): 95-125

Smith, Tony (1994). *America's Mission: The United States and the Worldwide Struggle for Democracy in the Twentieth Century*. Princeton, NJ: Princeton University Press

Smith, Tony (2007). *A Pact with the Devil: Washington's Bid for World Supremacy and the Betrayal of the American Promise*. New York: Routledge

Snyder, Jack (1991). *Myths of Empire: Domestic Politics and International Ambition*. Ithaca, NY: Cornell University Press

Snyder, Jack (2000). *From Voting to Violence*. New York: Norton

Sobek, David (2005). "Machiavelli's Legacy: Domestic Politics and International Conflict," *International Studies Quarterly*, 49 (1): 179-204

Sørensen, Georg (1992). "Kant and Processes of Democratization: Consequences for Neo-Realist Thought," *Journal of Peace Research*, 29 (4): 397-414

Souva, Mark (2004). "Institutional Similarity and Interstate Conflict," *International Interactions*, 30 (3): 263-281

Souva, Mark, and Brandon Prins (2006). "The Liberal Peace Revisited: The Role of Democracy, Dependence, and Development in Militarized Interstate Dispute Initiation, 1950-1999," *International Interactions*, 32 (2): 183-200

Spalding, Nancy L. (1988). "Democracy and Human Rights in the

Third World." In *Human Rights: Theory and Measurement*, ed. David L. Cingranelli, Chap. 10. New York: St. Martin's Press

Speier, Hans (1952). *Social Order and the Risks of War*. New York: Stewart

Spiro, David E, (1994). "The Insignificance of the Liberal Peace," *International Security*, 19 (2): 50-86

Stam, Allan C., III (1996). *Win, Lose, or Draw: Domestic Politics and the Crucible of War*. Ann Arbor: University of Michigan Press

Stannard, David (1992). *American Holocaust: Columbus and the Conquest of the New World*. New York: Oxford University Press

Starr, Harvey (1992). "Democracy and War: Choice, Learning and Security Communities," *Journal of Peace Research*, 29 (2): 207-213

Starr, Harvey (1997). "Democracy and Integration: Why Democracies Don't Fight Each Other," *Journal of Peace Research*, 34 (2): 153-162

Stedman, Stephen J. (1993). "The New Interventionists," *Foreign Affairs*, 72 (1): 1-16

Stoll, Richard J. (1984). "The Guns of November: Presidential Reelections and the Use of Force," *Journal of Conflict Resolution*, 28 (2): 231-246

Storey, Norman, *What Price Cod: A Tugmaster's View of the Cod Wars*. Beverley, North Humberside, UK: Hutton Press

Stouffer, Samuel A. (1955). *Communism, Conformity, and Civil Liberties: A Cross-Section of the Public Speaks Its Mind*. New York: Wiley

Streit, Clarence (1935). *Union Now: A Proposal for a Federal Union of the Democracies of the North Atlantic*. New York: Harper & Bros

Stuyt, A. M. (1972). *Survey of International Arbitration*, 2nd edn. Leiden: Sijthoff

Sweetman, Jack (1968). *The Landing at Veracruz: 1914*. Annapolis, MD: Naval Institute Press

Talentino, Andrew Kathryn (2010). "The Forgotten Element of Democratization: Bringing the Citizen Back In." In *Democratic Peace in Theory and Practice*, ed. Steven W. Hook, Chap. 6. Kent, OH: Kent State University Press

Tanter, Raymond (1966). "Dimensions of Conflict Behavior Within and Between Nations, 1958-1960," *Journal of Conflict Resolution*, 10 (1): 41-64

Taylor, Charles L., and Michael C. Hudson (1972). *World Handbook of Political and Social Indicators*, 2nd edn. New Haven, CT: Yale University Press

Tebbel, John, and Keith Jennison (1960). *The American Indian Wars*. New York: Harper & Row

Terrell, Louis M. (1977). "Attribute Differences Among Neighboring States and Their Levels of Foreign Conflict Behavior," *International Journal of Group Tensions*, 7 (1-2): 89-108

Thompson, William R. (1990). "The Size of War, Structural and Geopolitical Contexts, and Theory Building/Testing," *International Interactions*, 16 (3): 183-199

Thompson, William R. (1996). "Democracy and Peace: Putting the Cart Before the Horse?," *International Organization*, 50 (1): 141-174

Thompson, William R., and Richard Tucker (1997). "A Tale of Two Democratic Peace Critiques," *Journal of Conflict Resolution*, 41 (3): 428-454

Tillema, Herbert K. (1991). *International Conflict Since 1945: A Bibliographic Handbook of Wars and Military Interventions*. Boulder CO: Westview

Tilly, Charles (1985). "War Making and State Making as Organized Crimes." In *Bringing the State Back In*, eds. Peter E. Evans, Dietrich Rueschemeyer, and Theda Skocpol, pp. 169-191. New York: Cambridge University Press

Tomz, Michael, and Jessica L. Weeks (2013). "Public Opinion and the Democratic Peace," *American Political Science Review*, 107 (4): 849-865

Traub, James (2008). *The Freedom Agenda: Why America Must Spread Democracy (Just Not the Way George Bush Did)*. New York: Farrar, Straus, and Giroux

Tures, John A. (2001). "Democracies as Intervening States: A Critique of Kegley & Hermann," *Journal of Peace Research*, 38 (2): 227-235

Tures, John A. (2005). "Operation Exporting Freedom: The Quest for Democratization Via United States Military Operations," *Whitehead Journal of Diplomacy and International Relations*, 6 (1): 97-111

Ungerer, Jameson Lee (2012). "Assessing the Progress of the Democratic Peace Research Program," *International Studies Review*, 16 (1): 31

Utley, Robert M, and Wilcomb E. Washburn (1977). *The American Heritage History of the Indian Wars.* New York: American Heritage

Valentino, Benjamin A., Paul K. Huth, and Sara E. Croco (2010). "Bear Any Burden? How Democracies Minimize the Costs of War," *Journal of Politics*, 72 (2): 528-544

Van Belle, Douglas A. (1993). "Domestic Imperatives and Rational Models of Foreign Policy Decision Making." In *The Limits of State Autonomy: Societal Groups and Foreign Policy Formulation*, eds. David Skidmore and Valerie M. Hudson, pp. 151-183. Boulder, CO: Westview

Van Belle, Douglas A. (1997). "Press Freedom and the Democratic Peace," *Journal of Peace Research*, 40 (4): 405-414

Van Belle, Douglas A. (2006). "Dinosaurs and the Democratic Peace; Paleontological Lessons for Avoiding the Extinction of Theory in Political Science," *International Studies Perspectives*, 7 (3): 287-306

Van Belle, Douglas A., and John R. Oneal (2000). "Press Freedom and Militarized Disputes." In *Press Freedom and Global Politics*, ed. Douglas A. Van Belle, pp. 47-75. Westport, CT: Praeger

Van Den Berghe, Pierre L. (1981). *The Ethnic Phenomenon.* New York: Elsevier

Van Evera, Stephen (1992). "American Intervention in the Third World: Less Would Be Better." In *The Future of American Foreign Policy*, eds. Charles W. Kegley, Jr., and Eugene R. Wittkopf, Chap. 21. New York: St. Martin's Press

Vanhanen, Tatu (1993). "Construction and Use of an Index of Democracy." In *Monitoring Social Progress in the 1990s: Data Constraints, Concerns, and Priorities*, eds. David G. Westendorff and Dharam Ghai, eds., pp. 301-321. Aldershot, UK: UN-RISD/Avebury

Vanhanen, Tatu. (1997). *Prospects of Democracy: A Study of 172 Countries.* New York: Routledge

Vanhanen, Tatu (2000). "A New Dataset for Measuring Democracy, 1810-1998," *Journal of Peace Research*, 37 (2): 251-265

Vasquez, John A. (1995). "Why Do Neighbors Fight? Proximity, Interaction or Territoriality," *Journal of Peace Research,* 32 (3): 277-293

Vasquez, John A., and Colin Elmon (2011). *Realism and the Balancing of Power: A New Debate.* Upper Saddle River, NJ: Prentice-Hall

Verdier, Daniel (1994). *Democracy and International Trade: Britain, France, and the United States, 1860-1990.* Princeton, NJ: Princeton University Press

Verdier, Daniel (1998). "Democratic Convergence and Free Trade," *International Studies Quarterly,* 42 (1): 1-24

Vincent, Jack (1987a). "Freedom and International Conflict: Another Look," *International Studies Quarterly,* 31 (1): 103-112

Vincent, Jack (1987b). "On Rummel's Omnipresent Theory," *International Studies Quarterly,* 31 (1): 119-125

Vronsky, Peter (2011). *Ridgeway: The American Fenian Invasion and the 1866 Battle That Made Canada.* Toronto: Penguin Canada-Allen Lane

Wallace, Michael, and J. David Singer (1970). "Intergovernmental Organizations in the Global System, 1815-1964: A Quantitative Description," *International Organization,* 24 (2): 239-287

Wallensteen, Peter (1973). *Structure and War.* Stockholm: Rabén and Sjögren

Wallerstein, Immanuel (1984). *The Politics of the World Economy: The States, the Movements and the Civilizations.* New York: Cambridge University Press

Wallerstein, Immanuel (1993). "The World-System After the Cold War," *Journal of Peace Research,* 30 (1): 1-6

Waltz, Kenneth N. (1979). *Theory of International Politics.* Reading, MA: Addison-Wesley

Waltz, Kenneth N. (1993). "The Emerging Structure of International Politics," *International Security,* 18 (2): 44-79

Ward, Michael D., and Kristian S. Gleditsch (1998). "Democratizing for Peace," *American Political Science Review,* 92 (1): 51-61

Ward, Michael D., Randolph M. Siverson, and Xun Cao (2007). "Disputes, Democracies, and Dependencies: A Reexamination of the Kantian Peace," *American Journal of Political Science,* 51 (3): 583-601

Wayman, Frank (2002). "Incidence of Militarized Disputes Between Liberal States, 1816-1992." Paper presented at the annual convention of International Studies Association

Weart, Spencer R. (1994). "Peace Among Democratic and Oligarchic Republics," *Journal of Peace Research*, 31 (3): 299-316

Weart, Spencer R. (1998). *Never at War*. New Haven, CT: Yale University Press

Weede, Erich (1983). "Extended Deterrence by Superpower Alliance," *Journal of Conflict Resolution*, 27 (2): 231-253

Weede, Erich (1984). "Democracy and War Involvement," *Journal of Conflict Resolution*, 28 (4): 649-664

Weede, Erich (1989). "Extended Deterrence, Superpower Control, and Militarized Interstate Disputes, 1962-76," *Journal of Conflict Resolution*, 27 (2): 231-254.

Weede, Erich (1992). "Some Simple Calculations on Democracy and War Involvement," *Journal of Peace Research*, 29 (4): 377-383

Weede, Erich (1995). "Economic Policy and International Security: Rent-Seeking, Free Trade and Democratic Peace," *European Journal of International Relations*, 1 (4): 519-537

Weede, Erich (1996). *Economic Development, Social Order, and World Politics: With Special Emphasis on War, Freedom, the Rise and Decline of the West, and the Future of East Asia*. Boulder, CO: Rienner

Weede, Erich (2003). "Globalization: Creative Destruction and the Prospect of a Capitalist Peace." In *Globalization and Armed Conflict*, eds. Gerald Schneider, Katherine Barbieri, and Nils Petter Gleditsch, Chap. 16. Lanham, MD: Rowman and Littlefield

Weede, Erich (2004). "The Diffusion of Prosperity and Peace by Globalization," *The Independent Review*, 9 (2): 165-186

Weede, Erich (2007). "Capitalism, Democracy, and the War in Iraq," *Global Society*, 21 (2): 219-227

Weiss, Thomas G., David P. Forsythe, and Roger A. Coate (1994). *The United Nations and Changing World Politics*. Boulder, CO: Westview

Werner, Suzanne (1998). "Negotiating the Terms of Settlement: War Aims and Bargaining Leverage," *Journal of Conflict Resolution*, 42 (3): 321-343

Werner, Suzanne (2000). "The Effect of Political Similarity on the Onset of Militarized Disputes, 1816-1985," *Political Science Quarterly*, 53 (2): 343-373

Werner, Suzanne, and Douglas Lemke (1997). "Opposites Do Not Attract: The Impact of Domestic Institutions, Power, and Prior Commitments on Alignment Choices," *International Studies Quarterly*, 41 (30: 529-546

White House (1994). *A National Security Strategy of Engagement and Enlargement.* Washington, DC: Government Printing Office

Widmaier, Wesley W. (2005). "The Democratic Peace Is What States Make of It: A Constructivist Analysis of the US-Indian 'Near-Miss' in the 1971 South Asian Crisis," *European Journal of International Relations*, 11 (3): 431-455

Wilkenfeld, Jonathan (1968). "Domestic and Foreign Behavior of Nations," *Journal of Peace Research*, 5 (1): 56-69

Wilkenfeld, Jonathan (1972). "Models for the Analysis of Foreign Conflict Behavior of States." In *Peace, War and Numbers*, ed., Bruce M. Russett, pp. 275-298. Beverly Hills, CA: Sage

Wilkenfeld, Jonathan, Michael Brecher, and Sheila Moser (1998). *Handbook of International Crises in the Twentieth Century*, vol. 2. New York: Pergamon

Wilkinson, David O. (1980). *Deadly Quarrels: Lewis F. Richardson and the Statistical Study of War.* Berkeley: University of California Press

Williams, Michael C. (2001). "The Discipline of the Democratic Peace: Kant, Liberalism, and the Social Construction of Security Communities," *European Journal of International Relations*, 7 (3): 525-553

Wilson, Matthew T. (2013). "A Discrete Critique of Discrete Regime Type Data," *Comparative Political Studies*, June 9

Wolfson, Murray, Patrick James, and Eric J. Solberg (1998). "In a World of Cannibals *Everyone* Votes for War: Democracy and Peace Reconsidered." In *The Political Economy of War and Peace*, ed. Murray Wolfson, pp. 155-176. Boston: Kluwen

Wright, Jonathan (2010). "Locarno: A Democratic Peace?," *Review of International Studies*, 36 (2): 391-411

Wright, Quincy (1942). *A Study of War.* Chicago, IL: University of Chicago Press

Xenias, Anastasia (2005). "Can a Global Peace Last Even If Achieved: Huntington and the Democratic Peace," *International Studies Review*, 7 (3): 357-386

Yom, Sean L. (2010). "Washington in the Mideast: A Doctrine, a Dilemma, and Durable Despotism." In *Democratic Peace in Theory and Practice*, ed. Steven W. Hook, Chap. 10. Kent, OH: Kent State University Press

Yoon, Mi Yung (1997). "Explaining U.S. Intervention in Third World Internal Wars, 1945-1989," *Journal of Conflict Resolution*, 41 (4): 580-602

Young, Oran R. (1989). *International Cooperation: Building Regimes for Natural Resources and the Environment*. Ithaca, NY: Cornell University Press

Young, Oran R., ed. (1999). *The Effectiveness of International Environmental Regimes: Causal Connections and Behavioral Mechanisms*. Cambridge, MA: MIT Press

Zakaria, Fareed (1997). "The Rise of Illiberal Democracy," *Foreign Affairs*, 76 (6): 22-43

Zinnes, Dina A., Robert C. North, and Howard E. Koch (1961). "Capability, Threat and the Outbreak of War." In *International Politics and Foreign Policy*, ed. James N. Rosenau, pp. 469-482. New York: Free Press

Zinnes, Dina A., and Jonathan Wilkenfeld (1971). "An Analysis of Foreign Conflict Behavior of Nations." In *Comparative Foreign Policy: Theoretical Essays*, ed. Wolfram Hanrieder, Chap. 6. New York: McKay.

Index

Abu Ghraib. *See* Iraq
Achaean League, 8
action-reaction theory, 95
Aetolian League, 116
Afghanistan, 37, 84, 104, 188; Bagram Air Force Base, 108
Africa, 8, 24, 63, 64, 117, 122, 123, 124,
African Americans, 21
aggression, 26, 36, 39, 70, 75, 101, 102, 111
aggressiveness, 26, 34, 100. *See also* personality factors
Al-Qaeda, 6
Albright, Madeline, 100
Alker, Hayward, 30
Allee, Todd, 66, 72, 89
alliances, 8, 9, 26, 32, 33, 61, 79, 82, 83, 84, 86, 91, 102, 103, 113, 115; pseudo-alliance, 83; solidarity of, 57-58, 63-64
Allison, Graham, 94
American-Philippine War (1898-1901), 118
Amphipolis, 115
Anglo-American hegemony, 5
Anglo-Dutch War (1780-83), 35, 116

Anglo-French Wars (1782; 1792-1802; 1896), 35, 116
anocracies, 7, 9, 18, 20, 116, 119
anomalies. *See* deviant cases
Antholis, William, 8, 19, 21, 24, 31, 33. 48, 83
Appenzell, 116
Arab Spring, 99
arbitration, 30, 89
Arendt, Hannah, 107
Argentina, 123, 124
Argos, 115
aristocracy, 65. *See also* nobility
Armenia, 118, 124
Asia, 30, 61, 63, 64, 82
Asian and Pacific Cooperation, 30
Asian Way, 61
Association of South-East Asian Nations (ASEAN), 61, 63, 65, 66, 67, 82
assassinations, 28,
Athens, 21, 34, 35, 48, 77, 93, 105, 115, 116
attack on 9/11, 21, 66
audience costs, 53. *See also* public opinion
Austria, 120

Austria-Hungary, 118
autocracies, 6, 7, 9, 18, 20, 28, 51, 60, 62, 71, 79, 85, 90, 91
Azar, Edward, 27, 29
Azerbaijan, 118, 124

Babst, Dean, 5, 13, 33
Bachteler, Tobias, 21, 67
Bagram Air Force Base. *See* Afghanistan
Bahrain, 124
Baker, James, 98
Baker, William, 70
balance of power, 83, 95
Balkan Wars (1912-13),
Bangladesh, 125, 126
Baum, Matthew, 53
Baumann, Robert, 29
Belgium, 26, 35, 112, 117
Bell, Duncan, 5
Berbaum, Michael, 71
Bern, 116, 117
Bickers, Kenneth, 70
birthrates, 76
"black box," 31, 51, 60, 88, 90, 94
black operations, 28
black sites, 21
Blair, Tony, 104
Boer Wars (1880-81, 1899-1902), 33, 117, 118
Boeotian League, 8
Bolivia, 119
Bollen, Kenneth, 18
Boot, Max, 104, 105
borders, territorial, 34, 37, 38, 61, 62, 82, 87
Bosnia, v, 125
Botswana, 121, 122, 123, 124
"bounded competition." *See* competition
Brazil, 29, 34,
Brecher, Michael, 120
Britain, 25, 33, 34, 35, 37, 39, 51, 52, 65, 94, 100, 105, 114, 116, 117, 118, 119, 120, 121, 123, 124, 125,
Brock, Lothar, 52

Bueno de Mesquita, Bruce, 7, 84, 90
bureaucracy, 15
Burkina Faso, 121
Burma. *See* Myanmar
Bush, George H. W., 84, 101
Bush, George W., v, 84, 98, 104, 105
Butterworld, Robert, 30
Buzan, Barry, 77

Cambodia, 8, 37, 54, 64, 67, 82, 101, 105, 120, 121, 126; Khmer Rouge, 54, 101
Campbell, Sally Howard, 51
Canada, 62, 116, 117, 122, 124, 125
capabilities, 8, 82, 87; mediatory, 65; military, 85, 86
capitalism, 42, 43, 73, 74-75, 78-79, 103,
capitalist peace. *See* peace
Caribbean, 103
Caroline incident (1837-41), 62, 117
Carthage, 119
case study research, vi, 2, 7, 8, 23, 24, 28, 31, 32, 33-38, 39, 48, 55, 65, 78, 90, 91, 105, 106, 109, 111, 112, 113,
Casper, Gretchen, 17
Castilian League, 8
Castlereagh, Lord, 89
Cederman, Lars-Erik, 83
Central America, 103
Central Europe, 24
Cesarini, David, 104
Chan, Steve, 19, 31
Cheibub, José, 17
Cherokee Nation, 36, 117
Chesapeake Affair (1807), 116
Chile, v, 29, 34, 101, 117, 121
China, 6, 21, 101, 108
Choi, Seung-Choi, 52-53
Chomsky, Noam, 28, 108
civil liberties, 13, 114
civil rights, 12, 17, 43, 107, 108. *See also* International Covenant on Civil and Political Rights
civil society, 49, 52
civil wars, 37; Sri Lanka, 82; Switzer-

land, 35, 117; United States, 33, 117
civilian control of the military, 50, 53
"clash of civilizations," 61
Cleveland, Grover, 36
Cod Wars (1958, 1960, 1972-73, 1974-76), 63, 120, 121,
coercion. *See* diplomacy, coercive
Cohen, Raymond, 2, 20
coherent regimes, 13
Cold War, 6, 9, 10, 24, 28, 30, 33, 43, 48, 61, 63, 65, 75, 77, 78-79, 80, 82-83, 87, 89, 100, 102, 103, 104, 108, 113, 121
Colombia, 123, 124
colonialism, 6, 19, 21, 24, 25, 26, 28, 31, 33, 37, 43, 66, 91, 92, 93, 107,
Comache Nation, 36
Comanchería, 36, 117
Communism, 28
Communist countries, 105
Communist bloc, 64. *See also* Soviet bloc
communitarianism, 12
Community of Democracies, 100
competition, ; "bounded competition," 56, 60; economic, 68, 94; fair competition, 68; in elections, 14, 17, 19, 50, 51, 60
Concert of Europe, 65-66
concession making, 83, 89
conflict initiation, 7, 51, 84, 887
conflicts, internal, 8, 44, 59, 60, 69-72, 76, 83, 108, 113. *See also* civil wars; coups d'etat
conflict resolution, 30, 60, 64, 65, 75, 79, 86, 89, 92
conficts, international, 6, 7, 9, 10, 20, 26-31, 32, 39, 42, 44, 45, 47, 51, 53, 55, 60, 61, 62, 63, 64, 65, 66, 66, 67, 68, 69, 70, 71, 72, 77, 78, 82, 84, 85, 86, 87, 89, 90, 101. *See also* Appendix
contiguity, geographic, 8, 9, 25-26, 32, 53, 62, 63, 77, 81, 87, 93
Cool War, 101
Cooper, Richard, 75-76
cooperation, international, 2, 21, 65, 66, 77
cooperation, regional, 2,
Copeland, Dale, 78
Coppedge, Michael, 13
Correlates of War Project, 28, 31
correlations, vi, 11, 14, 17, 18, 30, 31, 38, 41, 42, 43, 44-46, 51, 60, 61, 62, 63, 69, 72, 75, 76, 78, 88, 93, 95
cosmopolitanism, 59, 68
Costa Rica, 28, 120, 122, 123
coups d'etat, 60, 64, 69, 107, 118, 121
covert action, v, 21, 28-29, 31, 36, 53, 54, 65, 68, 92, 100, 101, 102, 107-8, 112, 113
crises, 7, 9, 31, 35, 51, 65, 84, 89, 118
Croatia, 125
cross-sectional analysis, 32
cross-temporal analysis, 33, 45
culture, 56, 65-66, 68-69; cultural commonality, 57, 60-61, 83; cultural differences, 25; cultural similarity, 57, 61; democratic culture, 55-56, 59-60, 61, 64; diplomatic culture, 61; economic culture, 69, 74-75, 95; international organization culture, 58, 64-65; operationalizations, 59; liberal culture, 56, 59-60, 67; regional culture, 62. *See also* alliances; cosmopolitanism; indigenous cultures; national culture theory
culture-bound research, 25
Cuna people, 34, 119
Cyprus, 64, 120, 121, 122, 124
Czechoslovakia, 118, 199

Dahl, Robert, 12, 17
Daily Show with Jon Stewart, The, 104
Danzig, 116
David, Stephen, 76
Davies, Graeme, 72, 93
de Tocqueville, Alexis de, 1
de Vries, Michiel, 79
de-escalation, 7
decapitalization, 107
Declaration of the Rights of Man, 103
Delahunty, Robert, 104
Delian League, 67

democracies, types of:
Anglo-American, 13; capitalist, 103; clear, 13; coherent, 38; communitarian, 12; consociational, 12; deep, 18; developed, 78; developmental, 12; economic, 12; elitist, 12; Eropean, 92; fledgling, 106; full-fledged, 105; Greek, 19; Herrenfolk, vi, 12, 19, 21, 24, 68, 107; illiberal, 12, 21; inchoate, 21; institutionalized, 69; liberal, 13; libertarian, 13; mature, 20, 38, 87; open, 53; pacifist, 60; participatory, 12; peaceful, 6; polyarchic, 12; pluralist, 12; political, 14; premature, 122, 124; procedural, 3, 12, 13, 14-16, 42, 48, 55, 56; protective, 12; proto-democracy, 20; recently-established, 6-7, 20; semi-democracy, 21; social, 12, 13, 20, 22, 42, 108; stable, 38; substantive, 3, 12, 13, 16, 42, 50, 53-55, 56; transitional, 71, 72, 99-100, 113; well-established, 20
democracy, v, vi, 5, 10, 24, 28, 56; definition, 11-13, 14-23, 33, 34, 42, 48, 53, , 11256, 60, 66, 91, 94
democracy impostion, 103-5
democracy promotion, 99-100, 106, 107
democracy restoration, 103
democratic constraints, 12; constitutional, 49, 50-52; institutional, 19, 23, 48, 49, 53
democratic enlargement, 100, 104
democratic republics, 19
democratization, 20, 51, 72, 86, 99, 100. 104-5, 106
dependency theory, 75
deterrence, 9, 28, 43, 80-81, 82, 85-86, 102, 108-9
Deterring Democracy, 28
Deutsch, Karl, 61
deviant cases, 8, 11, 21, 32, 33-38, 39, 47, 91, 93, 112, 115-26
Diamond, Larry, 104
"dictators' club," 61

diplomacy, 61, 63, 79, 101; coercive diplomacy, 85
diplomatic propensity, 88, 89-90. *See also* negotiation propensity
diplomatic protests, 26
displays of force, 9, 30
disputes, territorial, 24, 30, 61, 63, 84; trade, 60. *See also* militarized international disputes
diversionary theory, 69-72, 76, 90, 92
Dixon, William, 30, 60, 75, 78, 89
domestic conflict. *See* conflict, internal
domestic stability, 69-72
Dominican Republic, 28, 101, 121
Domke, William, 18, 77
Doyle, Michael, 5, 17, 19, 33, 93, 94
drone attacks, 102
Dutch League, 8
dyads, 5, 8, 10, 19, 26, 31, 32, 33, 35, 38, 39, 42, 44, 45, 48, 53, 60, 62, 77, 86, 87, 89, 107, 112

East, Maurice, 28
economic competition, 68, 94
economic culture, 69
economic development, 43, 73, 75, 78, 82
economic downturns, 69, 70, 76
economic factors, 60, 68, 72-79, 83, 95, 118
economic growth, 8, 73, 75-76, 82, 107
economic inequality, 75
economic institutions, 62
economic interdependence, 64, 74, 75, 77-79, 93
economic liberalism, 59, 67, 68, 73-75
economic liberty, 13-14, 15, 52
economic norms theory, 94
economies: clientelist, 43, 67; contract-based, 43, 94; global, 78, 106, 109; market, 17, 67; regulated, 51; social market, 68
Ecuador, 28, 33, 35, 117, 119, 120, 122, 123, 125
Egypt, 37, 38, 104, 119, 120, 122, 123, 125

El Salvador, 64, 121, 122
elections, 17-18, 34, 36, 37, 52, 54, 60, 89, 92, 118, 119; campaigns, 54, 92; competitive, 14, 16, 19, 50, 51; direct, 13, 14, 16, 19, 36; defeat in, 54, 69; fair, 15, 16, 17; free, 13, 19, 37; indirect, 14, 16; regularity of, 13, 14, 16, 17, 19, 50; victory in, 37, 61, 62, 70
Elis, 115
Elman, Miriam, 112, 113
Ember, Carol, 19, 55, 69
Ember, Melvin, 19, 55, 69
Emmons, Juliann, 18
empirical research, canons of, 3, 12, 47
England. *See* Britain
English School, 68
Enola Gay, 101
escalation, 9, 29, 32, 51, 55, 84, 85, 86, 89
Estonia, 125
Etzioni, Amitai, 106
Europe, 21, 23, 24, 25, 26, 34, 35, 61, 66, 68, 77, 79, 92, 93, 103. *See also* Concert of Europe
European integration, 79
executions, 66, 108
executives: directly elected, 13, 14, 16, 19, 51; indirectly chosen, 14, 16; powers of, 15-16, 19, 23, 34-35, 48-52, 70, 99, 117, 118, 119
expected utilities, 80, 84
experimental research, 93, 100, 101
extraordinary rendition, 66, 112

facet theory, 42
factor analysis, 23
Facts on File, 29
Falklands/Malvinas War (1982), 64, 123
Farber, Henry, 9, 18, 32
Fashoda Crisis (1898), 35, 118
Fatah, 38
federal system, 51
Feierabend, Ivo, 17
Feierabend, Rosalind, 17
Feldman, Noah, 101

Ferejohn, John, 34
Ferris, Wayne, 27
Finel, Bernard, 53
Finland, 119
First World, 106
Florence, 116
Flotilla Raid (2010), 126
Football War (1968), 64, 121
force, military, 9, 27, 28, 29, 34, 36, 51, 52, 70, 82, 83, 119. *See also* diplomacy, coercive
foreign aid, 31
foreign policy, control of, 68, 107, 108, 111; research, 2, 101; voter interest in, 54, 92
France, 25, 34, 35, 55, 65, 94, 103, 116, 117, 118, 123, 124, 125
France, Vichy, 119
franchise. *See* rights, voting
Franco-British Crisis (1846), 51,
Franco-Prussian War (1870-71), 117
Franco-Thai War (1940), 34, 119
Freedom House, 13-14, 16, 17, 18-19
Freedom at Issue, 27
freedoms
    assembly, 15, 17
    economic freedom, 13-14, 15, 17, 52, 67, 72, 73, 77, 78, 79
    political, 13, 17, 18, 19, 25, 27, 37, 51
    press, 13, 15, 17, 18, 52, 53
    religion, 15
    speech, 13, 15, 17, 19
Freud, Sigmund, 94
Friedman, Gil, 65, 68
functionalism. *See* integration theory

Gabon, 124
Gambia, 123
game theory, 65
Gandhi, Jennifer, 17
Gar, Azar, 21, 75
Gartner, Scott, 56, 86
Gartze, Erik, 22, 44, 52, 62, 75, 76, 79, 113
Gastil, Raymond, 14
Geneva Accords (1954), 36

Genoa, 116
George, Alexander, 94
Georgia, 126
Germany, 20, 21, 32, 33, 35, 52, 55, 65,
   82, 103, 117, 115, 119, 121
Gibler, Douglas, 24, 30, 43, 87
Gleditsch, Kristian, 19
Gleditsch, Nils Petter, 2, 42, 87
Goldsmith, Benjamin, 68
governments: change of, 19, 34, 36,
   112; coalition, 37, 52; cost of, 53,
   54, 73, 76, 89, 108-9; head of, 13,
   33; local government, 15, 17; repre-
   sentative, 17, 72, 94; scope of, 13,
   16, 48, 50, 52, 55. *See also* regime
   types
Gowa, Joanne, 9, 10, 18, 32, 54, 68, 76,
   77, 89, 100
Greece, 19, 24, 31, 34, 83, 120, 122,
   123, 124. *See also* Athens and other
   Greek cities
Gregg, Phillip, 28
Grenada, 104, 123
Guatemala, v, 21, 29, 101-2, 119, 123
Gulf War (1991), 84, 101
Gurr, Ted Robert, 13, 17, 18, 25, 34,
   51, 60
Guttman, Louis, 42
Guyana, 28, 119

Halperin, Morton, 106
Hamas, 38
Hanseatic League, 8
Hawai'i, 25, 36, 102, 118
"hawks," 92
Hayek, Frederick, 67
Hayes, Jerrod, 47
Hearst press, 53
hegemony, 5, 28, 81-82, 83, 95, 114
Hegre, Hårvard, 75
Henderson, Errol, 6, 53, 93, 112
Henderson, Gordon, 94
Henderson, Gregory, 38
Herman, Frank, 30
Hermann, Charles, 27, 94
Hermann, Margaret, 6, 9, 13, 18, 28,

91, 94
Hewitt, Joseph, 52
Hitler, Adolf, 65
Holsti, Kalevi, 108
Honduras, 64, 121, 122, 123, 125
human rights, 45, 66, 93, 101, 106, 107,
   108, 109, 113; commitment to, 59,
   66. *See also* International Covenant
   on Civil and Political Rights
Hungary, 118. *See also* Austria-
   Hungary
Hussein, Sadam, 101
Huth, Paul, 66, 72, 89

Iceland, 119, 120, 121
ideologies: centrism, 2, 54; Communism, 28, 64, 108; elitism, 12;
   fascism, 65; humanism, 114; individualism, 13, 57, 61-62; liberalism,
   13, 47, 67-68, 75; nationalism, 54,
   99, 112; neoconservatism, 105; neoidealism, 2, 47; neorealism, 2, 47,
   79; pacifism, 60; pluralism, 12; realism (realpolitik), 2, 47, 79-87, 113;
   socialism, 8, 33, 79. *See also* cosmopolitanism
in-groups, 91
India, 82, 119, 120, 121, 124, 125, 126
indigenous peoples, 8, 19, 25, 29, 31,
   34, 35, 55, 69, 103. *See also* Native
   Americans; Native Hawaiians
individualism. *See* ideologies
Indonesia, 29, 37, 61, 93, 120, 121,
   122, 126; Kalimantan, 37; West Papua, 93
intergovernmental organizations
   (IGOs), 58, 64, 65, 79, 100. *See* specific IGOs
integration,
   economic, 79
   military, 80, 83
integration theory, 2
interdependence, *See* economic interdependence
International Convenant on Civil and
   Political Rights, 22

International Crisis Behavior database, 30
international law, 30, 36, 59, 66-67
International Military Intervention dataset, 29
international relations research, 1, 36, 37, 47, 108, 113, 114
international trust, 58, 65, 66, 91
interventions, 6, 9, 31, 72, 102, 104, 105
covert, 21, 28-29, 30, 100, 102, 113
overt, 28, 113
United Nations, 64, 105
Iraq in Kuwait War (1991), 84, 101, 125
Iraq War (2003), v, 37, 53, 84, 98, 104, 105, 106
Iran, 21, 29, 37, 100, 102, 119
Ireland, 119, 123
Ireland, Michael, 56, 86
Iron Curtain, 8
irredentism, 84
Islamic fundamentalism, 105
Israel, 33, 34, 37, 38, 98, 100, 119, 120, 121, 122, 123, 124, 126
Issue Correlates of War Project, 30
Italy, 35, 117, 120, 125
ivory tower research, vi, 11, 105, 108-9

James, Patrick, 52-53, 72
Japan, 21, 30, 55, 103, 120, 124
Jervis, Robert, 53, 93
jihadists, 102. *See also* Islamic fundamentalism
Jim Crow, vi
jingoism, 53, 61
Job, Brian, 54
Johns, Robert, 93
Johnson, Lyndon, 92
Jordan, 119
Journal of Conflict Resolution, The, vi, 98, 99
judiciary, independence of, 16, 17

Kacowicz, Arie, 63, 67
Kant, Immanuel, 1, 17, 39, 48, 56, 68, 72, 86, 93-94

Kashmir Wars (1947-48, 1963-65), 34, 119, 121
Keesing's Contemporary Archives, 29
Kargil War (1999), 125
Kegley, Charles, 6, 9, 13, 18, 28, 91
Keynes, John Maynard, 67
Khmer Rouge. *See* Cambodia
Kisangani, Enizet, 71
Koga, Jun, 28
Kosovo, v, 98, 100, 101, 105, 125
Kuwait, v, 84, 101, 125

Lai, Brian, 61, 79
Lake, Anthony, 98
Lake, David, 85
Lakota Nation, 36
Lalman, David, 84
lateral pressure theory, 94
Layne, Christopher, 2, 7, 30, 31, 32, 33, 35, 55, 89, 90, 91, 92, 95, 100
leadership, 85, 87-89, 94
league of republics, 68
Lebanon, 34, 119, 121, 122, 123, 126
legislatures, 13, 15, 16, 17, 19, 23, 51, 117. *See also* parliamentary systems
Lemke, Douglas, 19
Leng, Russell, 19
Li, Quan, 79
Lifton, Robert Jay, 101, 108
Lijphart, Arend, 24
Lili'uokalani, Queen, 36
limited government. *See* governments, scope of
Lipson, Charles, 51-52, 68, 75
Lithuania, 119
Lithuanian League, 8
Locarno Peace Pact, 63, 66
logit analysis, 23
longitudinal analysis. *See* cross-temporal analysis
Lord, Kristin, 53
Lucca, 116
Lucerne, 116, 117
Luria, A. R., 94

Machiavelli, Niccolò, 34, 65
Malaya, 37

Malaysia, 37, 61, 121, 122, 124, 125, 126; Sabah, 37; Sarawak, 37
Mali, 121
Malolos Republic (Philippines), 34, 118
Malta, 123
manifest destiny, 103
Mansfield, Edward, 24, 77
Mantinea, 115
Maoz, Zeev, 26, 30, 31, 51, 59, 63, 69, 126
Mapuche people, 34
mass society theory, 94
Marxian theory, 94, 95
Mauritania, 124
McKinley, William, 36
Mearsheimer, John, 2, 32, 100
mediation, 64, 65, 67, 89
Megara, 115
Mende, 115
mercantilism, 79
mercenaries, 28
Metternich, Klemens von, 89
México, 36, 103, 117, 123
Middle Ages (Europe), 35
Middle East, v, 77, 98
Milan, 116
military-industrial complex, 77
military regimes, 70
Miletus, 115
militarization, 9, 86
militarized international disputes (MIDs), 6, 9, 29-30, 35, 37, 39, 51, 87, 115
Miller, Paul, 104
mini-states, 25
Mintz, Alex, 100
misperceptions, 53, 91
Mitchell, Greg, 101, 108
Mitchell, Sara, 67
Moldova, 125
Momsen, Joseph, 13
Moon, Bruce, 78
morality, 53, 58, 65-66, 76, 108, 113
Morgan, T. Clifton, 51, 70
Morgenthau, Hans, 47, 63, 108

Mormons, 117
Morocco, 35, 118, 122
Moser, Sheila, 30
Mousseau, Michael, 43, 62, 67, 68, 69, 75, 78, 94
Mueller, John, 84, 106
Müller, Harald, 101
Munich Crisis (1938), 65
Myanmar, 120

Napoléon Bonaparte, 103
Napoleonic Wars, 94
national culture theory, 94
Native Americans, 116
Native Hawaiians, 36
negotiation propensity, 58-59, 66. *See also* diplomatic propensity
negotiation styles: reciprocation, 66; tit-for-tat, 66
Netanyahu, Benjamin, 98
Netherlands, 24, 26, 93, 112, 116, 117, 118
New York Times, 29
New Zealand, 123
Nicaragua, 29, 102, 122, 123, 125
Nobel Peace Prize, 98
nobility, 54. *See also* aristocracy
nondemocracy, 20, 21, 44, 45, 53, 60, 81, 101
normative critique, 3, 97-109, 111, 112
North, Robert, 94
North America, 35, 103
North Atlantic countries, 20, 68
North Atlantic Treaty Organization, 83
North Borneo. *See* Indonesia, Kalimantan
North Vietnam, 36
Norway, 118, 121, 123
Nye, Joseph, 7

Obama, Barack, 98
oligarchy, 60, 115, 117, 119
Oneal, John, 64, 70, 72, 76
open system, 13, 52, 53
operational code, 61
operationalization, 13, 14-16, 17, 20,

23, 59, 66, 67, 113
Opium War, First (1839), 21
Orange Free State, 118
Oren, Udo, 20
Oslo Accords (1993), 37
Ostrom, Charles, 54
out-groups, 91
outlaw states, 103
Owen, John, 13, 19, 30, 31, 35, 42, 55, 56, 91

Pacific countries, 30, 68, 93
pacific settlement, 59, 66-67
pacifism. *See* ideologies
Paine, Thomas, 1
Pakistan, 34, 82, 102, 119, 120, 121,
Palestine, 38; Gaza Strip, 38, 126
Palmer, Glenn, 51
Panamá, 34, 104, 119, 124
Papua New Guinea, 124, 125
paradigms, 3, 38, 47, 48, 93-95, 112, 113
parliamentary systems, 16, 33, 37, 52, 54, 71, 115
Paraguay, 119
Park, Johann, 83
Partell, Peter, 51
Pastry War (1838-39), 117
peace, types of: autocratic, 60, 62; capitalist, 42, 73, 75, 78, 94; Caucasian, 93; democratic, v, vi, 1-114; dyadic, 5, 8, 10, 19, 25-26, 31-32, 33, 35, 38, 39, 42, 44 45, 48, 53, 60, 62, 77, 86, 87, 89, 107, 112; liberal, 60, 62, 73, 77; monadic, 5-8, 48; oligarchic, 60; regional, 63; socialist, 8
peace, zones of, 66-67
Peace of Westphalia (1648), 66
Peceny, Mark, 21, 105
Peloponnesian Wars, 8, 115-16
Pennamite-Yankee War (1784), 116
people's power, 103
personality factors, 88, 90-91; aggressiveness, 67, 75, 91; cautious, 53, 90; conciliatory, 91; ideological, 90, 91; inner-directed, 90; outer-

directed, 90; pig-headed, 91; pragmatic, 90; reasonable, 91; respectful, 58, 65; sensitive, 90; sociable, 91; suspicious, 91; task-oriented, 90; trusting, 58, 65, 66, 91
Perú, 33, 35, 117, 119, 120, 122, 123, 125
Perugia, 116
Philippines, 21, 34-35, 61, 91, 103, 106, 118, 121, 122, 124, 126. *See also* Malolos Republic
Pickering, Jeffrey, 71, 105
Pisa, 116
plebiscite, 36, 37, 67
Polachek, Solomon, 77
Poland, 32, 116, 119
Polanyi, Karl, 43, 94
policy making, effectiveness of public on, 16
policy relevance of research, vi, 2, 3, 97-109, 111-112
political fission, 69
political parties, 51, 52, 70-71, 99
political science, 12, 22, 114; behavioralist, vi, 114; postbehavioralist, 114
political stability. *See* domestic stability
political suppression, 16
polyarchy. *See* democracy, types of
popularity of leaders, 54, 88, 92, 99, 105
post-Cold War era, 28, 61, 78, 108
post-industrial society, 75-76
Potter, Philip, 53
Powell, G. Bingham, 17
power. *See* balance of power; realpolitik; soft power
power calculations, 80, 83-85, 87
power status, 79-; major powers, 9, 25-26, 51, 81, 82, 85, 86, 87; superpowers, 26, 82
power transition theory, 80,
preliterate cultures. *See* indigenous peoples
presidential systems, 34, 36, 37, 52, 54, 65, 70, 71, 84, 92, 98, 100, 101, 104
Pride, Richard, 16
prime ministers, 33, 98, 104, 116, 118

Prins, Brandon, 71
profit, 43, 68, 72, 77
prosperity, 72-74, 75, 76
public opinion, 16, 17, 22, 39, 48, 52, 53-54, 55, 59, 61-62, 65, 70-71, 76, 83, 85-86, 89, 90, 92, 102, 104. *See also* audience costs; survey research
puppet rule, 105

Qatar, 124
Quackenbush, Stephen, 17, 22, 26
quantitative research, 1, 2, 48, 93

racism, 92-93, 107
Rasler, Karen, 22
Ralston, Jackson, 30
rank disequilibrium theory, 95
Rao, Mohan, 83
Rawls, John, 47
Ray, James Lee, 19, 20, 25, 34, 56, 60, 64, 91
Raymond, Gregory, 30, 86, 89
Reagan, Ronald, 54, 104
Real World Order, The, 106
realpolitik. *See* ideologies
regional affinity, 62-63
regulations, governmental, 51, 60
Reinecke, Wolfgang, 13
Reiter, Dan, 51, 61
relationships, logical: necessary but not sufficient, 42; sufficient, 41-42
relationships, statistical: bivariate, 1, 3; exogenous, 43; intervening, 43; inverse, 45; probabilistic, 44; recursive, 45; reverse, 44-45; simultaneous, 45
repression, 67, 70
responsibility to protect, 101
revolutions: political, 51; sexual, 76
Rhodesia, 123
Richardson, Lewis, 24, 61, 95
rights, 12, 65; civil, 12, 13, 17, 21, 43, 107, 108; economic, 13; equality of, 15, 19; juridical, 17; minority, 12, 43; nonpoverty, 22; political, 12, 13, 15, 17, 19, 21; privacy, 107; proper-

ty, 78; to run for office, 15, 17; voting, 16, 17, 21, 37, 107, 117; women's, vi
See also freedoms; human rights; International Covenant on Civil and Political Rights
Risse-Kappen, Thomas, 56
Rome, 34, 116, 117
Roosevelt, Franklin Delano, 65
Rorschach test, 97
Rosato, Sebastian, 46, 48, 60
Rosenbluth, Francis, 34
Rousseau, David, 55, 94
royalty, 36, 60
rule of law, 43
Rudy, Michael, 17, 22, 26
Ruhr Crisis (1923), 35, 119
Rummel, Rudolph, 6, 13, 16, 23, 27-28, 32, 33, 52, 86, 105
Russett, Bruce, 8, 12, 13, 17, 18, 19, 20, 21, 24, 26, 298, 30, 31, 33, 39, 41, 42, 43, 45, 48, 51, 52, 53, 55, 59, 63, 64, 65, 66, 69, 71, 72, 76, 83, 91, 92, 98, 100, 101, 102, 103-4, 105
Russia, 125, 126. *See also* Soviet Union

Salmore, Stephen, 27
Samoa, 35, 117, 118
sampling, vi, 2, 11, 23-39, 62, 64, 78, 87, 91, 63, 101, 102, 106, 107, 111
Scandinavia, 13
Schneider, Gerald, 77
Schultz, Kenneth, 55
Schultze, Gunther, 77
Schumpeter, Joseph, 67
Schwebach, Valery, 51
Schweller, Randall, 19, 26, 85, 86
Schwyz, 116
Scione, 115
secret raids, 22
security communities, 45, 67
selectorate theory, 88, 90
Sénégal, 123, 124
Senese, Paul, 7, 30
separation of powers, 49, 50, 51

Serbia, 98, 100, 118, 125
SERFACS database, 29-30
Siena, 116
Singer, J. David, 5, 19, 25, 28, 31, 38, 104, 112
Singer, Max, 106
single-party regimes, 70
Siverson, Randolph, 18
Six-Day War (1967), 37, 121
slavery,
Slovenia,
Small, Melvin, 5, 19, 25, 27, 31, 38, 104
Smith, Alistair, 71, 92
Smith, Tony, 104, 105
Snyder, Jack, 24
social constructionism, 3
social contract, 94
social market, 59, 68
social sciences, 24, 34, 41, 98, 99, 111
socialist countries, 8, 79, 121
soft power, 76
South Africa, 24, 33, 117, 118, 122, 123, 124
South African League, 8
South America, 63
South Asia, 82
South Korea, 103, 120
South Pacific, 68, 93
Southeast Asia, 63
sovereignty, 6, 17, 25, 33, 37, 38, 66
Soviet bloc, 33, 75, 79, 113. *See also* communist bloc
Soviet Union, 35, 64, 67, 82
Spain, 21, 34, 53, 91, 118, 123, 124
Spanish-American War (1898), 21, 63, 118
Sparta, 34
spillover hypothesis, 60
Spiro, David, 31, 32, 35
Sprecher, Christopher, 71
Sri Lanka, 82, 124
stable regimes, 8, 9, 20, 24, 28, 38, 69-72
Starr, Harvey, 2
statistical methods, 2, 18, 23, 24, 39, 44, 45, 48, 78, 88, 107, 109, 112,

113
Statistics of Deadly Quarrels, 24
Stewart, Jon, 104
Streit, Clarence, 5
superpowers. *See* power
surveys. *See* public opinion
Sweden, 119, 125
Swiss League, 8, 34, 117
Switzerland, 35, 117
Stuyt, Alexander, 30
survey research, 38-39, 53, 54, 59, 60, 65, 67, 75, 76. *See also* public opinion
Syracuse, 21, 115
Syria, 119, 120

Taiwan, 126
Talleyrand, Charles Maurice de, 89
Terrell, Louis, 53
Thailand, 34, 82, 119, 120, 122, 126
theories. *See* specific theories
Third World, 24, 92, 99
Thompson, William, 22
threats, military, 6, 7, 26, 27, 29, 37, 44, 45, 63, 72, 82, 84, 85, 86, 90, 99, 100
Tibet, 6
Tillman, Erik, 51
Tir, Jaroslav, 24, 30, 43, 87
Tomz, Michael, 39
torture, 22, 66, 104
trade, 43, 52, 60, 64, 94
trade communities, 74, 79; common markets, 79; customs unions, 79; free-trade agreements, 72, 78, 79; monetary unions, 79; preferential trade agreements, 79
trade dependency, 77
trade disputes, 30, 60
trade interdependence, 43, 75, 76-79
transitional states, 6, 45, 71, 72, 79, 99, 113
transparent politics, 49-50, 52-53
Transvaal, 117, 118
Trent Affair (1861), 35, 117
Tucker, Richard, 9
Tufis, Claudiu, 17

Tule Republic, 119
Tunisia, 117, 124
Turkey, 64, 118, 119, 120, 121, 122,
　123, 124, 126

Ukraine, 116, 119, 125
unitary system, 51
United Arab Emirates, 125
United Nations (UN), 38, 100, 101;
　voting patterns, 62, 78
United States of America (USA): allies,
　9, 21, 37, 65, 83, 103; Cold War
　role, 82; colonies, 24, 25, 34, 91,
　118; Congress, 36, 62; covert opera-
　tions, v, 21, 28-29, 30, 36, 54, 65,
　92, 100, 101-2, 108, 112, 113, 119,
　121, 123; "democracy," vi, 20, 21,
　24, 28, 37, 108; Democratic Party,
　104; foreign disputes, 30, 35, 37,
　100, 102, 117, 119, 120, 121, 122,
　124, 125; Georgia, 36, 117; Guantá-
　namo, 108; human rights, 21, 66,
　108; National Security Council, 104;
　public opinion, 39, 55; Supreme
　Court, 21; Texas, 36; Times Square,
　102; trade, 30, 78; University of
　Missouri, 13; Utah, 117; Voting
　Rights Act (1965), 21, 37; wars and
　military interventions, v, 28, 30, 34,
　35, 36, 62, 67, 91, 92, 100-1, 102,
　103, 10, 117, 118, 121, 123, 124,
　125, 126. *See also* indigenous peo-
　ples in North America; presidents of
　the United States
unstable regimes, 9, 29, 72, 102, 105
Upper Volta. *See* Burkina Faso
USS Liberty, 33, 121

Van Belle, Douglas, 18
van den Berghe, 6
Van Evera, Steven, 28
Vanhanen, Tatu, 17, 22
Venezuela, 34, 35, 118, 123, 124
Venice, 116
Vietnam, v, 8, 26, 36-37, 54, 64, 67,
　82, 100-1

Vincent, Jack, 27, 32
voting: level of, 16; regulations, 12, 15,
　107. *See also* rights, voting; UN,
　voting patterns

Waltz, Kenneth, 9, 47
War of 1812, 33, 116
war casualties, 24, 26-28, 62, 87
war crimes, 112, 114
war declaration, 62
war duration, 31, 85
war initiation, 7, 8, 32, 39, 55, 66, 100
war mobilization, 50;
war, nuclear, 28
war technology, 86
Ward, Michael, 19
wars (defined), 26
wars, costs of, 53, 54, 72, 73, 84, 108
wars, types of : big, 26; colonial, 6, 24,
　30; definition of, 27; diversionary,
　70-72, 76, 90; extrastate, 6; imperi-
　al, 6; independence, 34, 35; internal,
　31; interstate, 108; limited, 83; mi-
　nor, 78; national liberation, 31; pre-
　ventive, 26
quasi-war, 116; systemic, 25. See al-
　so civil wars; Cold War; world wars,
Warsaw bloc, 78
Washington Post, 105
wealth, national, 8, 75, 77
Weart, Spencer, 8, 19, 35, 60, 92
Weede, Erich, 9, 17, 26, 32, 43, 72, 78,
　82
Weeks, Jessica, 39, 53
welfare states, 16, 22, 108
West Africa, 63
"white man's burden," 103
Wildawsky, Aaron, 106
Wilkenfeld, Jonathan, 30
Wilkinson, David, 24
Wilson, Woodrow, 44, 103
Wilsonianism, 103
World Event/Interaction Survey, 27
*World Handbook of Political and So-
　cial Indicators*, 18
World Trade Organization, 60

World War I, 20, 38, 52, 65, 75, 76, 77,
    82, 84, 118
World War II, 32, 35, 65, 75, 82, 84,
    103, 119
Wright, Quincy, 5, 87

Xenias, Anastasia, 99

Yanomano people, 34
Yemen, 102, 108; North Yemen, 125;
    South Yemen, 125
Yoo, John, 104
Yugoslavia, 24, 35, 87. *See also* Serbia

Zaporozhian Cossacks, 116
Zimbabwe, 121, 122
Zone of Peace, Freedom, and Equality
    Declaration (1971), 67
Zürich, 117

Publications of Michael Haas

Approaches to the Study of Political Science
International Organization: An Interdisciplinary Bibliography
International Systems: A Behavioral Approach
International Conflict
Basic Documents of Asian Regional Organizations, 7 volumes
Politics and Prejudice in Contemporary Hawai'i
Fundamentals of Asian Regional Cooperation
Basic Data of Asian Regional Organizations
Korean Reunification: Alternative Pathways, 1st edn.
The Pacific Way: Regional Cooperation in the South Pacific
The Asian Way to Peace: A Story of Regional Cooperation
Cambodia, Pol Pot, and the United States: The Faustian Pact
Genocide by Proxy: Cambodian Pawn on a Superpower Chessboard
Polity and Society: Philosophical Underpinnings of Social Science Paradigms
Institutional Racism: The Case of Hawai'i
Improving Human Rights
Deconstructing International Relations Theory
Racism, Sexism and Heterosexism
The Political Film Today
Multicultural Hawai'i: The Fabric of a Multiethnic Society
International Human Rights
The Singapore Puzzle
American Government in Turmoil
Discrimination, American Style
The Politics of Human Rights
Comparing Governments and Global Policies
Discrimination and Public Policy
Human Rights Imperiled
Choices: An American Government Reader
International Relations: Arena of Terror
International Human Rights in Jeopardy
International Human Rights: A Comprehensive Introduction, 1st edn.
George W. Bush, War Criminal? The Bush Administration's Liability for 269 War Crimes
America's War Crimes Quagmire, From Bush to Obama.
Looking for the Aloha Spirit: Promoting Ethnic Harmony
Barack Obama, The Aloha Zen President: How a Son of the 50th State May Revitalize America, Based on 12 Multicultural Principles
Modern Cambodia's Emergence from the Killing Fields: What Happened in the Critical Years?
Mr Calm and Effective: Evaluating the Presidency of Barack Obama
Korean Reunification: Alternative Pathways, 2nd edn.
Asian and Pacific Cooperation: Turning Zones of Conflict into Arenas of Peace
International Human Rights: A Comprehensive Introduction, 2nd edn.

www.ingramcontent.com/pod-product-compliance
Lightning Source LLC
Chambersburg PA
CBHW052129270326
41930CB00012B/2808